P9-CFL-442

Elkins Park Free Library
563 East Church Road
Elkins Park, PA 19027-2499

A
BORDER
PASSAGE

ALSO BY LEILA AHMED

Women and Gender in Islam:
The Historical Roots of a Modern Debate

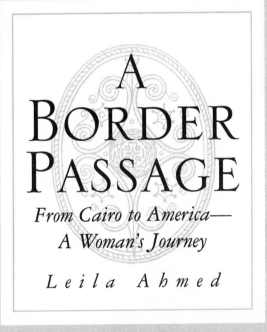

A
BORDER
PASSAGE

From Cairo to America—
A Woman's Journey

L e i l a   A h m e d

FARRAR, STRAUS AND GIROUX

NEW YORK

Farrar, Straus and Giroux
19 Union Square West, New York 10003

Copyright © 1999 by Leila Ahmed
All rights reserved
Distributed in Canada by Douglas & McIntyre Ltd.
Printed in the United States of America
Designed by Lisa Stokes
First edition, 1999

Library of Congress Cataloging-in-Publication Data
Ahmed, Leila.
   A border passage / Leila Ahmed.
      p. cm.
   ISBN 0-374-11518-4 (alk. paper)
   1. Ahmed, Leila. 2. Women—Egypt—Biography. 3. Muslim
women—Egypt—Biography. 4. Women in Islam—Egypt.
5. Egyptians—United States—Biography. 6. Feminism. I. Title.
HQ1793.Z75A55   1999
305.42'092—dc21
[B]   98-39027

The quotations from Rumi on pages 1, 130, 155, and 306 are taken
from *Rumi: In the Arms of the Beloved*, translated by Jonathan Star
(New York, 1997); the web page of Handan Oz; and *The Essential
Rumi*, translated by Coleman Barks with John Moyne, A. J. Arberry,
Reynold Nicholson (San Francisco, 1996).
   Grateful acknowledgment is made to Rhonda Cobham and Merle
Collins for permission to quote from "Strangers in a Hostile Land-
scape" by Meiling Jin, first published in *Watchers and Seekers: Cre-
ative Writing by Black Women in Britain* (London: The Women's
Press Ltd., 1987).
Elkins Park Free Library
563 East Church Road
Elkins Park, PA 19027-2499

$\mathscr{A}$CKNOWLEDGMENTS

I want to thank the University of Massachusetts at Amherst, and Clare Hall, the University of Cambridge, for a Samuel F. Conti Faculty Fellowship and for a Visiting Fellowship, respectively, both essential to the completion of this book. Thanks also to friends and family on both sides of the Atlantic whose interest and support were just as essential.

Many thanks to my editors at Farrar, Straus and Giroux, Jonathan Galassi and Lauren Osborne.

Some names and the details of people's lives have been changed to protect privacy.

CONTENTS

Part I
   IN THE HOUSE OF MEMORY   1

· 1 ·
   EGYPT: THE BACKGROUND   3

· 2 ·
   FROM COLONIAL TO POSTCOLONIAL   32

· 3 ·
   IN EXPECTATION OF ANGELS   47

· 4 ·
   TRANSITIONS   68

· 5 ·
   HAREM   93

· 6 ·
   SCHOOL DAYS   135

· 7 ·
   SUEZ   158

· 8 ·
   THE HAREM PERFECTED?   179

Part II
   "RUNNING FROM THE
   FLAMES THAT LIT THE SKY"   195

· 9 ·
   PENALTIES OF DISSENT   197

· 10 ·
   IN THE GROVES OF WHITE ACADEME   206

· 11 ·
   ON BECOMING AN ARAB   243

· 12 ·
   FROM ABU DHABI TO AMERICA   271

Epilogue
   CAIRO MOMENTS   299

IN THE HOUSE OF MEMORY

"To hear the song of the reed
Everything you have ever known
must be left behind."

Rumi

$\mathcal{E}$GYPT: $\mathcal{T}$HE $\mathcal{B}$ACKGROUND

I T WAS AS IF there were to life itself a quality of music in that time, the era of my childhood, and in that place, the remote edge of Cairo. There the city petered out into a scattering of villas leading into tranquil country fields. On the other side of our house was the profound, unsurpassable quiet of the desert.

There was, to begin with, always the sound—sometimes no more than a mere breath—of the wind in the trees, each variety of tree having its own music, its own way of conversing. I knew them all like friends (when we left in the summers for Alexandria I would, the last day, make the round of the garden saying goodbye to the trees), although none more intimately than the two trees on either side of the corner bedroom I shared with Nanny. On one side was the silky, barely perceptible breath of the mimosa, which, when the wind grew strong, would scratch lightly with its thorns at the shutters of the window facing the front of the house, looking out onto the garden. On the other side was the dry, faintly rattling shuffle of the long-leaved eucalyptus that stood by the window facing the street. On hot nights the street lamp cast the shadows of the slender twirling eucalyptus leaves onto my bedroom wall, my own secret cinema. I would fall asleep watching those dancing shadows, imagining to myself that I saw a house in them and people going about their lives. They would appear at the door or windows of their shadow house and talk and come out and do things on the balcony. I would go to bed looking forward to finding out what had happened next in their lives.

I loved the patterns of light cast by leaves on the earth and I loved being in them, under them. The intricate, gently shifting patterns that the flame tree cast where the path widened toward the garden gate, fading and growing strong again as a cloud passed, could hold me still, totally lost, for long moments.

Almost everything then seemed to have its own beat, its own lilt: sounds that distilled the sweetness of being, others that made audible its terrors, and sounds for everything between. The cascading cry of the *karawan*, a bird I heard but never saw, came only in the dusk. Its long melancholy call descending down the scale was like the pure expression of lament at the fall of things, all endings that the end of light presaged.

Then there was the music of the street beyond the garden hedge in the day, not noisy but alive, between long intervals of silence, with the sounds of living. People walking, greeting one another, the clip-clop of a donkey, sometimes of a horse. Street vendors' calls—"tama-a-tim" for tomatoes, "robbabe-e-eccia-a" for old clothes and furniture. And the sound, occasionally, of cars, though rarely enough for us to be able to detect the horn and the engine even of our own car. Our dog, Frankie, could detect it long before we could, when the car was still almost two miles away. That was how Frankie died in the end, running out as he always did to greet my father when he arrived in the car driven by a uniformed government chauffeur. Frankie's front paw got run over, leaving him whimpering about in a cast that he soon chewed through. Father put a guard on his mouth but it was too late; Frankie got gangrene and died. More precisely, he was put down, although this was kept from me at the time.

Then there was the sound sometimes, in the earliest morning, of the reed piper walking past our house. His pipe sounded private, like someone singing to himself. A simple, lovely sound, almost like speech, like a human voice. He would say "good morning" with his pipe and one knew it to be "good morning." When he passed, it would feel as if something of infinite sweetness had momentarily graced one's life and then faded irretrievably away.

Years later I'd discover that in Sufi poetry this music of the reed is the quintessential music of loss and I'd feel, learning this, that I'd always known it to be so. In the poetry of Jalaluddin Rumi, the classic master-poet of Sufism, the song of the reed is the metaphor for our human condition, haunted as we so often are by a vague sense of longing and of nostalgia, but nostalgia for we know not quite what. Cut from its bed and fashioned into a pipe, the reed forever laments the living earth that it once knew, crying out, whenever life is breathed into it, its ache and its yearning and loss. We too live our lives haunted by loss, we too, says Rumi, remember a condition of completeness that we once knew but have forgotten that we ever knew. The song of the reed and the music that haunts our lives is the music of loss, of loss and of remembrance.

That's how it was in the beginning, how it was to come to consciousness in this place and this time and in a world alive, as it seemed, with the music of being.

And yet also, as I sit here now, in these halls, in this house of memory, it is not in those days and those moments that my story begins. Rather, it begins for me with the disruption of that world and the desolation that for a time overtook our lives. For it was only then that I'd begin to follow the path that would bring me—exactly here.

And so it is with those years and their upheaval and with the politics that framed our lives that I must begin.

I grew up in the last days of the British Empire. My childhood fell in that era when the words "imperialism" and "the West" had not yet acquired the connotations they have today—they had not yet become, that is, mere synonyms for "racism," "oppression," and "exploitation."

Or, at any rate, they had not yet become so among the intellectual, professional, and governing classes of Egypt. In Cairo it was entirely ordinary, among those classes, to grow up speaking English or French or both, and quite ordinary to attend an English or French school. It was taken for granted among the people who raised us that there was unquestionably much to admire in and learn from the civilization of Europe and the great strides that Europe had made in human advancement. No matter that the European powers were politically oppressive and indeed blatantly unjust; nor did it seem to matter that the very generation which raised us were themselves locked in struggle with the British for Egypt's political independence. There seemed to be no contradiction for them between pursuing independence from the European powers and deeply admiring European institutions, particularly democracy, and Europe's tremendous scientific breakthroughs.

This was the common ethos among other Middle Easterners, too. My schoolmates at the English School in Cairo included Syrians, Lebanese, and Palestinians from the same broad class background as mine, and their attitudes toward English, like mine, no doubt reflected the attitudes of our parents. One of my two best friends through my school years was Jean Said, who would later write *Beirut Fragments*; she was the younger sister of Edward Said, the well-known theorist and literary critic. They were Christians of Palestine and we were Muslims of Egypt, but their attitudes were not discernibly different from ours. Our very names—Edward, Jean, and my own school name, Lily, an anglicized version of my given name—plainly suggest our parents' admiration of things European.

At home my parents' heroes were Gandhi and, to a lesser extent, Nehru, as well as the leaders of Egypt's own struggle for independence, such as Saad Zaghloul. Egypt in the decades of my parents' youth and young adulthood—that is, the 1920s, 30s and 40s—was, in fact, slightly ahead of India in its pursuit of independence and democratic rule. By the early twenties Egypt had won partial independence from Britain, established itself as a constitutional monarchy, and installed its first democratically elected government. The new government believed that education was key to ensuring Egypt's stability as a democracy and began at once to open more free schools, for girls as well as boys. By the late twenties Egypt's first modern university opened its doors.

For three decades the country was a democracy. Then came the Egyptian Revolution of 1952, which drove the old governing classes out of power and put an end to their dreams. Democracy was abolished and Egypt was declared a socialist state, drawing its political inspiration now not from the democracies of the West but from the Soviet Union. The revolution had inaugurated a new and fiercer type of anti-imperialist, anti-Western rhetoric, which would become the dominant rhetoric of the postrevolutionary age.

Already in the thirties and forties events had begun to prepare the ground for revolution as well as for a deepening anger at and disillusionment with the Western powers.

Egypt, like many countries, was caught up in the eddies of the Great Depression, which overtook Europe and America and which came in Egypt just as the new graduates of the expanded schooling were entering the workforce, looking for the professional opportunities their education had promised. Already, even before this, Egypt had been experiencing its first glut of school and college graduates. Frustrated in their hopes of upward mobility, increasingly alienated from the government and its rival parties, these aspiring members of the middle and lower-middle classes began to turn to alternative organizations of opposition. They turned, above all, to the Muslim Brotherhood. The Brotherhood, founded in the late twenties, aimed to institute Islamic government in Egypt and free the country from lingering and still-palpable British domination. The Brotherhood grew rapidly through the thirties, in particular among those educated and alienated lower-middle classes. While the government merely talked about improving conditions, the Brotherhood got down to work raising charitable funds from its members and establishing free health clinics and other much-needed centers providing vital assistance and relief. As the Brotherhood's influence grew, its profoundly negative view of imperialism and the West became more familiar and widespread.

In the thirties, too, Egypt, which had hitherto kept its distance from the Arab East, began to find itself more and more drawn into negotiations around the question of Palestine. European immigration to Palestine surged with the rise of Fascism in Europe, and reports of Palestinian uprisings and brutal British reprisals were more and more frequently in the news. Egyptian sympathy for the Palestinians grew, as did outrage at the flagrancy of imperialist injustice. The Muslim Brotherhood also took up the Palestinian cause.

Already, then, Egyptian attitudes toward the West were beginning to radically change. Then, in the forties, cataclysmic events cast an altogether bleaker and more lurid light on Europe and its civilization. Postwar revelations about the death camps in Germany and America's dropping of atom bombs on Hiroshima and Nagasaki now called into question the very notion of European and Western civilization. Many, including people of the class and generation who had once so admired the West, found themselves compelled to ask in what human values, indeed in what garbling of human values, this civilization of Europe was after all grounded. Toward what abyss was this flagship civilization leading humanity?

Such events precipitated a sense of shock and revulsion. Probably no one gave voice to this sense more succinctly than Gandhi, wrestling as he was with Western civilization and the new order of violence. "There have been cataclysmic changes in the world," he said, responding to news of the atom bomb. "It has been suggested by American friends that the atom bomb will bring ahimsa [nonviolence] as nothing else can. It will, if it is meant that its destructive power will so disgust the world that it will turn it away from violence for the time being. This is very like a man glutting himself with dainties to the point of nausea and turning away from them only to return with redoubled zeal after the effect of nausea is over. Precisely in the same manner will the world return to violence with renewed zeal after the effect of disgust is worn out." Hiroshima and the gas chambers of Germany were not merely distant events without effect on Egyptian lives. Egyptian memoirs from that era record how these events indelibly marked the writer's consciousness. In our house they had a direct impact on my mother. She became a pacifist. She required my brothers to take a solemn oath, which we were all summoned to witness, that they would never serve as combatants in any war. It was an oath they kept. In the Suez conflict, when one of my brothers was drafted, he served at the front as an ambulance driver.

The final blow that would trigger the revolution in Egypt would come with the founding of Israel, swiftly followed by Egypt's and the Arabs' defeat by Israel in the war of 1948. Egypt's defeat, profoundly galling to the army, was rumored to have been caused by corruption at the highest levels of the military establishment, members of which, it was said, in collusion with the king, had pocketed the funds intended for military supplies, procuring instead, and passing off on the army, cheap, defective equipment.

The revolution of 1952 was planned in the aftermath of that defeat by a group of young, bright, capable army officers smarting from the humiliation of a defeat suffered, they believed, entirely because of the corruption of the establishment.

One of these young officers was Gamal Abdel Nasser. Another was Anwar al-Sadat.

Egyptians would take pride in the fact that Egypt's revolution was a bloodless one. While other revolutions in the region—the Iraqi revolution, for example, which came soon after the Egyptian—would carve out a bloody path, in Egypt the royal family was treated with civility. The deposed King Farouk even received a twenty-one-gun salute as his yacht sailed out of his palace harbor in Alexandria to exile in Italy. I recall following its progress across the horizon. Violence, Egyptians said with pride back then, was not the Egyptian way. Egyptians, they said, had a tradition of abhorring violence. Even people who would eventually come to hate Nasser and the Egyptian Revolution would give the revolutionaries credit for having honored this tradition of nonviolence.

Following the revolution, the state took control of the media and set in motion a propaganda machine that tirelessly disseminated its new message of socialism and anti-imperialism, and also of something quite new to Egypt at the time, Arab nationalism.

Today we are so used to the idea of Egypt as "Arab" that it seems unimaginable that Egyptians ever thought of themselves as anything else. In fact, I made this assumption myself when I first began writing this memoir. It was only when my own discordant memories failed to make sense that I was compelled to look more carefully into the history of our Arab identity. Eventually I began to see the constructed nature of our Arab identity as it was formed and re-formed to serve the political interests of the day. For example, during the years of my adolescence and early adulthood, Egypt underwent several changes in name, reflecting the shifting definitions of our identity. Under Nasser, when the idea that we were Arab was incessantly hammered home in the media, the word "Egypt" was removed altogether from the country's name—and we became the United Arab Republic as we united, briefly, with Syria. Through the Nasser era the country retained that name, even though the union with Syria dissolved within a couple of years. Eventually, in a sign of shifting political winds, Sadat brought back the word "Egypt" and we became the Arab Republic of Egypt. Of course, the issue of identity, a profoundly ambiguous matter for Egypt, was inescapably and deeply political. Sadat, who published his autobiography during his presidency, actually called his book *In Search of Identity*.

If the president of Egypt himself, no less, was searching for his identity, no wonder that I, crossing the threshold into my teenage years in that era of revolution, would find myself profoundly confused and conflicted and, forever after, haunted by feelings of deep uncertainty and a mysteriously guilt-ridden sense of ambiguity. Identity was not simply a matter of rhetoric and politics but something that directly touched my own life in personal if unarticulated ways. While Jean Said was a Palestinian Christian, my other best friend, Joyce Alteras, was an Egyptian Jew. The new definition of our identity that was being crystallized in those years had direct implications, as I am sure I sensed, for the Jews of Egypt.

But how else might Egyptians define themselves, if not as Arab? Were Egypt not hostage, as it has been in our time, to a politics that so firmly fixes its identity as Arab, we might easily see that, on the basis of the country's history and geography, there are in fact quite a number of other ways of conceiving of Egyptian identity.

Egyptians, for instance, might, with equal accuracy, define themselves as African, Nilotic, Mediterranean, Islamic, or Coptic. Or as all, or any combination of, the above. Or, of course, as Egyptian: pertaining to the land of Egypt.

Pertaining to the land of Egypt. Pertaining—to use the indigenous ancient Egyptian word for this land—to Kemi. "Mizraim," as it is called in the Bible. "Musur" to the Assyrians. "Aigyptos" (from Hi-kuptah, one of the names of Memphis), as the Greeks called it, when Egypt became a province of their Hellenic Empire. "Aegyptus" to the Romans, when we became part of their empire. "Misr" to the Arabs, when they, too, conquered Egypt. "Masr," as we Egyptians call it. "Masr," as we call our capital too. Masr. "Cairo" to English speakers, "al-Qahira" to Arabs. A city founded, in fact, by the Arabs a little over a thousand years ago, soon after they conquered the country. Founded on a site fifteen miles or so north of Memphis, the ancient capital of Egypt—a city dating from about 3000 BCE. "Memphis" from "Mennufer," City of the Good.

⤙

They came in, the revolutionaries, with high ideals and good intentions. They simply wanted, they said, to cleanse society and bring the corruption with which it was rife to an end. The revolution, they said, would sweep out the old corrupt order and end the injustices of class oppression that had forever plagued this country, with its extremes of wealth and poverty. This would be a new era, they said, an era of equality and opportunity for all. Democracy, they said, had failed; socialism now was the only answer. The old, unscrupulous rich would have their wealth stripped from them; their properties would be nationalized and put to use for the benefit of all the people. The land they owned would be taken from them (anything over two hundred *feddans*—about two hundred acres) and distributed to the peasantry. And the factories they owned would be taken over and run by the government for the benefit, now, of all the people.

Of course the old upper classes and propertied middle classes did not like losing what they had owned and did not like the revolution and the new laws nationalizing this and that and stripping them of the wealth they had inherited or themselves built up. But there were many members of those classes, too, who disliked and feared what the revolutionaries were doing, not out of greed but out of political conviction. They believed that the revolutionaries' first act, of suspending and then abolishing democracy, augured ominously for the country's future.

The revolution did in fact bring about some positive and important changes. It immediately instituted free schooling for all and free college education for all who qualified, both men and women. Although even this policy had its costs, in the enormous overcrowding of schools, colleges, and universities and a resulting dramatic decline in educational standards, it had the extremely significant effect of opening up educational and professional opportunities for all classes, and it brought about a class mobility and a democratization of wealth unprecedented in Egypt's recent history. Even more fundamentally, perhaps, it effected a transformation of consciousness and expectation by making equality of opportunity a basic assumption of society. To be sure, though, Egypt continues to be a society marked by vast inequalities—no less vast today, perhaps, than in the old days.

But gradually it became apparent that there was a more somber side to the revolution. Soon enough it became a blatant dictatorship, with Nasser emerging from the initial group of revolutionaries as the sole ruler, whom no one could challenge or defy. Soon, too, corruption became the order of the day at the hands of a new ruling class, many of them military men, who had come in on the coattails of the revolutionaries. Political repression became the norm and Egypt's prisons began to bulge with political prisoners. The *mukhabarat*, a Soviet-style network of informers and secret police whose purpose was to ferret out critics and dissidents, became a pervasive presence in society.

This was not what the young revolutionaries had meant to happen. But here it was; it had happened.

～

This darker side of the revolution would in due course affect my own family. The problems that were just beginning to touch our lives when I left for college in England in the late fifties had become, by the time I returned, full-blown. These years following my return to Egypt were to be, for me, quite crucial. They marked the end, in important ways, of the enormously privileged life I had until then taken for granted. They changed me forever. At once turning point and crucible, they fundamentally shaped my life and my work and who I became. The story of my life, then, begins with these crucible years and the circumstances and politics of these years.

～

In the changed Cairo world to which I returned, those undergraduate years at Cambridge would quickly come to seem idyllic. A time when "work" was the pleasure of immersing myself all day in reading, thinking, and writing. A time when I discovered the riches of English literature. As I remember, it was Thomas Hardy, above all, whose books I immediately loved. It must have been autumn when I first read him, holing up in my room with an armful of his books, for I remember trudging, damp leaves underfoot, back and forth from the bus stop at the corner of the Girton woods in between hours of reading him. There were squirrels in the woods, red squirrels always fleeing, vanishing at the sound of a footfall. And in the spring the woods rang with the call of cuckoos, which I could hear in my room—E22. Dark and narrow, its one virtue was that it looked out on a lovely courtyard. A great tree stood to one side, changing with the seasons, and in the center were rose beds that filled with color in spring and summer. The rooms below me were occupied by Muriel Bradbrook, the Shakespearean scholar, who was also my director of studies. I'd been told when I arrived, by way of warning perhaps and as a piece of college legend, that the previous occupant of my room had one day unthinkingly emptied a teapot out her window, only to learn that Miss Bradbrook, sitting out on a deck chair, had been down below.

The way Hardy wrote of nature, the earth, the trees, as if they were living beings, gave voice to a sense I'd had of them growing up, a rather lonely child in a house encircled by a garden whose variety of enfolding trees had given me nurturance, companionship, and solace. Perhaps it was also Hardy's acute sense of the loveliness of England that drew me to him. The sheer physical loveliness of England, the way the earth here transformed itself through the seasons, subtly and moment by moment and yet also spectacularly, was to me quite new and marvelous. Even winter with its snows and early nightfalls was mysterious and lovely.

Other things too had made Hardy particularly resonant for me. His sense of some force—nature, society, something—inexorably set against man, fundamentally primed to crush and defeat him, gave voice to my own sense, then, of our puniness before blind and stupid forces, before which we were as nothing. Often too, in Hardy, it is sex or something to do with society's rules about sex that is at the heart of the destruction that unfolds through the book. And that too conformed to the pattern and understanding of life that had etched itself in me.

In earlier years it had been Somerset Maugham whose books I had loved for the same sorts of reasons. I'd come on them among all the other English books that lined our shelves at home: scientific books, novels, the works of Dickens, Thackeray. I don't know how I would have survived the loneliness of my teenage years without the companionship of such books, read to the sound of only the wind in the trees, alternately dirge and solace. I remember moonlit evenings, leaning on my windowsill, when all that stood between me, the spell of the moon, and the pull of some vast abyss below was a book that I could turn to and bury myself in.

Sometimes from my window I saw, across the stretch of wasteland between us and the next neighbors, men crouching by the railway line, defecating. And the dead, borne on litters, passed by on that side of the house toward some burial ground beyond sight on the desert side. Sometimes there would be no one following the litter, the dead person being someone destitute and without kin, the bearers in that case literally jogging with their burden, hurrying, the customary rhythmic chant *"innana min Allah wa illayhi ragi⁽un"* ("We are from God and to him we return") pounded out of them with each breath. (That was how I heard that phrase, which, as I now know, is different in its "correct" form—but of course memories are the stories of our consciousness rather than just "objective" facts.)

But it was in the years when I returned from Cambridge that what had been only vague forebodings took on reality in the gloom that overtook my parents' lives and the air of desolation that now permanently overhung Ain Shams, our family home.

Ain Shams (the name of the suburb in which we lived as well as the name of our house) had already in that era begun to change for reasons that had nothing to do with politics. What had been in my childhood a remote, sparsely populated suburb was, by the time of my return, being rapidly assimilated into the chaotic, crowded urban sprawl of Cairo. Previously our house had been bordered by lush and tranquil countryside on one side and by desert on the other, the dreamlike outlines of palm groves lightly gracing the horizon. A single road, lined with a scattering of garden-enclosed houses, linked it to the city.

What we had most loved about our house, its most remarkable feature in our own eyes and everyone else's, had been its garden. Besides being enormous by Cairo standards, it was marvelously rich in its variety of shrubs and trees—pine, eucalyptus, apricot, mango, tamarind, oleander—and in its winding paths and arbors and its clambering plants, brilliant and fragile—roses, bougainvillea, wisteria. It was, among family, friends, and even casual visitors, one of Cairo's legendary gardens. On the other hand, the suburb where we lived, which made it possible for us to have so large a garden, was on the remote and distinctly unfashionable edge of the city. Nearly all my schoolmates lived in elegant apartments in the fashionable districts of central Cairo or else in villas with town-sized gardens in the similarly exclusive Heliopolis—districts that were the equivalent, say, of Park Avenue in Manhattan or of Scarsdale, whereas we lived, as it were, in Brooklyn. Cairo, of course, is not New York. With its medieval core, its ancient sites, and its great spiritual hubs—shrines to

which people have flocked over centuries as they flock to Lourdes—
it is a city whose geography, spiritual and historical, is complexly layered; and all of this somehow, even if subliminally, is part of the
experience of growing up in Cairo. At Ain Shams we had, each within
ten minutes' walk of our house, the obelisk of ancient Heliopolis,
standing in the place in which it had stood since it was erected
thousands of years earlier, and the ancient tree, a great, spreading
sycamore (with, beside it now, a small church), where, legend has it,
Mary halted to rest with Jesus and Joseph on their flight into Egypt.

Our house, then, standing as it did at the intersection of country,
desert, and city, stood also at the edge and confluence of these many
worlds and histories. It seems entirely apt now, as I look back, that
Ain Shams was in this way quintessentially a place of borders and
that even geographically it was so placed as not quite to belong to any
one world. Or rather to belong, at once, to all of them.

The original conception of this garden had been my father's. It
was he for whom having a wonderful garden had been a priority and
he who, before his marriage, had bought the land and planned and
planted the garden. Throughout our childhoods my parents bickered,
albeit always in friendly fashion, over the subject. Mother would com-
plain that she wanted to live in a more central location, and Father
would ask if it wasn't worth the inconvenience of living where we did
to have such a garden. Then he would appeal to us, the children, and
we invariably took his side. But even Mother was less than halfhearted
in her protests, for she herself was by then an avid gardener. More
than that, the garden and the cultivation of its loveliness, and indeed
the entire meditative mood of Ain Shams, a mood of garden and reading and imagination, became her domain, a realm sustained by her
involvement.

It was hard, returning from Cambridge, to see how disheveled the
garden had become as my parents' home subsided into decay. Nevertheless, while they were alive, Ain Shams would continue to retain
its air of enclosure and seclusion as if holding off the encroaching
urban sprawl beating like a sea against it.

Within the house my parents lived from day to day, disoriented, like people whose ship had foundered. My mother in particular often looked as if she didn't quite recognize the world in which she found herself. And it was indeed a quite different world, for the revolution affected my family in fundamental and irreparable ways. Most critically in this period, my parents' difficulties were the direct consequence of the position my father had taken on the building of Aswan High Dam.

A distinguished engineer, Father, previously chairman of the Nile Water Control Board, was chairman of the Hydro-Electric Power Commission when he opposed the building of the High Dam. Nasser and the government rejected Father's views, but Father would not be turned away nor would he be silenced. In fact, he went on to write a book about his views, which the government then promptly impounded, ordering him neither to speak nor to write any further on the subject. My father's reasons for opposing the dam were what we would today call ecological. But in those days there was no ecology movement and the very word had not yet acquired the meaning and power it now has. It was in the mid-1950s that Father began his efforts to stop the building of the dam. Rachel Carson's *Silent Spring*, which would become the first well-known work to sound a warning note about ecological destruction, was not published until 1962. And so my father, with his forecasts about the consequences of the dam —most of which, incidentally, have proved to be correct—was a lone voice in the wilderness.

There were many reasons that he opposed the construction of the dam. The first was that Egypt would lose the Nile silt, that silt of proverbial fertility brought annually by the fast-flowing waters of the Nile in flood, spread on its banks, and left there by the receding waters. With the dam this silt would sink to the bottom of the lake, the world's largest man-made lake (to be called, of course, Lake Nasser). Henceforth, consequently, Egypt would have to rely on artificial chemical fertilizer, as indeed it does today. In addition, before the dam, the swift-flowing waters of the Nile in flood brought with them organisms that fed the fish of the eastern Mediterranean and contributed to sustaining the very livingness of the sea and its plant and animal life. All of this, too, would be held back by the giant dam. A series of smaller dams, on the other hand, which Father recommended, would have had all the benefits of one colossal dam while causing none of its problems. Father's plan would have made possible the control and regulation of the flooding river, but without disrupting its vital and life-sustaining processes. With the Aswan High Dam, Father also argued, there would be a dramatic rise in the snail-borne disease bilharzia among those whose livelihoods required them to work with water—the Egyptian peasantry. The fast-flowing waters of the Nile in flood had kept the disease in check by annually flushing the snails out to sea. Furthermore, according to Father's calculations, there would even be an enormous loss of water because of the dam, for it would create a huge lake, a body of water with a vast surface, in what was one of the hottest, driest regions of the world; the rate of water loss through evaporation would be enormous. In addition, the geological composition of the earth south of Aswan, where the lake would form, was such that the lake's walls would seep as a result of the enormous pressure on them, causing further significant water loss. And so on, for this is only a partial list of the damage Father foresaw.

He felt he could not obey Nasser's ban against his speaking out on the matter of the Nile: the cost of his silence to Egypt, he felt, was too high. He believed it was his duty to alert people, particularly the scientific community, to these catastrophic problems and to do everything in his power to stop the dam's construction. Prevented from publishing in Egypt, he took the only other course open to him: he went to London, where he delivered a paper with his findings at the Institute of Civil Engineers, of which he was a long-standing member. The institute published it forthwith.

To Father's mind, his paper, full of mathematical calculations, measurements of water volume, evaporation rates, soil erosion, and so on, was a presentation of meticulously calculated scientific evidence important to the future of Egypt, not a political attack on Nasser. For Nasser, however, the dam was a political symbol, a symbol, among other things, of Egypt's defiance of imperialism and of Nasser's own important role in Egypt's political future. His nationalization of the Suez Canal in 1956, that supreme act of challenge to imperialism, had been undertaken, as he had declared in his nationalization speech, in order to use the canal's revenues to build the High Dam (once America had reneged on its promise to finance it). Moreover, for Nasser, the dam's very size and grandiosity was emblematic of Egypt's rebirth as a great nation, a nation venturing once more, as in ancient days, on monumental projects—projects as grand as the pyramids. That was how the dam was touted in the press in those days: it was new Egypt's great pyramid. For Father, it was Egypt's great disaster.

Finally, of course, Nasser's own political stature and glory were at stake. Weighed against these matters, what did environmental damage or the illness and premature deaths of a few thousand more peasants from bilharzia matter? Father believed that Nasser cared not at all about the Egyptian peasantry or about what happened to Egypt in the long run, only about his own power and prestige. And so at any rate Father's defiance of Nasser's ban on publishing further provoked Nasser's fury. On their return to Egypt my parents found themselves living under a palpable cloud of government censure and displeasure. In daily life this translated into small habitual harassments that made their lives bleak, difficult, anxious, debilitating.

This was how things were when I left England and college to return home to Egypt.

Soon my father became ill with chronic pneumonia. He had days of respite, but more and more regularly now when I visited my parents I would find Father prostrate, his body puny as a child's under the sheet. He would open his eyes fleetingly to look acutely, intensely, then close them again, breathing with the aid of an oxygen mask, each rasping breath harsh and labored, drawn, one could hear, in pain.

Sometimes my entire visit (in my last couple of years in Cairo I moved out of my parents' home to a flat of my own) would be taken up with sitting or standing at his side, holding the oxygen mask over his mouth. Wearing it was uncomfortable for him, and my mother or Fat-hia the maid or I would relieve him for a while by holding it gently over his mouth.

The smells, the sights, the paraphernalia of illness.

Sitting in the darkened room, my arm aching from holding the mask, listening in the silence to Father's labored breath, I turned over and over in my mind all that was happening to us. How Father had struggled on the right side and how he had been crushed by this political giant, this great hero of our Arab world. And I thought of the years of careful, devoted, meticulous thought and calculation about the Nile that had gone into his work and his understanding of this river, and of his heroic attempt to avert catastrophe and preserve for future generations the riches that Egyptians had enjoyed, and depended on, for their lives and their civilization since the beginning of time. And I thought about England and of how I longed to return there and take up my own life. And I thought about justice and injustice. I see now how my sense of a troubled division between cultures, places, even civilizations took its particular cast and color and form first of all from this—those moments sitting here at this bedside. And I see how my self-understanding and my understanding of the history I was living through would be forever marked and scored by the thoughts I had sitting here listening to Father struggling to breathe, aware of his pain and of his ebbing life.

But here they were anyhow and this was how their life was now. Living from day to day, my mother tended to Father and in between would sit exhausted in front of the flicker of the television, she and her faithful Fat-hia sometimes sitting together and sometimes separately, taking turns.

There was nothing really for which to hope.

Father's illness and the fact, unspoken by anyone, that he was dying occupied the forefront of our thoughts. Unspoken but near the surface, evident in our eyes whenever they met.

For me there was another, deeper, more obscure dread in those visits, a dread I am sure I barely acknowledged. It was the dread that

I, like my mother, would never have a professional life. This possibility was particularly real and acute in those days because the Nasser government was refusing to grant me a passport. They were refusing to grant me the means to leave Egypt not because I'd had any significant political activity myself but because I was my father's daughter, and this was a way of further harassing my father. Captive in Egypt, unable to return to England to begin graduate studies as I had hoped, I began to think my own dream of pursuing a professional life was doomed to come to nothing.

My mother's life, a life in which (in my eyes in those days) she had "done" nothing, pursued no profession, focused for me all those fears about my own future. I remember, as I was leaving one evening, coming out of Father's room and looking into the room adjoining my mother's bedroom, which she used now as her main living area. I found her and Fat-hia watching television, an Arabic film. She looked up, startled, as I came in. Her face, gray and exhausted, had the passive, almost stunned look of absolute weariness. I went up to her, bending to kiss her goodbye—always with her a formal gesture, a careful kissing of the air, for my mother, unusually in this society, always shrank from touch. And I remember thinking as I left them sitting together in the flicker of the black-and-white television, the dusk outside closing in, how terrible it must be to do nothing with one's life, to just sit there, passively watching television.

But of course Mother was not doing nothing. Nursing my father was certainly not doing nothing. And in truth it fell mostly to her now, in the face of Father's illness, to cope with the daily problems arising from the government's ongoing harassment and political oppression. Having to borrow money, for instance, when the government froze their bank account, scrambling to find a way to pay for their basic needs and for Father's medication. And the worry of it all, the constant anxiety as to what the government might do next fell on Mother's shoulders, not on Father's, as he lay desperately ill and dying. Mother had from the start supported him in his stand and she steadfastly and unreservedly continued to do so even when the consequences began to affect their lives and the lives of all of us deeply.

Nevertheless, the act of conscience was Father's, and it was he rather than Mother who would have had the satisfaction of knowing that he had done what he believed he had had to do. Even the fact that Mother was much younger than he and, as far as anyone knew then, healthy made this time harder for her, because of the bleakness of the future confronting her, a future in which she would be bereft of the people she had loved and the resources and status that had once been hers.

All of this, of course, I understand quite clearly now—far more clearly than I did then, when I might have been more of a comfort to Mother. Back then I gave little thought to how it was she on whom the brunt of their difficulties fell and that it was she, ministering, coping ("doing" nothing), who sustained their life, such as it was, through these most difficult times. What I remember now from those days is the constant look of apprehension in my mother's eyes.

And so a mood of gloom and a sense of fallen fortunes engulfed Ain Shams. On those days when Father was better our spirits would lift. On good days Father would sit on the sofa in his bedroom by the radio, writing, a stack of pads and pencils beside him, the warm winter sunlight streaming in. Wrapped in his brown checkered dressing gown, pausing sometimes to enjoy a sip of weak tea or just relish the sweet air, he looked cheery and even radiant when he glanced up, then utterly engrossed again in the act of writing, his hand moving slowly but determinedly across the page, pausing to erase, rephrase. Sometimes, too, on those days he would sit simply listening to the Quran. He listened to it often in those last months and always with a look of keen appreciation, sometimes exclaiming out loud in sheer pleasure at the marvel of its words.

It was to me at once incomprehensible and riveting that one could know oneself to be dying and yet so enjoy, unperturbed, the passing, precious moment.

I assumed that Father was writing one of the scientific papers that I was used to seeing him write, but he was in fact writing his memoirs. I have with me now those yellowed, faded pages. They came into my possession in chaotic, jumbled form more than twenty years after Father's death, having been set aside in the houses of relatives, among things one day to be "gone through." Alas, they are almost indecipherable to me, for I do not have the easy mastery of the cursive Arabic script that my father had. At the best of times I find cursive Arabic hard to read, and these pages are in the slurred handwriting of someone ravaged by illness and nearing death.

～

But how did it happen, I've sometimes found myself wondering, that someone like Father, who loved the Quran, as he clearly did, had somehow neglected to see to it that his children would have as sure a command of its language—written Arabic—as he had? English too, by all means, since it was the language of the globally dominant and the language, therefore, of knowledge and professional advancement. But why not also classical, written Arabic? We were completely fluent in spoken Arabic, but not in the written language.

For me now there is no doubt that, at least implicitly, English was valued above Arabic in ways that would have marked it, in a child's mind at least, as being somehow innately a "superior" language. English was, to begin with, the language we spoke at school, where we were prohibited even in the playground from speaking Arabic. And it was the language of the people we looked up to at school, namely, our British teachers. And the language of the movies we went to and of the glamorous worlds in which they were set, and of the books we read and *their* enticing imaginary worlds.

At home we spoke Arabic and French as well as English. At home, too, though, English soon became the favorite language of us children for speaking among ourselves—chiefly because the adults around us, except Father, could not understand it. And so, since Father was often not home, English was from the start for us a language of subversion and a way of circumventing and baffling the adults around us and of communicating around them. Sometimes we spoke English with Father. With our mother we almost always spoke Arabic and, if not that, French.

Nor was it only the Arabic language that became implicitly

marked as inferior (and presumably marked as *native* and inferior). I think we heard Arabic music, too, as somehow lesser. It is probably for this reason that I do not now remember any, not a single one, of the songs my mother sang. She had a lovely voice. I remember how its sweetness arrested me, held me still. I remember other songs, other musics of childhood, but I can't recall even one of the lyrics my mother sang.

Father admired Mother's voice enormously and would say that she could have been a professional singer. "But Mother was not a professional anything!" I find myself involuntarily thinking, in a thought that is really only an echo or ghost of an old thought that I once harbored intensely and angrily as an adolescent. Such thoughts live on and shape how we see our past, even when we know them to be products of false perceptions and old, unexamined prejudices— prejudices even against our own kind and the most cherished people in our lives.

When my mother listened to the Egyptian singer Um Kulsum, the singer whom she and everyone else in Egypt admired, or to others (Asmahan was another favorite), she listened mostly alone. Sometimes, though, she and her sisters and other women relatives would gather together to make an evening of it, listening to one of Um Kulsum's concerts the first Thursday of every month. They would sit, consuming coffee and lemonade, smoking, relishing this singing as if it were some rich and subtle feast. To us children, it sounded like endless monotonous wailing. And we took care to make this plain to our schoolmates, sighing and rolling our eyes when we heard it. They did much the same, particularly the children of Egyptians and other Arabs attending the English School. It was common, this show of looking down on Arabic music, among English Schoolers. Arabic music was the music of the streets, the music one heard blaring from radios in the *baladi*, the unsophisticated folk regions of town.

But Mother was not, in our eyes, *baladi*. She quite distinctly and also quite self-consciously belonged to a culture and background quite different from the folk culture around us. Still, the fact that Mother loved Arabic music and sang in Arabic, and even the fact that we nearly always spoke to her in Arabic, undoubtedly marked her, too, in some way silently, silently in my child's mind, as inferior.

It would be decades before I would come to reflect on these issues in my own life. When I began to look in my academic work at issues of colonialism and began to unmask the colonialist perspectives and racism embedded in texts on Arabs and on the colonized, steeping myself in writings on internalized colonialism, I began to realize that it was not only in texts that these hidden messages were inscribed but that they were there, too, in my own childhood and in the very roots of my consciousness. I had grown up, I came to see, in a world where people, or at any rate my father, had not merely admired European civilization but had probably internalized the colonial beliefs about the superiority of European civilization. My mother, who always distinctly kept herself at a distance from Europeans and their ways and who always also explicitly cherished and honored her own heritage, never became suspect in my mind for having had a colonized consciousness in the way that my father did.

It was excruciatingly hard to find myself having to conclude that my father, whom I had admired for his integrity, clarity of vision, and open-mindedness, had after all, and in spite of himself, had a colonized consciousness, cherishing things European and undervaluing the very heritage that had shaped him. Now I no longer struggle with this. I have been through many revolutions in my understanding of my father, my mother, and my own consciousness—understanding them now this way, now that, convinced at one moment that they are this and at another that they are that. For the truth is, I think that we are always plural. Not either this *or* that, but this *and* that. And we always embody in our multiple shifting consciousnesses a convergence of traditions, cultures, histories coming together in this time and this place and moving like rivers through us. And I know now that the point is to look back with insight and without judgment, and I know now that it is of the nature of being in this place, this place of convergence of histories, cultures, ways of thought, that there will always be new ways to understand what we are living through, and that I will never come to a point of rest or of finality in my understanding.

Once I had arrived at this point I began to be able to reflect on, and for the first time to see, events in the past with clarity and even to remember things that I had forgotten. For example, I remembered that my parents had arranged when I was a child for my uncle to tutor me in Arabic (which he did, albeit without, for all his valiant efforts, inspiring in one much enthusiasm for Arabic grammar). And that in adolescence I'd been given a professional private teacher of Arabic. I learned very little from him because I was chiefly occupied during our sessions with figuring out how to stay beyond reach of his wandering hands groping at me under the table as I inched my chair away from him. Feeling somehow shamed by his behavior, I was unable to tell anyone what was happening but announced one day that I was not going to take any more Arabic lessons; I remained adamant on the subject. But for many years I had forgotten that I had this teacher and had forgotten that I had myself stopped the lessons and had forgotten why I had done so, my mind attributing my lack of fluency in written Arabic to my parents' neglect of that language.

And then, fortuitously, a little later I came to learn why we had not been sent to the *kuttab*, the traditional Quranic school, for a few hours each week, as some of my schoolmates had been, to learn classical Arabic and the Quran. A friend visiting me from Cairo, more skilled than I at deciphering cursive Arabic, looked through my father's memoir and read me a few pages in which he described his own experience of the *kuttab*. Daily he dreaded going because the teacher kept a thick stick at his side with which he would whack the boys if they were not properly memorizing their lessons. Father himself could recite the entire Quran by the time he was eight, but he had no idea at that age what any of it meant. When he grew up, he vowed never to subject his own children to such an experience. He decided, too, that the one thing he wanted them to have was a garden, a place where body and imagination could run free. Listening to my friend read these words I found myself intuitively understanding that English and all the English books with which Father had surrounded us had been intended to serve exactly the same purpose as the garden: to nourish and free imagination.

~~

This, then, was what I returned to. Ain Shams under a pall of gloom, my father dying, the best of the past vanishing in decay, in disarray, turning, like the bitter fruit of the fabled *al-zaqqum* (the tree that grows in the bottommost pit of hell), to dust in one's mouth.

Unable to leave, I took a teaching position at the newly opened women's college at al-Azhar University. But almost every moment I wasn't teaching I'd be at the Mugammaa, trying desperately to secure my passport and a way out of Egypt. The Mugammaa, a vast building dominating Tahrir (Liberation) Square, was the country's bureaucratic center, where all the bits of paper that ruled people's lives were processed. In the Nasser era, at least in my experience, it became a place of nightmare, where the country's already notoriously complicated bureaucratic system became one of the tools with which the government controlled and punished dissidents and others it disliked by denying their applications without explanation or simply stalling under endless pretexts. It became, with its innumerable cell-like windows dominating Tahrir Square, the emblem and, for me, the very heart of the revolution's abuse of power and of its concealed, diffuse malevolence.

Every day I would be referred from office to office to office and from one floor to the next and the next, then told to come back *bokra*—tomorrow—or next week. Some further signature was required and the relevant person was not there that day, some bit of paper was missing, or, as I was told eventually, my application was on the minister's desk but for some reason—no one knew why—he was not signing it. For four years I was put through this. It was not that I was denied a passport. I was simply unable to get one. It was obvious that it was not merely bureaucratic convolutedness that stood in my way but an intentional political will to deny my father's daughter her freedom.

I refused to give up. It was not a choice for me. As month after month and then year after year passed, I simply would not give up. Everyone around me began to urge me to face reality, resign myself to the inevitable, settle down and accept what I was obviously going to have to accept—that I was not going to be able to leave and not going to be able to continue my studies abroad. Relatives and friends remonstrated with me and treated me as unreasonable for being so utterly and relentlessly determined to leave—everyone, that is, except my father. My father alone seemed completely to empathize with my yearnings and my refusal to give up, even though, as time wore on, that refusal was in some sense "unreasonable" or, at any rate, unrealistic.

I've never been sure why I could not take no for an answer. Being compelled to stay in Egypt, being compelled to give up my studies, felt to me like a sentence of doom. There's no doubt that my family's difficulties in Nasser's Egypt and the bleakness of the future I myself now faced there were key in my determination to get out, as were my hopes and ambitions for professional and intellectual development. But it was more than that. I needed to understand myself and I believed that the path to understanding lay in returning to England and to graduate studies there. I believed, moreover, that I would not find that same understanding in a university in Egypt.

There was something else, too, a shadow always there, adding to my sense of desperate resolve. My aunt Aida had committed suicide a few months after I had come home to Egypt. I had grieved at her death, and now her despair became hauntingly real to me. I feared that a despair like that might overtake me if I found myself trapped in Egypt forever, unable to go on with my life. Aunt Aida had felt trapped in a life that she did not want and that finally became completely unendurable to her.

Her example, always there before me, terrified me and made me all the more resolute.

I was going to leave, no matter what. Once it was obvious that it was not just inefficient bureaucracy that was holding me up (I had the required scholarship—from the British Council—and had fulfilled every other condition that the government officially required for a passport), I began trying other avenues. Resorting to the *wasta* approach of getting things done through connections, one of the normal ways of pursuing one's affairs in Egypt, I begged and badgered relatives and family friends to inquire into my case or get me appointments myself with this undersecretary or that minister.

It was one of those meetings that would lead finally to my release. A man who was an engineer by training and who privately though not publicly supported my father over the High Dam became a minister, and I managed to obtain a meeting with him. At the end of it, as we shook hands, his eyes alive with sympathy, he said that if I was anything like as brilliant as my father it would be a crime to prevent me from pursuing my studies. The following day my exit permit was signed.

This man remained in office only a few months. I had been struck at our meeting by his courage in even indirectly acknowledging the value of my father's work and his service to the country. Nobody wanted to be known to be supporting, or even to be respectful of, someone who was the object of Nasser's fury. Occasionally in those days when I was introduced or gave my name somewhere, someone would react with visible emotion—shaking my hand fervently, telling me how deeply they admired my father and how much it meant to them that my father had taken the stand that he had. But always when this happened we would be in some private venue, not in a public place—and certainly not in a government office.

This resolution to my passport difficulties had a further blessing. It helped dissolve Father's sense that, as he once said to me, my future had been the sacrifice made to his conscience. While so many others had insisted that I be more "realistic" and set aside the dream of continuing my studies abroad, while so many others had urged me to reconcile myself to the fact that I was not going to be able to study abroad, never for a moment had Father wavered in his support for my efforts, sharing with me always the hope that perhaps this time I would manage to get a passport and sharing, too, in my despair when, time after time, I failed. I remember how one morning when things

had gone particularly badly at the Mugammaa and I went out to Ain
Shams with my story, Father began to cry as I told him of my plight.
He asked me to forgive him: he had not meant to do this to my life
and he hoped that some day when I was older I'd understand why he
had done what he had done. But of course I told him I already
understood.

I also remember vividly the last meeting he and I had. I'd come
to say goodbye. He was well enough to be out of bed and was sitting
in the upstairs hallway, looking somewhat gray. He would not look at
me and was extraordinarily offhand, gruff even, he who was usually
so warm and so openly affectionate. I was taken aback and a little
hurt, until I encountered his eyes, casting me a quick, brief glance
from under his lashes. And then I understood. It was in his eyes, the
acknowledgment that he and I would never see each other again and
that this was no ordinary goodbye.

The last time I heard his voice was about a year later. I was in
England working desperately hard to get myself registered quickly for
a doctoral degree instead of the M.Litt. that beginning students are
registered for until they prove their worth. I so hoped to be able to
tell him before he died that I had succeeded in this. But it did not
happen, not in time. The call came through from Cairo, my mother's
voice saying that Daddy wanted to talk to me.

"Hello, Nana darling," I heard him say, his voice so tender. That
was all. She must have held the phone for him.

He died the following day.

On March 9. Or maybe it was March 11. My mother died exactly
two years later. Or almost exactly. On the ninth, or the eleventh, or
the twenty-somethingth. Later, when I could not remember the exact
day, I tried to calculate it, to think what day of the week it had been
and so what day of the month. I could never quite get it straight, and
there was no one to ask. No one in the place where I lived then knew
them. No one mourned, at least not in the world around me. And
without mourning and without the visible grief of those like me who
had been left behind, my parents' deaths felt quite unreal for a long
time, as if they had not died at all but just somehow vanished.

"I was never certain that mother had died," wrote Emily Dickinson in a letter to a friend. Except, she went on, in those moments when she listened to the choir singing, their voices so clearly coming "from another life."

Sometimes even when we have heard the choir sing it is still hard to believe that the dead are dead.

2

*F*ROM *C*OLONIAL TO *P*OSTCOLONIAL

THE SUEZ CRISIS of 1956 would come to be thought of by those who lived through it and also by historians of empire as the pivotal moment that heralded the final passing of the European empires, when the world moved irrevocably from the colonial to the postcolonial age. In fact, there still were many countries under European domination, but Suez became a symbolic and important date above all because it marked the moral defeat of the European powers and the public exposure, on the world stage, of their hectoring tyranny toward countries under their dominion. It also made plain their open greed, their brazen abuse of power, and their moral bankruptcy.

Nasser, who had precipitated the crisis, would emerge as its hero. The sequence of events is well known. In June 1956, Nasser announced in a speech that he was nationalizing the Suez Canal and appropriating its revenues for Egypt—revenues that had been going, unjustly, to Britain and France. The British and French denounced his act and issued threats, and in October, joined by Israel, they launched a military attack on Egypt. The spectacle of two of the world's mightiest powers combining to attack the small nation of Egypt, in collusion with Egypt's new neighbor, had the effect of demonstrating to the entire watching world how unjust and bullying, and how immoral, the European imperial powers actually were. The outcry was worldwide. Not only were Third World nations unanimous in their condemnation but there were huge demonstrations in Britain and France, and in Britain, at any rate, resignations by major political players. American action brought the attack to a halt and compelled the withdrawal of the aggressors.

In Egypt Nasser emerged triumphant as the leader who had dared to stand up to the imperial tyrants. Even prior to Suez his call for Arab nationalism had begun to gain him a considerable following outside Egypt. Now, his heroic stature enormously magnified throughout the Arab world and beyond, he became politically unassailable within Egypt. Henceforth he ruled openly as dictator and his government became more and more overtly repressive.

Besides transforming Nasser into a national and Arab hero, Suez seemed also to give new impetus to the struggles against imperialism already under way around the globe and to spur opposition to imperialism within the imperialist nations themselves. In the late fifties and through the sixties, struggles against imperialism grew fiercer and more determined everywhere, and country after country in Africa and elsewhere gained independence. In Britain and France, leftist intellectuals supported the struggle against colonialism. In France, for instance, as the savage battle for Algerian independence moved toward its climax, leftist intellectuals—Sartre, Camus, and de Beauvoir among them—came out in support of the Algerians. By the time I finally obtained a passport and returned to college in England in the late sixties, Frantz Fanon, the philosopher and theorist of the colonial condition, was among the most admired voices among intellectuals, while anti-imperialism, Marxism, and socialism had become the politics and the intellectual positions of the avant-garde.

Thus began the era that would give rise to the critiques of colonialism that would lay bare its huge costs—psychological, cultural, political, and economic. And we began, through the new lenses and insights of figures such as Fanon, as well as Paolo Friere, Alberto Memmi, and Edward Said, analysts all of colonialism and its consequences, to interrogate, reinterpret, and reevaluate the lives and work of the generations that preceded us. And we began also to look with new eyes at the lives of our parents and grandparents, the generations in which our own lives were rooted, and to see what they apparently had not seen, the psychological consequences of colonialism and that silent, insidious process of internalized colonialism.

Reflecting on all this and thinking back to my father, I had a sense of how enormously complex these issues were. The members of his own and of the preceding generation had undoubtedly internalized colonialism, possibly more fully than we had, and certainly in any case they had been less analytically conscious of the psychological processes they were subject to than those of us of Fanon's and of subsequent generations. I thought, for example, not only of my father but of the man whom Father had admired above anyone else, Gandhi. I thought of how Gandhi himself, when he had started out as a young man, had dressed not in the familiar loincloth but in the starched collar and suit of the English gentleman that he had at first striven hard to become. And yet, for all that, it is they far more than we who had remained more deeply rooted in their own heritages and their different ways of seeing. Gandhi, for all his exposure to and assimilation of European ideas, did end his days in a loincloth and he came to draw fully and explicitly on the understanding of life, both Hindu and Jain, in which he had been nurtured.

Similarly Hasan Fathy, the Egyptian architect who in the forties pioneered the return to the use of traditional materials and to ecologically sound as well as aesthetically satisfying indigenous forms in architecture—an approach eventually adopted globally, particularly in Third World countries—seems to have done so by tapping into another heritage, a way of seeing other than that of the modern West. Thoroughly versed in Western architectural ideas, he developed his innovative views and methods in reflecting on the fact that, as he wrote, "the peasant built his house out of mud, or mud bricks, which he dug out of the ground and dried in the sun. Here, for years, for centuries, the peasant has been wisely and quietly exploiting the obvious building materials, while we, with our modern school-learned ideas, never dreamed of using such a ludicrous substance as mud for so serious a creation as a house."

Father, too, quite possibly owed his own innovativeness—antici-
pating, as he did, the ecological understanding that was to become
an ordinary way of seeing in our day—to his rootedness in his own
tradition and perhaps even to his thorough immersion in the language
and thought of the Quran, with its sense of the profound connectedness of all life and all the processes to which we are subject. Thinking about a dam, he considered earth, river, sea, fish, organisms, and
people and thus came up with an "ecological" understanding long
before "ecology" was a common concept. Interestingly, those who
have studied Rachel Carson, Barbara McClintock, and other women
pioneers of Western scientific thought have suggested that the origi-
nality of these women sprang in part from their rootedness in a different cultural ethos—a women's ethos of connectedness—different
from the ethos of competitiveness and individualism of the men of
their culture.

No doubt about it, though, my father did love science.

He grew up in a world in which the inventions of science and the
ways of the West were quite visibly transforming the world around
him. Cairo in the late nineteenth and early twentieth centuries was
exuberantly surging forward in acquiring these "modern" ways. Already a few decades before my father was born, the Khedive Ismael,
ruler of Egypt (*khedive* is a Turkish title for "sovereign"), after a visit
to Paris, had ordered the construction of a new section of Cairo—
today the heart of the modern city—to be laid out with boulevards,
wooded parks, and streetlights. He was eager to show the European
royalty who were coming to Egypt to attend the celebrations for the
opening of the Suez Canal in 1869 just how modern and "European"
Egypt was.

The Khedive Ismael was by no means alone in his attitude. In
those days the Egyptian elite and intelligentsia pursued and believed
in the idea of Egypt as a rapidly advancing nation, as dedicated to
"progress" and to becoming fully "modern" as any of the "civilized"
nations of Europe. Consequently, they believed (much as the intelligentsia of Turkey today believe of their country) that Egypt should

take its place and be accepted by the European Powers as, to all intents and purposes, a "European" nation. European domination was still new to Egyptians. They had not grasped or even remotely begun to surmise that in European eyes there was one thing that defined them as unalterably and ineluctably different, unalterably and ineluctably *unlike* Europeans and unalterably and ineluctably inferior—their race. They had not yet understood that this was what defined them in the European gaze and that nothing would make them "civilized" and "modern" in European eyes. They did not know that nothing else counted, not "progress" or "development" or "modernity," just race.

In any case, by the mid–nineteenth century, Egypt had indeed already been forging rapidly forward in the adoption of modern ways and technologies, leading the way among Muslim and eastern Mediterranean countries, ahead even of Turkey. It had begun to make enormous strides in the acquisition of European know-how under its dynamic ruler, Muhammad Ali, who had become governor of Egypt in 1805. He opened schools and colleges staffed by Europeans and sent student missions to Europe to acquire and bring home its sciences. By mid-century, Egypt was on a par with European nations like Italy and indeed ahead of others. Trains, for example, linked the vital centers of Cairo and Alexandria before railways were introduced in Norway. By then, too, the country had begun to move forward in the establishment of industries, until Britain, alarmed at the prospect of an industrialized Egypt capturing Middle Eastern markets away from British exports, exerted pressure on the Ottoman sultan to put a halt to Egypt's developing capabilities.

By midcentury, a growing body of Egyptian intellectuals who had studied in Europe and were familiar with Western ideas were coming to constitute a significant political and intellectual leadership in the country and to advocate various reforms. By the time my father was a young man, there had been two or three generations of such intelligentsia, among whom there was a consensus as to the kind of society Egypt should aspire to become: a fully modern European-style country, committed to freedom of speech and free public education, to the modernization of the role of women and the ending of the practice of veiling, and to government by democracy. This tradition of thought, a dominant tradition within Egypt when my parents were young, would shape their generation. And in my own family anyway, they would remain deeply committed to these ideals and aspirations all their lives.

While Egypt had begun its march into modernity under its Turkish rulers, by the end of the nineteenth century it was the British who were in power. The British Occupation of Egypt began in 1882, when the Khedive Tewfiq appealed to the British for help in putting down a native rebellion. In response, the British bombarded Alexandria and landed their troops in the country. The rebellion that the British helped suppress had been led by Colonel Urabi, one of only two native Egyptians who had risen to the rank of colonel in the Egyptian army. In those days, when Egypt was still part of the Ottoman Empire, not only was Turkey and its imperial capital of Istanbul the ultimate political authority over Egypt, but within Egypt, too, the ruling class was essentially Turkish. And according to the laws of the land, native Egyptians were prohibited from holding senior positions in either the government or the army. All such positions could be held only by Turks. But Urabi and the other native Egyptian colonel had risen to their rank because these laws had begun to fall into disuse. The government, controlled of course by Turks, was now proposing to reinstitute laws prohibiting Egyptians from holding senior positions. It was this that had triggered the rebellion.

Thus, in any case, had begun the official British Occupation. Once the British troops were on Egyptian soil, Egypt began in effect to be governed by the British, though it continued officially to be considered not a colony of Britain but what it had been for several centuries, a province of the Ottoman Empire. While some in the country would always hate the infidel British presence, others, and in particular a growing number of the intelligentsia, did not. For one thing, Egypt in some ways prospered economically under the British. The British invested Egypt's resources in projects, such as irrigation and road construction, that brought prosperity, at least for some, and that developed the country as a producer of raw materials, in particular cotton, for British industries. But conversely, the British continued their policy of not allowing Egypt to develop as an industrial nation, a policy whose costs to the country are more obvious to us now than they were to the people of those earlier generations. And the British held back and even cut funding from other projects, such as education, essential for Egypt's long-term prosperity.

But at the time what was obvious and palpable to Egyptians, especially the elite and the rising middle classes of Cairo, was that Egypt was becoming prosperous. In addition, although Lord Cromer, the British consul general in Egypt and in effect the country's governor from 1882 to 1907, was distinctly autocratic, British rule was still more benign and more beneficial to the country (or so some of the intelligentsia believed) than despotic rule by one Ottoman sultan or another or by the local monarch who served as his representative. Moreover, under the British, Egypt enjoyed for the first time ever a free press, chiefly because Cromer believed that what Egyptians thought did not matter and that, on the other hand, having a free press would be useful because it would provide a safety valve. Cairo was the only capital in the Ottoman world with a free press, and consequently it became a magnet for the literati of the Arabic-speaking world. Major publishing houses in Damascus and Beirut moved their presses to Cairo. The result was that Egypt enjoyed a thriving press vibrantly alive with free debate, and it became the venue of an outpouring of books, newspapers, and magazines that included fierce criticism of the British, on the one hand, and open criticism of the traditional system of despotic rule, on the other.

Egypt's prosperity, rapid modernization, and open society attracted many immigrants, not only from the Ottoman territories but also and particularly from Europe. For under the British the laws were skewed in favor of Europeans. They were exempt from paying taxes and could not be prosecuted by any local court—even for murder. Not surprisingly, Italians, Greeks, and Maltese, as well as French and British, flocked to Egypt.

Not everyone, though, benefited from the country's prosperity.

Middle-class people like my father, who managed to get a modern education and thus to join the professional classes, did well, and so did the landed classes, who benefited from the improved irrigation projects and transport systems in which the British invested the country's revenues. But for common working peasants it was a time of dire hardship and dispossession. They were heavily taxed, and many of those unable to pay fled their land, making their way to the capital, where they found refuge in the abandoned areas of Old Cairo, with its winding medieval alleys, or in the ramshackle constructions put up on the outskirts to house them. The ever-expanding modern Cairo, with its handsome new apartment blocks and gardened mansions on the Nile, was where the Europeans, the old upper classes, and the rising professionals made their homes. The luckier ones among the destitute country migrants found domestic work in the houses of the well-to-do in the new, other Cairo.

It was, then, for some, an exhilarating time to be young. It was a time of hope, when all sorts of ideas—democracy, women's rights, new personal freedoms for men and women, the casting off of the veil—were in the air and being freely discussed in a press avidly read by the young. And it was a time when everywhere there were signs of the improvements that the coming of the West and its modern ways was poised (apparently) to bring to all of humanity. Pipes were being laid for internal plumbing in people's houses, streetlights were going up, and tramways began running. Cars made their appearance on Cairo's streets almost as soon as they did in the capitals of Europe. And Egypt was prosperous.

A moment in my own memory connects me with that era and with the sense of a new world that young people like my father must have had. I was sitting in the car with my father and we were driving in from the outskirts toward the center of Cairo. Our route took us past the king's Ubba Palace. As we drew nearer, the rough potholed road turned into a smooth, elegant avenue running the length of the palace gardens—gardens that were invisible to us behind their high ochre walls except for a luxuriance of foliage that here and there spilled over. A couple of cars, no more, passed us, going in the opposite direction, their headlights in the gathering dusk picking out the rare figure of a trudging pedestrian. As we reached the end of the avenue, I noticed a not-unfamiliar sight in the Cairo of those days: a young man standing on the median leaning against a lamppost, reading by its light. My father, at this point in his life a solidly established member of the middle class, chairman of the Nile Water Control Board, former dean of the Faculty of Engineering, said to me, "That's how I did my homework at his age." It was obviously not an unhappy memory, for he chuckled to himself as he added, "In those days I thought I was lucky to live in a district where there were streetlamps to study by."

My father's older brother had taken him in when their father died. That brother, who was himself scarcely more than a boy, finding himself now having to provide for the family and perennially short of cash, had considered it a waste of money for his younger brother to burn lights at home, reading.

Their father had been a qadi, a judge. Just months before his death he had been appointed to a prestigious new post on the Islamic High Court in the capital. My father remembered traveling to Cairo from his native Alexandria and moving into a house arrestingly lovely, with its vivid, glowing carpets and its fine, dazzling chandeliers. Then, suddenly, his father died.

But for my grandfather's death, my father, his brightest son, might have followed in his footsteps and become a mufti (a religious leader and scholar of the law), the profession that the men of the family had practiced in a tradition going back (according to family legend) to the time when they had fled the Spanish Inquisition, settling first in Morocco and then making their way to Alexandria. But soon after his father's death my father transferred to a modern school. It was there that my father had his first encounter with things English, in the person of a British teacher.

Gazing at this figure, embodiment, in his complexion, language, and dress, of the different world and its enticing ways now palpably encroaching on the local world, the child would be immensely taken by the man's impeccable "modern" dress (as he would later recall in the faded pencil-scrawled pages of his memoir). All his life my father would himself be an impeccable dresser, in European-style suits, which soon became the ordinary dress of the professional as well as the upper classes. Only the tarboosh, the fez that my father wore to work, would be retained of the old ways. My grandfather, on the other hand, must have dressed in the kaftan and turban that were traditional for a mufti and scholar. My father does not set down how old he was when he first donned this new and evidently much-coveted attire. One can imagine him, however, standing, adjusting it, looking at himself in the mirror, now the very embodiment himself of the new and "modern" man.

I believe that my father, from a very young age, fell in love with science and with the world that it unveiled. He would one day hang in his study a portrait of Isaac Newton that encapsulated, even for me as a child, the wondrousness of science. Newton stands in a library, holding a prism in the path of a beam of light, which emerges on the other side split rainbow-like into a band of colors.

Father would devote his life to harnessing these invisible forces that science had revealed. He would do so in the service of the community, through the construction of dams and the development of irrigation and electrification projects linked to the Nile. A huge geological map of the Nile in its entire course hung on the wall beside his desk. He had explored the river, too, in its full length, by steamer. Photographs in our family album recorded that journey: in the backgrounds of photos of himself and of the more numerous ones of his assistants were the sails of feluccas and the fertile riverbanks, the black granite boulders of Aswan, palm trees, and barren hills in the distance; and then jungles, a dead lion and a man holding a gun, and waterfalls and lakes. The map, in contrast, was mostly sand-colored, its empty, pale ochre spaces marked here and there with swaths of deeper ochre and cut into by the contours and traceries following out the flow of river.

Eventually, too, as I said earlier, Father would spend his last days trying to prevent the catastrophic destruction that the insensitive, unimaginative misuse of these forces could wreak.

I wish that he had lived to know that he had, in fact, been in the forefront of a new kind of thinking. But he did not. The only consolation he enjoyed in that last period was the entirely meager one afforded by the fact that certain words in the Bible seemed to offer confirmation of his views. The Egyptians would build dams, the passage said ("turn away the rivers"), and this would bring destruction. The passage occurs in Isaiah. Once or twice, when he was well enough to sit up in his room wrapped in his dressing gown, quietly enjoying the winter sunlight, he asked me to find them for him again and read them to him. These gloomy prognostications would give him brief pleasure, but pleasure evidently—and of course inevitably—that was at best a mixed, ambiguous pleasure, accompanied always also by a shaking of the head at the folly and tragedy of it all.

There was only one other picture in Father's study of someone who was not a family member. This was a photograph of Mahatma Gandhi, lying on his funeral pyre and covered with flowers.

~

Christians' hatred for Muslims is as intense and fanatical today as it was in the days of the Crusades. Fanaticism still abides in their tissues, permeates their entrails, and circulates in their veins.

Ahmad Amin, an Egyptian contemporary of my father's, wrote these words in the early 1950s, when disillusionment with the West had begun to set in deeply, even among this earlier generation of intellectuals who, whatever reservations they had, nevertheless still admired the West and believed that Egypt should follow in its footsteps. (Amin, a conservative Muslim thinker, had from the start both admired the West and cautioned against too wholesale an imitation of Western ways.)

But these are words such as I never heard—and cannot imagine—my father uttering. Although I often heard him speak critically of British political duplicity and injustice, I never heard him speak in this comprehensively dismissive way of Christians or of the West generally. Possibly this was because in his own life and in the battles he had to fight, Egyptians as well as British had been corrupt, and Muslims as well as Christians had been tyrannical, unjust, and destructive. Years before tangling with Nasser, Father had run into difficulties with King Farouk. Father had refused to endorse some engineering scheme that a British firm had put forward with the support of the king, a scheme from which both the firm and the king stood to make a lot of money and that was essentially, my father believed, a scam. Father was fired from his job on trumped-up charges to make way for someone who would endorse the scheme. For a number of years then, in the 1940s, he had to earn his living abroad. The rest of us stayed in Egypt and he would come back every few months to see us, arriving with suitcases filled with gifts. In Cairo, meanwhile, the charges against him were investigated and he was eventually reinstated and fully exonerated.

Certainly my father had himself personally suffered British injustice. It had been the British who, in his youth, had nearly put an end to his dreams of becoming an engineer. After graduating from the College of Engineering in Cairo, he had won a scholarship to continue his studies in England. The British Administration had demanded, as a condition of his taking up the scholarship, that he abandon engineering and study geography. He had no choice, and so he agreed. And he did for a time study geography. He might even have obtained a degree in the subject, though that I am not sure of. But somehow he managed to get back to the subject he loved and not only obtained a degree in it but also distinguished himself at his university— Birmingham—as a singular and brilliant student. Father's reading of why the British had tried to obstruct his training as an engineer was that they wanted to prevent natives from acquiring such skills so that the country would have to continue to depend on British know-how. That was the way the British were in those days, he said. Unjust in their dealings with Egyptians, trying one way or another to hold onto the country for themselves.

I know also that the events of Dinshwai, which occurred when
he was a youngster, were landmark events in his consciousness, as
they were for that entire generation. I remember hearing him and
others talking of the great tragedy of Dinshwai one evening when we
were sitting in our beach cabin in Alexandria. I was too young to
follow what they were saying and had to look up recently what exactly
happened in Dinshwai, a small village in the Delta. It had all begun
when some British officers decided that they wanted to go out pigeon
shooting. This sport of the British was not popular among the villagers
because to them pigeons were creatures they kept and bred in dovecotes on the roofs of their mud-brick huts. The shoot, in any case,
went forward, and in the course of it a barn in the village caught fire.
The villagers, blaming the officers, came out and began to beat them
with sticks. One officer escaped and, running back to camp in the
heat of noon, collapsed and died. A passing peasant, seeing him fall,
ran up to help him. At that moment a group of British soldiers
emerged and, seeing the two figures, assumed that the peasant had
killed the officer—and killed him.

No one was ever tried for the death of the peasant. The death of
the officer, however, was treated by the British as a heinous crime
against the Occupier, and they created a special tribunal to deal with
it. From the start they seemed determined to use the trial to make an
example of the villagers. Fifty men were charged with premeditated
murder—rather than manslaughter. The defense tried to no avail to
show that the circumstances had been fortuitous and the attack un-
planned. Long before the court reached its verdict the British Administration, as the papers reported, ordered the erection of gallows
outside Dinshwai. The villagers—men, women, and children—were
to be compelled, the Administration had decided, to watch the pun-
ishment and execution. When the verdict came in, amid the tears and
screams of the villagers, four men were hanged, and seventeen others
savagely and repeatedly whipped before being taken off to serve sen-
tences, some of penal servitude for life.

The drama unfolded, followed daily by everyone in the country,
through June—and then the whole country plunged into mourning.

All Egyptians, it seemed, would remember where they were and what they were doing when they heard the news of Dinshwai. Ahmad Amin was at a dinner party on the roof terrace of a friend's house in Alexandria. It was June 27, 1906. When the news arrived, "the banquet turned into a funeral and most of us wept." Salama Musa, another contemporary of my father's, also was in Alexandria. He had gone out for a walk with his brother and they had stopped to eat at a restaurant. There, purchasing a newspaper, he read the verdict and was overcome. For days, he wrote, he was unable to eat because of the rage he felt at those "who had so brutally wronged our people." Even the British, wrote Musa, seemed ashamed of what they had done, though in England the British foreign secretary, as Musa recalled, tried to justify Cromer's conduct by stating that such tough action had been necessary because "Islamic fanaticism was flaring up all over North Africa." Musa, a Copt, was thoroughly disgusted at the fabrication of a nonexistent Islamic enemy to justify savagery, injustice, and inhumanity.

In the ensuing years, Egyptian politicians would go on to negotiate with the British for Egypt's independence and, by the end of World War I, would bring about a partial British withdrawal. It was soon thereafter that Egypt's experiment in democracy would begin.

There was one further major change under way that would critically affect my father's life, and indeed my own. This was the ending of the old system of separation between the Turkish upper classes and native Egyptians.

Through the first decades of this century intermarriage between these two groups became more and more common. As the new class of Egyptian professional men rose through the ranks to positions of power and authority, they consolidated their new status by marrying the daughters of the Turkish upper classes. They themselves sought out such marriages, but they, too—able, hardworking men distinguishing themselves in their professions and clearly on their way up in society—were sought out by the Turkish elite. Ambitious Egyptians pursued educations and professional lives with a zest and dedication that many of their aristocratic Turkish brothers, secure in their inherited wealth, lacked.

Rising through the ranks, establishing himself in life, helping his younger brother get an education, my father, too, consolidated his status in life by marrying the daughter of an upper-class Turkish family. Aziz—"beloved," "dear one"—my mother would call him, abbreviating his full name, Abdel Aziz. Her own name, Ikbal, was unusual, a gender-neutral one as often a man's as a woman's. Mother's family's wealth, like that of most such families in Egypt, was in land. They owned a fine estate, devoted mainly to growing fruit—grapes, oranges, tangerines, bananas—in the fertile oasis of al-Fayyum.

$\mathscr{I}$N $\mathscr{E}$XPECTATION OF $\mathscr{A}$NGELS

I REMEMBER IT AS A TIME, that era of my childhood, when existence itself seemed to have its own music—a lilt and music that made up the ordinary fabric of living. There was the breath of the wind always, and the perpetual murmur of trees; the call of the *karawan* that came in the dusk, dying with the dying light; the reed-piper playing his pipe in the dawn and, throughout the day, the music of living: street-vendors' calls; people passing in the street, talking; the clip-clop of a donkey; the sound of a motor car; dogs barking; the cooing of pigeons in the siesta hour.

Night too had its varieties of music. The clack of the wooden clogs of village women returning home, sometimes singly, sometimes in pairs, from work or from errands among the shops in the suburb of Matariyya. And the sound, as much a part of summer nights as the croaking of frogs, of the neighbors' waterwheel creaking gently, turned by an ox whose eyes were blinkered so he would not know he was going round and round rather than forward. The neighbors had a mango grove within the dried mud walls of their land. Along one of those walls, directly opposite my bedroom window, was a stream bordered on its other side by the mud wall and fruit garden of the next neighbors. The stream, dark and still and edged with reeds, disappeared beyond the walls into open fields. It was all that remained, I was told, of the canal that had run parallel to our house until just before I was born. The canal was filled in and a road built at about the time that a railway line was laid down on the other side of our house, linking the suburbs and the distant country centers beyond our house with Cairo and with Maadi on the other side of Cairo.

In the depths of the night, one also sometimes heard hyenas somewhere out on the distant edge of the villages, in the heart of the countryside, and very occasionally but so faintly that they were like a beat on the membrane of night, one could hear drums: a village wedding. There would be pipe music, too, but only a note here and there carried to us; what one heard, or sensed rather, were the drums. The drums, I do not know why, awoke in me a kind of obscure terror. I did not think, I am frightened of the drums. Instead they seemed to bring alive in me the hidden and muffled terrors that inhered in and threaded our ordinary living. Terrors above all about death, whose presence was there in our lives in myriad ways, but also of other things, the vagaries, for instance, of why things were the way they were—the beggars, the blind, the cripples, or even just the poor and the villagers themselves, and what it was that kept us on one side of the line and them on the other.

Privilege, in a setting where the deprivation of others is glaringly obvious, no doubt produces its own mesh of anxieties and perhaps also of guilt. What does a child make of seeing another child, just like herself, on the other side of the hedge, looking in at her, hollow-eyed, in rags, as she stops in her play to stare back? I imagine that the sense of terror and precariousness that seemed to have pervaded my childhood was not unconnected with whatever conclusions I drew about the mysterious arbitrary line that divided our lives and that could quite possibly at any moment shift—people are struck blind, die, in an instant.

Sometimes the sheer pain and terror of existence would be right out in the open, in the screams, for instance, that tore through the night once, in the darkest time before dawn, when our neighbor's ox somehow fell into the well by the waterwheel. He was dragged out dead and the women's wails were shrill and endless, like the wails of villagers and poor people over the death of a person. Another time it was in the day that the screams went up from another house, farther away but still piercing. A son of the house, a young man in his twenties, had committed suicide by drinking a bottle of Lysol.

And once someone was run over by a train just outside the large, disused iron gate to our garden, a gate that had been the main entrance before the canal was filled in and the railway built. That day, unusually, the gate was open, and I saw bloodstains on the road and here and there bloodied newspapers covering something, or some things, the mangled scattered bits of a person. (No one could figure out why he was run over. It might, someone speculated, have been a suicide. Or maybe his foot got stuck.) I was five or six. I literally shivered for days after that, although it must have been early summer. I remember that I would squeeze myself in beside my mother in the stuffed easy chair near the radio where she habitually sat. She comforted me, I remember, but I must have taxed her patience because I remember her saying, "It's just too hot, dear, I can't have you sticking to me like that!"

Other one-time events also happened on that side of the house, at that gate, which seemingly opened only for those occasions. I remember standing there once watching a train full of smiling, red-faced English soldiers chug slowly by. They called out and waved to us and threw chocolates; given their cheeriness and their dispensing of chocolates, this must have been close to the end of the Second World War. I was five in 1945.

Besides the drums, there was a whole variety of other beats and rhythms that marked and threaded our days and nights, and most were not frightening. Even the trains, despite that dreadful accident, were not frightening. They mostly passed at a comfortable chug, occasionally blowing their haunting whistles. It did happen sometimes (for no better reason, I think, than that the engine driver took it into his head to put on a sudden burst of speed) that the chug would turn into a loud, gathering, hurtling sound, as if some unearthly monster would shortly be upon us. The sound would cause us children to drop whatever we were doing and race to the top or bottom of the garden or of the stairs. Safety lay in getting to wherever it was before the hurtling monster was fully upon us.

And there was the regular beat of *al-makana*, "the machine," which pumped well water to the house and to the pond and garden and the various canals and waterways of earth and concrete that ran through it. Turned on every morning, it would come on again in the afternoons when the weather grew hot, so that summer afternoons were filled with the sound of hoses, running water, the regular fall of a spade, and, in the background, the phut-phut-phut of the machine. All these, the *makana* and the running water, were good sounds, re-assuring sounds, sounds about everything going forward in the way it should. Sometimes, though, the *makana* would pick up and inter-weave with the sound of one's heart. And for some reason, perhaps because I imagined the absence of that sound, the possibility of its ceasing, the sound of my own heartbeat reminded me of death.

The regularity of my own breath did not frighten me the way the sound of my heart sometimes did, but I remember listening for Nan-ny's breath, in the bed beside me, to make sure she was still alive. Nanny was sixty when I was born. She sat at the foot of our bed every night, reading her Latin Bible, turning its silky leaves, moving her lips sometimes in prayer. Her Bible had a picture of Jesus coming on clouds of glory, the light streaming out in bands from the clouds in a way that I'd never seen it do. I didn't believe that light could ever look like that, but when I got to England I discovered that that was exactly how it looked sometimes. Nanny would pause in her reading sometimes and say meditatively, *"Tu sais, Lili, moi je mourirai bientôt"* ("You know, Lili, I will die soon"). At times I would cry when she said this, and always I would beg her not to. I don't know if she said it to me in part because the depth of my distress reassured her or simply because the thought was on her mind. Perhaps a little of both.

I think that quite often when Nanny appeared to be talking to me she was, in fact, talking to herself and I was overhearing her inner monologues as I attended to my own thoughts and games. "I earn my living by the sweat of my brow," she often said, perhaps as she hung some washing (delicate items that no one else might wash) there in the sunny backyard, a cat or two rubbing back and forth across her legs, "and that is nothing to be ashamed of." She said this as if defending herself, as if some invisible interlocutor were suggesting otherwise. In truth, she rarely had anyone of her own age or background to talk to.

Still, I don't think she knew the depth of the misery she caused me by her ruminations. Her dying was my one great and secret dread in childhood. My one prayer, which I added secretly to the prayers that my sister would make me go over with her at the bottom of the stairs before I went up to bed (prayers that consisted of a litany of the names of the people we were asking God to protect: Mummy, Daddy, all of us children, Nanny, Enayat the maid, etc.), was that Nanny would not die before I was old enough to bear it. I told God that I had to be fifteen at a minimum. I think I believed that adults —which in my assessment meant anyone about fifteen or older—had less feeling than children.

It was on one such occasion, waking up in the middle of the night and lying still, listening for Nanny's breathing, that I saw my guardian angel, the angel that, Nanny had told me, was always there to protect me. It looked something like a moonbeam, standing still, touching the mosquito net by the foot of the bed. I did not dare put my head outside the mosquito net to get a better view, lest I drive it away. Yet even with all my longing to believe in my guardian angel, as well as a host of other unseen things—fairies, for example, which the books said you would see if you believed, if you looked in foxgloves, which we didn't have—and even as I made my eyes as wide as I possibly could, trying to see what exactly this angel looked like, there was deep within me a center of disbelief. It was an angel, I really had seen it, I would say to myself later, but some part of me still always thought that it was a moonbeam.

It was Nanny in particular who in some sense entered with me into the realm I inhabited where the demarcations between the realities in one's head and those that were solidly outside were matters as yet to be circumspectly investigated. The world we shared, or that she at least pretended to share with me, included ghouls as well as angels. When I dawdled about getting into bed she would threaten to call the ghoul, and if I persisted she would stick her head out the window on the street side and call "Gho-o-oul! Gho-o-oul!" getting me immediately into bed. I never, fortunately, saw a ghoul, but I did know where it would come from—from somewhere near where the drums and the hyenas were. It was Nanny, too, who told me stories in the days before I could read and maybe also after. The usual fairy tales, or versions of them. One of our favorites—she would cry when she came to the moving bits at the end—was a version of the story I encountered years later as *King Lear*. It was about a king who had three daughters. The first two, when he asked them how much they loved him, said more than rubies and diamonds and so on. Only the youngest refused to flatter him. She really loved him but would only say she loved him as much as salt; rubies and diamonds were nothing to her, she said, compared with salt. He became angry and exiled her. Eventually he understood that salt and not rubies and diamonds gave taste to life and that it was she alone who really loved him, and of course they found each other again and lived happily ever after. I liked the story in part, I am sure, because it was about the triumph of the youngest, my own position among my siblings. But it also encapsulated something essential about Nanny and her values. It was a story about honesty and integrity, about valuing these qualities above everything else, and it implied a distrust of people who cared too much about money. It also implied that simplicity and hard work, salt, simple things were, in the end, the real prizes.

Nanny's sense of what mattered, what was good and what was bad, manifested itself in numerous ways—for example, in her solid support and admiration for my father as against another engineer, a man called Fahmy Pasha, whose grand, sumptuous mansion on the Corniche (the broad, sweeping avenue running the length of the Alexandria coastline) we would pass every day in the summers on our way to the beach. He had built his palatial villa with ill-gotten gains, Nanny would regularly say, and consequently he would not prosper, even if he seemed to now; there would be disasters, some way or other he would suffer, and if not him, then his children and his children's children, unto the seventh generation. Nanny was responding to that episode in Father's life when, long before his troubles with Nasser, King Farouk fired him from his job; obviously he was destined to find himself compelled to stand up to one corrupt Egyptian ruler after another. All this occurred in my earliest childhood and I have no memory of these happenings, except for my father's periodic returns from abroad with suitcases full of gifts. Among these, quite unforgettably for me, was a clock, out of which, to my constant fascination, flew a bird that announced the time by saying "cuckoo."

By and large there was a congruence between Nanny's actions and her values, both professed and implicit. But there were also moments of incongruence. Her enormous and somewhat simpering admiration for Grandfather, for instance. Grandfather, Mother's father, was a man of very substantial wealth who lived his life in commensurate style. He had three Mercedes of different sizes, and he used to order his valet to have the chauffeur bring one or the other car to the door according to where he was going: the larger one for ceremonial occasions, the small one for city errands, and so on. He dressed with impeccable style and elegance. Very tall, with an elegant, athletic frame, he was an imposingly handsome figure, with strong features, piercing blue eyes, and an air and habit of command. He was also, it is true, a fine farmer, passionate about the land he farmed and the quality of fruit he produced. But I think it was all the other things that had their effect on Nanny. She was openly partial to blue eyes—her husband had had blue eyes, she told us, and the younger of my two brothers was undisguisedly her favorite in part because he had blue eyes. She doted on this brother, Karim, and accepted from him things she would not have put up with from the three others of us. I was her next favorite. Nanny herself had brown eyes and dark, straight hair that she wore in a bun and that remained mainly dark and only lightly threaded with gray well into her seventies.

In retrospect, I do not doubt that besides blue eyes the other thing Nanny favored was men—or maleness, in infant, boy, or man. I knew this then, too, or more precisely sensed it, sensed that it was something about boyness as opposed to girlness that brought about this

abandonment of who she was, of her otherwise forthright and unde-
viating commitment to fairness and to judging things solidly for what
they were. Surprisingly, perhaps, she was the only person in my childhood environment in whom I sensed this preference. Neither of my
parents betrayed at any level a preference for boys; if anything, my
father possibly took slightly more delight in his daughters. My mother
would commonly say that she found people's prejudice toward boys
unintelligible. She would recount as illustration the story of a visitor
who came to our house when I was born and who exclaimed, when
Mother said she had not quite decided on a name for me, "What does
it matter what you call her? It's only a girl. Call her anything, call her
Figla [radish]!" The woman who said this was herself, in my memory
of the story, nameless. Certainly Mother never betrayed a partiality
for her sons over her daughters. She kept us all, I am tempted to say,
at an equal distance. But that comment is perhaps unjust. Mother
did have difficulty connecting with us, and with children in general,
but she did not, either in relation to her children or in talking about
or relating to men as distinct from women, communicate, as Nanny
did, that there was something innately preferable about the one sex
over the other. Nor did my grandmother or any of my aunts convey
this.

Nanny did not like Mother. This was one instance in which blue
eyes did not win her over. She was plain, at least with me, about not
liking Mother. *"Moi je ne peux pas mentir, je n'aime pas ta mere"* ("I
cannot tell a lie, I do not like your mother"). But, she would add,
Mother was the mistress, "and as the mistress I respect her." That
much I remember her saying. She did not directly discuss why she
disliked Mother. Still, she evidently let slip sufficient remarks to have
left me with the distinct impression that she regarded Mother as an
idle woman of the spoiled upper classes, someone who applied herself
to no useful work but wasted her days, after a few moments in the
morning instructing the servants and discussing the menu with the
cook, exchanging visits and chatting with her relatives. I wonder now
what it was that Nanny thought Mother should have occupied herself
with—embroidering perhaps, or baking, or charity work. Nanny was

herself a strict respecter of, someone even who deferred to, the conventions of life, including the hierarchies of class, so I cannot imagine that she thought Mother ought, for instance, to be cleaning the house herself or doing all the cooking.

She once hinted at something more somber, which to my child's understanding was somewhere between sinister and incomprehensible. This was that I had had another sister, born shortly before I was, who had been premature and had died within instants. I do not recall quite how she conveyed it, but something in the way she told me suggested that my sister's prematureness and consequently her death were somehow Mother's fault. Now, of course, I conclude that she was suggesting that sometime in the course of this pregnancy Mother had attempted to have an abortion; and that this somehow had later precipitated, at least in Nanny's eyes, the infant's premature birth. I have no idea if there was any truth to this. Nanny was a Catholic and to her any abortion or attempted abortion would have been abhorrent.

My own imagination supplied the detail that this sister was buried in the back garden by the Seville orange tree, close to where we had buried Mitso, our tabby cat, who had died of old age. We had held an elaborate funeral for Mitso and then had placed a cross over his grave, but Nanny, even though she had loved Mitso as she loved all cats, made us remove it. It was blasphemous, she said. Cats did not have souls like people, and in any case they were not Christians.

I think now that, apart from anything else, the fact that Mother was her employer *and* a woman would have strongly predisposed Nanny to dislike her. Nanny was someone who had her own clear, firm opinions on things and there was nothing in her makeup that would have made living as the subordinate of another woman—a man might have been a different story—a palatable situation.

Still, even though she might say to me that she did not much like my mother, it was a muttered, semi-covert dislike, not an open or a blazing defiance. And it may well be that I am exaggerating that dislike, because in daily life there was actually very little friction between them—most of the time, none. Looking after the children was Nanny's province and Mother was evidently perfectly happy to leave all the details of our lives to her. It was also always clear, however, that Mother was the supreme authority regarding us, and if there was any serious matter afoot or any major moral lesson with which Nanny thought we needed to be inculcated, Nanny would confer with Mother and then bring us before her. It was Mother who dealt with grave infractions. Not even Father superseded Mother in our house as moral authority. On the contrary, he would always say that it was she whose judgment and discernment had to be deferred to, that he himself deferred to her. And she was, when she was scrutinizing you, questioning, judging with her eyes, a very august and even a frightening presence. One would not, after being subjected to this, easily do something she had clearly interdicted.

It was evident, too, that whatever Nanny's views were of Mother, there was no disagreement between them as to the moral code to which we were to be held. Regarding how we should behave, what was permitted or not permitted, what was wrong and what was right, and the general moral framework within which we should live, there was no detectable difference in what they inculcated, in fact there was a profound and singular consonance between their views on those sorts of issues, and Father's too (although Father was less likely to defer to convention), despite the differences between their cultures, their religions. Those differences, in my experience of them, were rather nominal.

But I remember one terrible row. I remember that they shouted at each other and that I inserted myself between them, protecting Nanny. This disconcerted them only a moment and they resumed shouting over my head. Nanny said she would leave, resign, and Mother said, Yes, leave, leave, now, at once, out.

Of course Nanny did not leave, and it all blew over. But the incident left me with a fine legacy of anxieties. For one thing, Mother, in the course of their row, had said that it was disgraceful the way Nanny was using "the child," making me unnecessarily dependent on her, thinking that this would make it impossible to dismiss her. What did it mean that Nanny was using me? I didn't think she was using me. Nanny wasn't, I said, using me. But these words dropped into my life like a handful of dust, making me uncertain about yet more things, things I needed to be certain about. And what did it mean, too, that Nanny could be dismissed? Who else could be dismissed: could I be dismissed? Servants could be dismissed. Nanny wasn't a servant, but she wasn't a parent either. Were we, was I, more like a servant or a parent? Like Nanny? I think I felt that I occupied some marginal space, that I didn't belong quite at the center, where my parents and maybe even my siblings were. That I could be left out of things and maybe they wouldn't notice.

It may be, too, that it was in connection with this row that I was made to move into my own bed. I know that when this took place it happened at Mother's instigation and against my impassioned protestations, even though I was only being moved to another bed in the same room. I do not know what age I was—perhaps six or seven.

My confusion about categories and where exactly I belonged extended also to animals, or at least to cats. I believe I wondered, for instance, whether maybe I belonged in the category in which cats also belonged, the category of small beings. Or maybe somewhere between them and people? I vaguely remember spending a long time staring into a cat's eyes and feeling that it was like me or that I was like it. This moment and the conclusion it brought me to, which I confided to my father—that I thought that the cat and I were very alike, especially our eyes—amused and delighted him (what we said or did often delighted him) and for some while afterwards he would playfully say to me, "Come here, tell me, are your eyes really like the cat's eyes?" I think it was the fact that the cat only looked—looked rather than spoke—that made me feel we, and our eyes in particular, were alike. My father's nickname for me as a child was Wise Owl, because I spoke so little but looked always, he thought, with such an air of wisdom.

Our family, or rather Nanny, had numerous cats. She fed the cats, most of which were not strictly ours or hers but cats that simply came daily to eat the scraps on our back balcony, whose trellis was shaded with a vine and clematis flowers of the vividest blue. Usually a cat or two would be ours and would be allowed into the downstairs hallway, although nowhere else in the house. At least once or twice in my childhood a cat gave birth in the curtained-off portion under the stairs in that hallway, where empty suitcases and other odds and ends were stacked. It was here, when the kittens emerged from their lair behind the curtain, round-eyed, staggering and stumbling over themselves, absorbed in and exploring anything and everything, agog at life, that I got to know them.

Nanny, however, also sometimes drowned kittens the moment they were born. Not, as a rule, those born under the stairs, who belonged to special cats, but those she might find elsewhere, the litter of a strange cat in the garage or in the bric-a-brac room at the bottom of the garden. She said it was kinder to kill them than to let them grow up and starve or be abused by people, but I found it nearly unbearable and I would plead with her not to. She would hold them, newborn, eyes still closed, in a pail of water until they died. You could hear, I think, their squeals for a second or two. I cannot tell now whether I ever witnessed her drowning a kitten or just imagined that I did. I see her doing it in a pail by the pond in the garden where the hand pump was, a hand pump from which cascaded the sweetest, coldest water, water that had emerged only that instant out of the well, out of the depths of the earth. There were plants in the pond and goldfish that were not always easy to see in the dark waters. A vine grew over the trellis above it, putting forth small opaque green grapes that for some reason never ripened.

~

Nanny, her voice calling me in from the garden at nightfall, singing out my name into the dark in a music that was part of the music of childhood. Nanny, standing on the front balcony, calling, herself just a smudge of white, the whiteness of her apron all that could be made out as, tired and yet unwilling to end my play, I made my way at last to the safety of the lighted house.

It is first of all memories of my own childhood that come to me when I think of her, memories that, screening her, make it hard for me to discern who she herself was.

Nanny was a Yugoslav, a Croat, though I had remembered only

that she was Yugoslav until I happened fairly recently to see a television program about a Croat village in Yugoslavia to which people were flocking because the Virgin Mary had appeared to some children. I watched, riveted, scanning their faces intently to see what her people looked like. I could see resemblances.

Afterward I looked for her country in my atlas. It seemed, on the map, like a beautiful region, hills and mountains and close by the sea. And she did often say that her homeland was beautiful, and that strawberries there were four times the size of ours, and that they had snow.

She had left with her daughter during or immediately after the First World War, in which her husband had been killed. She went to Istanbul and took a position as governess with a Turkish family who wintered in Egypt. She left them to come to us when their one child was grown past needing a governess, and she was with us from the time my elder brother was born or a few months thereafter. (Among the upper classes most particularly, European nannies—the most prized among whom were the English—were not uncommon.) In another day, another age, Nanny, accomplished as she was, would have made her way to make a new beginning to America. But in the 1910s, when she found herself widowed and with a daughter to support, the place she thought of to make her way in life was Istanbul. Istanbul was the capital of what was still the Ottoman Empire, a familiar landmark in people's consciousness, as it had been for generations. (For four centuries it had dominated a considerable region of southeastern Europe as well as a good part of the Muslim world and the eastern Mediterranean). And so, setting out to create a new life, Nanny had made her way toward the center of a familiar old empire just as I, decades later, setting out to make a new life, would find myself heading toward the heartland of yet another fading empire.

Nanny's name was Clothilde. She spoke several languages— German and Italian as well as French—and was a fine embroiderer and a superb cook. She made kugelof and cannelloni and a superbly delicious dessert of chestnuts topped with cream called Mont Blanc, and she baked cakes and made wonderful strawberry and apricot jams whose tastes represent still for me the distillation of childhood. When we arrived ravenous from school we would come indoors just long enough to drop our satchels and take our sandwiches, which she would make as we waited in the pantry, filling them with fresh cream and jam. Her apricot jam, made with apricots from our garden, was unforgettable and through all these years is still unequaled. I've tried apricot jam in every country I've been to and sought out gourmet varieties in the hope of finding that taste again, and I never have.

She hated Tito and Communism and made bundles of clothes to send to her relatives, whose letters could only hint, because of censorship, at their sufferings under Communism. (She hated Hitler, too, and spoke of him as the devil.) When we protested about not wanting to eat this or not liking the taste of that, she would tell us that during the war children in Europe were so hungry they searched the bodies of dead soldiers for a crust of bread and were glad of anything, even if it was stained with blood. (At least in Nanny's stories it was not only dark-skinned children who made up the hungry and the destitute of the world.)

Nanny's daughter, Eugenie, was in her late thirties when I was a child. Unmarried, she too was a governess. She had attended a school run by nuns and was an able woman and an accomplished piano player, sometimes playing for us when she visited her mother. When she came for these visits, arriving perhaps at midday and spending the rest of the day at our house, Nanny, normally not a very talkative woman, would suddenly become very loquacious. They would speak in their own language, of which I understood not a word, and Nanny would talk, it seemed, nonstop, Genie for the most part just listening and nodding sympathetically. Occasionally Genie, growing conscious of me, would eye me reflectively and smile, but Nanny for the most part chattered on, oblivious. I knew of course that I was not Nanny's daughter and that it was entirely natural that they should talk in their own language. All the same I felt excluded and privately hurt that Nanny didn't know that she could say anything in front of me, anything even about my mother, and that I would never betray her.

That, in those days, was the worst that I could imagine her saying.

What if she were saying that she hated having to live in someone's house, hated having to make a living in this way?

Often during these visits Nanny would open the wardrobe in our room, which she kept locked. She would take things out and show them to Genie or perhaps put in there something Genie had given her. I do not know what exactly their transactions were around this wardrobe, but I remember that I was fascinated by its contents and that Nanny would allow me, on those rare occasions when she opened it, to look in, standing beside her, but not to touch anything. It had in it things I think not innately mysterious—her sewing kit, for instance, embroideries in progress, private papers probably, perhaps some jewelry—but it was crammed full. Among the objects that I could touch and that I found mysterious and interesting was a rosewood box, its wood stained dark and carved with red roses. And it smelled too—Nanny would open it and give it to me to smell—of roses.

That wardrobe was the only space in the entire house that was hers alone. Or that was the case, anyway, until I moved out of her room when I was about eleven or twelve.

Nanny relished her food and missed being able to enjoy pork, and in particular bacon, her descriptions of its delicate, complicated taste rivaling her account of the magical wonder of snow. Very occasionally she treated herself, privately, to some ham or a glass of wine. But the climate of Egypt, she said, was the best there was; she was always aware of how lovely the days were (they seemed to me, who knew nothing else then, nothing about how terrible the cold could be, just ordinary). She often thanked God, she would say, that she lived in such a climate; we were very fortunate, it was the perfect climate, and it was good for one's rheumatism.

She cried at movies like *Lassie* and hated, as well as disapproved of, the voluptuous kissing in some American films—she would turn away from the screen, making noises of repugnance. She regularly read, besides her Bible, the French edition of *Reader's Digest*, and she read books too sometimes, crying copiously, I remember, over *Uncle Tom's Cabin*.

She had one close friend, Zia (Aunt) Maria, who came from a place near Nanny's hometown, but on the Italian side of the border. Zia Maria was also a governess, with a family of Turko-Greeks in Alexandria, the Boyazoghlus. They were Christian Greek Orthodox by religion but also considered themselves Turkish, I do not recall now how or why. We all, the children at least, became friends because of our governesses' friendship. There were three girls the ages of my siblings and a boy, Manoli, who was my age. We would go to their house in the afternoons (during the summers, that is, which we spent in Alexandria) and play in the garden, and after dinner we would play the card game Crazy Eights. When they visited us, they would come to our cabin on the beach and spend the day there and we would go swimming together, sometimes to the island off Sidi Bishr No. 2— one of the beaches of Alexandria. They left Egypt about the time we did, they too destroyed by the revolution. Some of them, the children, now live in Greece, and some here in America. We exchange cards and occasionally my sister speaks to one or other of them on the phone (it is my sister, among us, who keeps up family connections). Like us, they look back with a vast nostalgia toward the Egypt that was and, like us, they feel at home nowhere.

Nanny was deeply religious, praying regularly and reading her Bible. Only my grandmother, in the circle of my childhood, prayed as regularly and was as religious as Nanny (and perhaps even more religious than she). Nanny attended church on Sundays, but not regularly. The church she attended, the one nearest us, was at Matariyya, about a ten-minute walk away. It had a vast, spreading sycamore tree beside it, an ancient tree said to have sheltered the Holy Family on their flight into Egypt. The name Matariyya means "sweet water," and, according to legend, that is what the Virgin Mary said when she first tasted the water there: sweet water, "Ma' tariyya."

Sometimes Nanny would take me with her when she went to church but would leave me to play under the tree while she went in to prayers. She was scrupulous about not inculcating us with Christianity, and she would say, too, that this was always something of great importance to her, never to influence us in the slightest degree toward

Christianity. And she always spoke of Islam with the same respect that she spoke of her faith. Moreover, though her Bible included pictures of Jesus and Mary, when she spoke of her beliefs she spoke only of God, *Le Bon Dieu*, and God was the same, she said, whatever religion you were, whether Muslim, Christian, or Jewish. There were no other religions in Egypt, and for Nanny, as for my parents and most everyone else, these three related monotheisms were, at least by implication, the only true religions.

Nevertheless, this matter of different religions was not, for a child, entirely comprehensible and was capable of inducing considerable anxiety, particularly when I was confronted with the assertions the servants made on the subject of Christians. Even on a purely rational level it was a little bewildering. For if God was the same God for all of us, then why were we different, why weren't we all Christians or Muslims or Jews? Moreover, although my parents, like Nanny, took the line that all three religions were equally good and that people were not all the same religion simply because one had to be of the religion into which one was born, the servants declared otherwise. Although I did not exactly seek out their opinions, they were inclined, particularly when they were angry at Nanny, to give vent to the view that all Christians were going to hell, Nanny among them. Nanny had strict notions as to the duties of the servants and would not hesitate to report them to Mother if they seemed to her lazy and inattentive to their responsibilities—and this of course made them furious with her. It was on those occasions that they would mutter against her and claim that she was bound for hell. Their words would have preyed on my mind far more than they did had my parents not categorically dismissed them. These were uneducated opinions, they said, and we should never ourselves utter such words, even to repeat what we had heard.

Nanny never knew fully what the servants were saying because she never mastered Arabic. Although she could express herself in it, and intelligibly enough, it was a broken Arabic that, to a child, was often, even when she was at her most serious, exceedingly comic. Its comicness arose above all from the fact that she always managed to address people as the wrong sex, and so there she would be, speaking to the *suffragi*, the man who cleaned downstairs and who served at table, haranguing him at length, telling him off about what he had failed to do, and addressing him all the while as if he were a woman! And she managed always to exactly reverse it if the person at whom she was directing her harangue was a woman. I found this sidesplittingly hilarious, and even the objects of her harangues would not uncommonly be distracted from the content of her speech and break suddenly into wide grins.

                                            ~

She was in many ways not only the person who looked after me but also my closest companion, the person with whom I spent the most time in childhood and in adolescence. Even before my siblings left for England, the age gap between them and me (the youngest of them was five years older than I) often meant that the three of them would be off doing things together while I would be left with Nanny. We would go for walks, just Nanny and I, walks that she had taken with my siblings before I was born.

The walk we most regularly took was down the shady lane branching off from the street on which we lived, a lane with villas and walled gardens, where Dr. Bo'tor (Boktor) and my schoolmate Lucy, the daughter of Sir Ronald and Lady Jane Fulton, lived. We would walk to the end of that lane, where there was an old stone fountain that had a spout for people to drink from and a trough for the animals, and then turn, where the lane ended, out into the open fields. In the fields, depending on the season, we would see cotton, bursting in soft clouds from its pods, or *barseem*, a lush, vivid green grass used to feed animals, or thick green pods of beans, or corn stalks, young still or full grown, dense and tall, rustling and heavy with heads of corn. And always, in the distance, villages, nestling among palms and sycamore trees, with only a minaret perhaps and the top of a dome, and some dovecotes on the roofs of houses emerging above the trees. The villages were never our destination, although sometimes we skirted them, walking close enough to see, usually across a stream separating the village from the path, into the village common area, where children played in the shade. Trees sometimes so closely enfolded the village that it felt, to the outsider looking in, as if they might not be letting in enough air. We would sometimes pass close enough even to see into the doorways of the very simple houses of dried mud brick, consisting perhaps of one or two rooms, with hard earth for a floor. And if it was dusk or approaching dusk, one would see in the openings to the homes the play of firelight, the light of an oil lamp perhaps or of a fire for cooking. In those days the villages had no electricity.

Our usual destination when we took that route was an obelisk standing, enclosed in railings, in the middle of fields. Once—in the days when the obelisk had first been erected—this area, these open fields, had been the ancient city of Heliopolis.

By the time we came back, as the dusk was closing in, the handful of small shops on the main road toward Matariyya would have their lights on, the dim yellowish electric lights of those days; and the street lamps, of the same dim yellow tinge, would also be on. If we turned in that direction we would pass the store that sold sweets and cigarettes, and next to it the shop to which we sent our ironing. Farther on, in the more populous area, people would be sitting or strolling outside their shops and homes, watching the world go by. The men would be wearing, for their evening leisure, their best, neatly pressed striped pajamas.

The walks I remember most of my many, many walks with Nanny were our daily afternoon walks in Alexandria. Taking the chalky white road from Siouf, where we spent the summers, past the Victoria tram station, we would walk along the Corniche toward a particular beach, almost empty except for ourselves, where we would stay until sunset. Nanny would sit with her thoughts, looking out to sea, and I would gather shells—pinks, reds, oranges, and the rare emerald green, which I would later string into necklaces—or play in the sand. And then, as the sunset colors grew more intense, I too would stop to watch the sun melt finally into the sea.

I loved those walks and remember still those sunsets, but there was also a core of sadness and loneliness, a sense of being left out of other things I'd have liked to do. In Alexandria we lived in our grand-

father's house, which we shared with my grandmother and aunts—
my mother's sisters—and their children, each family having its own
suite. But I slept in a separate part of the house, separate from my
mother and siblings (Father, like the uncles, generally came only for
weekends) and even from my aunts and cousins, a room downstairs
with its own bath and its own little balcony, which I shared with
Nanny. We were the only two who slept downstairs; everyone else
slept upstairs. This separateness carried over to other things. My
aunts and mother, when they went out in the evening, taking carriage
rides along the Corniche, going into town shopping or sightseeing or
attending the theater and rounding off the evenings with ice creams
from Délices, often took my siblings, considered old enough to join
in their activities, but not me or my younger cousins, children with
whom, although I could occasionally play, I was not close. And so I
felt left out, relegated to keeping Nanny company.

Nanny died when I was in my late teens and away in England. I
tell myself now that the reason I know so little about her is that she
died before I was old enough to want to know who she was, before I
was old enough to have quite left behind me the days when all that
mattered was that she was there for me, for *my* needs. Had she died
when I was just a little older I would surely have known the name of
the town or village she was from, and what her home and her parents
had been like, and if she had sisters or brothers, and what it was like
to leave home like that and live all one's life, every moment, among
strangers. And I would have asked her if it had been hard and if she
had been very lonely. And what she thought, looking back, and
whether she wished she had never left, hard as it might have been to
stay.

She died in our home, in her late seventies, of stomach cancer.
She had planned always to spend her last years among the nuns in a
convent in Cairo that she visited regularly throughout her life. I do
not know why she did not do so; perhaps she was planning to once I
had left home (she died about a year after I left for England) but did
not get around to it. I would not have known, in those days, how to
bring up such a subject, even if I had wanted to. Besides, the idea of

discussing where she would go after she had raised us and we were grown up—as if she were not as fully part of our home and family and as entitled to stay on as anyone—would have seemed to me then, as it still seems today, an outrageous absurdity.

She died, I heard, in great pain. And worse, even worse to think of, given how much she thought about death and prepared for it and how much she prayed, she died not wanting to die, crying out in her last days *"Je ne veux pas mourir! Je ne veux pas mourir!"* ("I don't want to die!"). Turning away the priest, refusing to receive him, refusing, several times, the last rites.

It was in the Alexandria house that I had my second brush with angels. It was a starlit night in Ramadan, the twenty-seventh of Ramadan. My grandmother told me that it was a very special, a specially blessed night, when God permitted his angels to descend freely, and if he wished, one would see them. We went up to the roof together to watch for them, taking with us a bowl of water because someone had told me (I think it was Aunt Aisha's young maid, Fatma) that if one left a bowl of water out on this night and an angel passed it would turn to milk. The roof of the Alexandria house had regular stairs going up to it and was laid out as a terrace with alcoves. We sat there, the two of us, under the lovely starlight until I fell asleep. I didn't see angels and the water did not turn to milk, but I have vividly with me still that night's enormous sense of wonder—sitting quietly in the starlight in expectation of angels.

4

TRANSITIONS

MY PARENTS went to Europe for their honeymoon. I have a photo of my mother on shipboard, a beautiful young woman, looking romantic, mysterious, a beret on her head at a rakish angle, a wisp of hair blowing across her face.

The man she married was pleasant-looking. He had warm brown eyes and a small mustache. But he was short, shorter than she was. That would not have come as a surprise; she would have been shown a photo of him before marriage and he would have been described to her and his shortness certainly commented on. He was also considerably older—she was twenty and he forty. That too, of course, would not have come as a surprise.

It was her first trip to Europe. By the time I was a child this was long in the past and they had by then been there many more times, so I never heard from her what it was like to see Europe for the first time or what it was like to be on a honeymoon with a man you had met only the day before, on your wedding day. Still, even had the years not intervened, I do not think I would have heard much. Throughout her life, at least in the years that I knew her, my mother was a reserved person. If a subject touching on the intimacies of life so much as hove into view, she lowered her eyes and flushed, a look of acute awkwardness coming over her, as if these were not things that she could speak of. She was quite different from her sisters in this. They looked as if among themselves they could discuss anything, whereas I imagine that even with them she would have been, in the discussion of certain subjects, awkward and reserved.

She was the eldest, which perhaps accounts for her difference from her sisters. As a child she would have had to come to her own conclusions about things and would have had no one, in the early years at least, with whom to compare notes. Perhaps too, being the eldest and a girl had been particularly burdensome—perhaps, that is, as a first child, a girl had not been particularly welcome and perhaps, then, coming into this world she had been confronted with some hard, sobering realities, and it is this that gave her the sober reflective air that she has in the one photo I have of her in childhood. She stands by a trellis, her father's austere ochre house behind her, aged about ten, great luminous eyes looking out, serious and diffident and lonely.

I remember playing under that trellis. It had a loofah plant growing over it, something we did not have in our garden. I remember tearing open the ripe loofah pods that hung down and investigating the mystery of how the sponges we scrubbed ourselves with in the bath and these plants were the same thing.

Among her family she was looked to, in the years that I knew her, as someone who could be counted on to think things out, to deliver a responsible opinion as to the proper course of action, this too perhaps a legacy of her being the eldest and having had, from early on, to think for herself.

Reserved though she was and forbidding and categorical in my experience of her, particularly in matters of sexuality, I knew from my second cousin Samia that she could be quite open-minded and sympathetic about other people's experiences. Samia, who was four years older than I, would come occasionally, in the period just before I left for college, to spend the day at Ain Shams. She came as my friend but she would always also set aside a couple of hours to talk with my mother, whom she called Bella. (This was the diminutive of her given name, Ikbal, which, until Samia began to use it, only Father had called her.) They would talk about two subjects. First was the current state of Samia's love life. Samia was separated from her husband and deeply in love with another man—and was alternately, depending on what their most recent exchange had been, in a state of great anguish and despondency or of lyrical ecstasy. Mother, Samia would tell me, was most sympathetic, and she was good, too, she said, at analyzing the details that Samia recounted, the import of words and silences, and what exactly it was that this remote, elusive man might have had in mind when he said this or that. Their other topic of discussion was books. Samia's reading, like Mother's, was in French (although Mother also read Arabic), and Samia, who had a B.A. in French literature, thought Mother was easily as acute a critic as she was herself. When Samia left us to return to her flat in Cairo, she usually carried off with her an armful of books culled from Mother's bookshelves, books that Mother had acquired and read since Samia's last visit.

This relationship always astonished me and I believed, as I maintained to Samia, that Mother was able to listen sympathetically and uncensoriously to her account of being in love with someone to whom she was not married only because Samia was not someone who was under Mother's moral jurisdiction. Had Samia been a close relative, I said, love and lyricism would have been dismissed as just so much nonsense, the indulgence of which could lead to the jeopardizing of one's honor and purity and the honor and purity of one's name and the family name—and nothing, absolutely nothing, was worth that.

The only remnant of their first trip to Europe, by the time I was a child, was my mother's memory of the marvelous beauty of the fjords, which I remember her telling me about, and of the northern lights. There was a framed certificate on the mantelpiece in Father's study, attesting that they had crossed into the Arctic Circle. The certificate bore the words "Norway, Land of the Midnight Sun" and across the top of it was a rainbow representing, I was told, the northern lights. A midnight sun! The very thought was quite magical, and perhaps I heard from my mother about the fjords only because I was so fascinated by that certificate and always asked to be told about Norway.

The other photos on that mantelpiece, besides the photo of Gandhi on his funeral pyre, were one of Father shaking hands with King Farouk, the old Aswan Dam behind them, and one of my parents— my mother in a polka-dot dress, looking at once both stern and dreamy, and Father, turned slightly toward her, looking serious in a tarboosh and glasses. A larger version of this photo hung in the family living room, by the radio.

Soon after they returned from their honeymoon came the news of her brother Fuad's death. He had been next to her in age and they had been very close. Mother was of course devastated. Just two months later, her first child was born. She would say in later years that she often worried as to the effect her grief might have had on that child, Omar, what shadow she might inadvertently have cast over his childhood. And it is true, there is an air of anxiety and aloneness about him in his baby photographs. In one in particular, his dark eyes, peering out from under his floppy baby hat, seem like great pools of sadness.

Their marriage, when we knew them, was a happy one. Their day began with drinking tea and reading the newspapers in Mother's bedroom, which adjoined Father's, sitting opposite each other at either end of her bed. On weekends and during vacations we would join them there, running to Mother's huge bed as soon as we woke and getting under the covers. Once there we might again fall asleep or talk quietly while they sipped their tea and exchanged newspapers and analyzed the news. Politics was not a matter of distant, irrelevant events. Who formed the cabinet, what party might get in, what the prime minister said, what the King was doing, and of course, when it came, the revolution—these were matters they analyzed carefully, as things that could closely affect their lives. At times my father was directly involved in politics, campaigning for candidates and himself running for office as a Saadi, a parliamentary reformist; for a number of years he served as a member of the Egyptian Senate. Even when he was not formally involved, his job was always closely affected by politics. These morning discussions, then, and my parents' analysis of the day's news served a practical purpose. Mother was adept, according to Father, at reading between the lines and figuring out what was really afoot behind the façade or the official line being presented in the papers. She always, he would tell us, proved right in the end, even when he had thought that she could not possibly be.

Over lunch (the midafternoon lunches of the Middle East) they would be absorbed in similarly lively discussions of what had transpired at work and what was going on in the world. Then they would retire for their siestas, waking after an hour or so and usually staying home the rest of the day, although they occasionally went out on visits. Sometimes in the evening Mother might receive guests in the garden or, in winter, indoors. Father would be in his study or in his own bedroom upstairs, where he often worked sitting on the sofa by the radio, emerging occasionally to greet the guests and spend a few moments with them.

Sometimes we had large dinner parties or, during Ramadan, huge *fitars*, the meals breaking the fast at sunset. These would be either for relatives or sometimes (and always separately) for father's foreign colleagues, men visiting from England and Switzerland, often with their wives. I do not remember Egyptian colleagues coming to dinner or calling, except for very brief formal visits to pay their respects and welcome Father home if he had been abroad, and in those instances only he would meet with them. I think perhaps it was not done to have nonsegregated visits other than with family or with foreigners. The interest of these dinner parties for us children was chiefly the wonderful foods that would be served: stuffed pigeons, a fish for which the Nile was famous called *arus al-Nil*, varieties of seafood, turkey and rice with raisins and pine nuts, a large variety of stuffed vine leaves and other stuffed vegetables—cabbage leaves, tomatoes, peppers—and varieties of salads. All would be home-cooked except for the desserts, elaborate gateaux from Groppi's, a famous Swiss patisserie in Cairo.

More usually, Mother's guests were relatives or connections of relatives, always women. Sometimes they included her sisters, but they did not come frequently, since they saw one another regularly anyway at Grandfather's house. Friendships with people who were not family connections were not common, although cordial exchanges of courtesy visits every few months or every year or two with acquaintances beyond that circle did occur. And there would be friends she would see more frequently. I remember a friendship she had with Madame Sultan, who lived in one of a cluster of villas nearby. She was widowed and had four sons who often came to play with us in our garden. She raised her sons, as they told us, with a view to making them capable of doing for themselves whatever they might need to do; she wanted them to be competent at all the practical skills and not to think that there was shame in doing any of them, even if people laughed. They explained this somewhat defiantly because we and the other neighbors' children who came to play in our garden were in fact astounded at what they did and would probably have laughed at them had we been less polite and less close to them as friends. The boys cleaned house, sewed, knitted, gardened, and attended to everything that needed attending to in their home. They had no servants; they and their mother did everything. I remember one of the sons, Husain, a strapping young man of about sixteen, bringing his knitting with him one evening, and how extraordinary it was to see him knit as he talked, even though we already knew he did.

I remember that when Madame Sultan came, she and Mother would sit out on summer nights, their cigarettes glowing, their voices a murmuring interplay, a jug of iced lemonade and glasses on the garden table between them. But their friendship eventually faded.

Most commonly, Mother spent her afternoons and sometimes her evenings reading. That is how we remember her: reading. Sitting, freshly bathed, on the chaise longue in her bedroom, wearing fresh cotton clothes, clothes with the sweet smell of cotton dried in the sun, the air blowing through them. Behind her, the garden. French windows open, pale green curtains, drawn back, billowing gently in an afternoon breeze. A book in her hand, a cup of Turkish coffee on the table beside her. Reading. Lighting cigarette after cigarette and reading.

Two moments in particular still live for me. One was on one of those afternoons when a breath of wind stirred the curtains and the sound of running water drifted in. She was half-reclined on the chaise longue, a book in her hand or perhaps lying face down beside her because I had come in and she had stopped reading and looked up, waiting to hear me speak, a cigarette between her fingers. I had wandered into her room, I do not know why. We must have had some conversation and I must have said—I was probably about fifteen at the time—that I wanted to be a writer. I do not remember saying it, nor can I now imagine why I would have said it to her; I was not at all wont in my memory of our relationship to speak to her of my secret desires. Still, I must have done so because I remember her looking up at me (a cup of coffee on the table beside her, black, no sugar) and saying, speaking with animation, that she too would have liked to have been a writer. It was too late for her now, she said, but sometimes she thought about her life and how interesting it had been and wished she could write it all. Maybe I could write it for her, she said, maybe I could write the story of her life. "I'd tell it to you and you could write it," she said. She spoke enthusiastically, eagerly, looking at me.

I was fifteen. Like many other girls that age, I was sure of one thing: I did not want to be like my mother. I was sure that I wasn't like her and would never grow up to be like her. I didn't want to think we were alike in anything, let alone in our deepest hearts' desires, and didn't at all want to think that I might indeed be her daughter.

How would I have known that the time would come, and not once but over and over, when I would think back to that moment in her room, the breeze rustling the curtains, her eyes looking luminously toward me, and wish that I could return to it, taking with me, preferably, just one piece of modern equipment, a tape recorder. Or that at the very least I had at once sat down with pad and pencil and said, "Mother, speak, I want nothing more in life right now than to take down your words, to know what you lived, what you thought, how you saw your life." How would I have known then that those who bring into their lives and into the shaping of the consciousness of others their own deepest thoughts and feelings and moral imagination, create out of their own lives texts, oral, evanescent texts that are every bit as rich and sustaining as the most celebrated written texts? How would I have known this then?

I did not know, I did not know, I did not know.

What wouldn't I give now for the gift of my mother's passing on to me, in her own voice, her own and her people's story.

And so of course I wasn't at all taken with her idea. Rather, anxious to distance my own desires from hers, I thought to myself that what she dreamed of doing, writing a memoir, telling the story of her life, was not at all what I wanted to do. There was nothing in the least interesting about writing the story of your life.

The other memory dates from about the same period, and again it was one of those tranquil afternoons, an afternoon that was turning, as we spoke, to dusk. And once more she seemed to be speaking from that space where one is who one is in oneself, that space where one is not, for that moment, daughter, mother, or wife but only a consciousness traversing life, existing beyond social trappings and gathering on its way what wisdom and insights it may. It is a space perhaps that one enters in reading or that reading somehow opens up, for she had again been reading when I came in.

The subject this time must have been God or religion. She did not as a rule pray or fast or observe what in our household were thought of as the outer trappings of religion—its formalities and rituals. But she talked of herself as a religious person. On this particular afternoon she was saying that she thought that the core of Islam, the core of all religions, was summed up in one particular verse of the Quran, a verse she then quoted: *"man qatala nafsan qatala al-nas gamicᶜan, wa man ahya nafsan ahya al-nas gamicᶜan."* "He who kills one being kills all of humanity, and he who revives, or gives life to, one being revives all of humanity." That, she said, is all one needs of religion. "If you follow that, harming no one and helping when you can, you will have done enough." And then, thinking for a moment, she added that if there was one piece of advice and one alone that she could give me, it would be never to harm anyone. In fact, she said, "even if your choice is between harming yourself and harming someone else, choose to harm yourself, because if you harm someone else you will have to live all your life with the knowledge that you have done that, and nothing that happens to oneself is worse than that."

She took her beliefs seriously, to the point of prohibiting my brothers, who were engineers, from working in any field that contributed in any way to weaponry, as well as from participating in any war as combatants. She had them swear this before her, as I mentioned earlier. She could not live, she said, with the thought that she had been responsible, through giving birth to them, for the death of another mother's son. It would make her, she said, as well as them, a murderer.

⁓

It is not, after all, true that my childhood, at least my early childhood, was lonely. Or if it was, then it was so in some profound existential sense rather than in any ordinary, tangible way. I am liable most of the time to think it was lonely because the loneliness of later childhood and adolescence—a loneliness that followed on two consecutive events that fractured my life—was of such pure and overwhelming intensity that it has tended in my mind to engulf the earlier years as well.

Among my playmates, there were two special ones. I played with Gina at home. At least in early childhood, Joyce, to whom I was closer, belonged chiefly to the world of school. Gina and I played together in our garden, acting out stories that were sometimes my inventions and sometimes hers or galloping on imaginary horses. We made ourselves necklaces and bracelets and tiaras out of flowers, joining stem to blossom in circlets that we threaded together. Or we climbed trees and pretended to be on ships. And sometimes we played with dolls. I had two favorites. One was an adult with perfect features and blond hair and bright blue eyes that opened and closed. The other, supposedly a baby, was almost half the size of the first doll, which I designated its mother. The baby had no hair and had little blue dots for eyes.

Gina's house adjoined ours at the bottom of our garden. Running to the bottom of the garden to call Gina to come and play was the second thing I did on coming home. The first was to go indoors to get one of Nanny's sandwiches. I would wait for it on the small balcony at the side of the house, watching the milkwoman milk her cow. She came every day with her cow, but not always at exactly the same time, so she might or might not be there when we got home. Or I would wait where Nanny usually made the sandwiches, in the small room that one entered from the side door. It was here that she kept, in a wire-net cupboard to which only she had the key, the wonderful cakes and biscuits that she baked, and her jams, and fruits from our garden, mangoes and apricots and guavas that had fallen off the trees or had been picked but had not quite ripened to perfection. The room always smelled delicious. And besides, over the top of the doorway there were panels of colored glass, and when the sun struck the side of the house, as it did in the afternoon when we came home from school, colored light, red and gold and rose and blue and green, would fall across the floor and the wall and over oneself if one stood in it.

Gina's family was Italian; her father worked in a hotel in Cairo. They had a small house whose balcony looked onto our garden, a part of the garden where there was a storeroom and the gardener's room and, on the other side, the garage. It was screened off from the rest of the garden by a hedge with variegated white-and-green leaves. Beyond, in the space between the hedge and the garden wall, was a huge sycamore fig tree with boughs that were wrinkled like skin where they branched off from the trunk.

I would run down there and stand and call, and Gina, who had short straight brown hair and brown eyes and freckles, would appear on her balcony and climb through the wood posts and over the garden wall, using the footholds we had made to come down on our side. Gina was one year older than I. She had a brother, Freddy, five years older than she, who would sometimes come over to play with my brothers or to join in the games we all played together with other neighbors. On weekends, for as long as there was enough light to see, it might be cricket. Or, in the dusk and early evening, cowboys and Indians or soldiers and thieves, or, on colder evenings when we wanted to be indoors, Monopoly.

At a certain point Freddy began coming over to play with me and Gina. We would play tag and he would always or almost always catch me. The penalty for being captured was to be taken, hands held behind one's back by the capturer, to the garage to be "tortured" and eventually released. We must have played this game on weekends, because the car was always there and "torture" consisted of Freddy's holding me jammed against the front of the car, my wrists gripped in his hands. He pressed himself against me and I wriggled, trying to escape, as I was supposed to be trying to do.

Gina did not like this game and complained to me about her brother's coming to play with us. She complained to him, too, but he would retort angrily in Italian and she would fall silent. I didn't like having her and my games disrupted either, but there was the mysterious pleasure I felt when I was captured and "tortured." I must already have felt some guilt and uneasiness about it, because I remember that Gina asked me what Freddy did to me when he tortured me and I would not tell her with the exactness she wanted. "He just tortures me" was all I would say.

And then once when he had captured me and marched me off to the garage, something different happened. Freddy did something with his pants, I could not see what, but I felt something strange and different and frightening, and then I felt him trying to get into my clothes. All I felt now was fear, a physical fear that hurt me in my stomach, and I began to struggle in earnest to break free and Freddy gripped my wrists harder and twisted my arms, hurting me.

I got away and afterward I refused to play the game. But Freddy did not give up. He said if I did not play he would tell everyone about our earlier games. I must have felt very guilty—I was about eight or nine. I do not know what I knew or thought I knew about sex or about those parts of one's body. I know that I felt dread at the thought of his telling people and that I was even more terrified of playing our old game and being taken by him into the garage. Either possibility gave me a pain in my stomach. I think sometimes my fear and my stomachache grew even greater because I imagined that it meant I was having a baby. I began avoiding Freddy, running off when he appeared and never being alone with him. He found a way to threaten me even when others were there. He would say, "Shall I open the newspaper?" meaning, Shall I tell everyone? If I didn't want him to tell people, I was supposed to go back to playing with him.

One of the Sultan boys, Basil (who would later be tortured in Nasser's prison) heard what Freddy had said to me and asked him afterward what it was all about. Freddy boasted to him about our games, swearing him, of course, to secrecy. As it happened, Basil, who was the same age as Freddy, regarded himself as my special friend. Of all the neighborhood boys the four Sultan boys were the ones who were closest friends with my brothers and who came over most often. Whenever there were games that entailed older children picking younger ones to be on their side, Basil would always choose me. He was himself a shy boy who was also very funny, and he was always very loving toward me.

Basil's response to Freddy's confidence was fury, and they had a fight. Then he spoke to his mother. His mother advised him to talk to my brother and tell him to let my mother know. Basil told me what he was going to do. I must have looked terrified, because he told me not to be afraid. My mother would not be angry with me, he said, she would only protect me.

I knew that evening that what I feared had happened, that my mother had been told. I looked into the family living room, where she usually sat in the evenings, and saw her talking to my elder brother, who was back from England for the holidays. I do not know how I knew they were talking about this thing that I dreaded and about me, but I knew, sensing it perhaps from their low voices—my mother doing most of the talking, my brother nodding—and from the pale- ness of my mother's face and the mixed seriousness and awkwardness of my brother's expression. I do not think they saw me.

I went up to bed.

I was woken the next morning by my mother pulling me upright by my arm, yanking me out of sleep. What transpired then and over the next few days was so confusing and so terrible to the child I was at the time that I have a muddled and still pained memory of it. I know that she asked me questions and that I answered and that she did not seem to believe me. I am sure it was in part that I did not understand what it was she was asking me, what it was that she kept wanting to know had or had not happened. I know that she hit me, the marks of her hand and fingers immediately turning red and coming up in welts on my thigh, and I remember looking up into her eyes and then down at the marks on my thigh in dazed shock—shock and confusion. My shock came firstly because our parents never hit us and because they had made clear it was one thing they would never do. And it came also, as did my confusion in that instant, from what I saw in my mother's eyes and sensed in how she was: as if she were doing what she was doing—hitting me—and, at the same time, were dissociated from herself and from what was happening. I had the peculiar feeling that the scene that she was playing out was something that she was enacting rather than really feeling: as if she were enacting anger and hitting me in some kind of obligatory ritual from which she was somehow herself abstracted.

I felt that my mother had violated something, broken something. And that she was unjust and stupid. I did not think these thoughts openly, and I probably did not even know I thought them, but they were thoughts that surfaced in me in later years, and I know that they were born in me at the moment when she hauled me up out of sleep and shook me, and when she questioned me and did not know how to question me and did not accept my answers, and when she hit me, her hand coming down over and over on my thigh, and said that had I been just a little older she would have gone down and got a kitchen knife and killed me, and I saw it in my mind as she said it, I saw her raising her arm, the knife in her hand, raising it above my head, ready to come down on me. And then she said that she would have had then to kill herself too, because a mother could not bear to kill her own child, but that she would have had to do it, kill us both, had I been a little older; the shame of what I had done was so great, she would have had to kill us both for the honor of the family. And she said I was lucky that Daddy was abroad, because he definitely would have killed me, young as I was.

This was only the beginning. Within a few days or perhaps that very day she took me to a doctor, not our usual doctor but a special doctor, who put me on a table and looked between my legs and told her I was fine, that I was just a little girl and that she should not make such an event of it, and in any case she had no ground whatever for her concerns.

And then I was no longer allowed to play outdoors, even with Gina, as if I were innately bad and were simply not to be trusted. And the games we all played together came to an end.

And my mother said that what I had done was so terrible it pained her to see me and that every time she saw me she remembered it and it made her unhappy. I did not want to give her pain, so I kept out of her sight as much as possible. I would edge out, slinking away when she was there. And if I could not, if we were having a meal, for instance, and I had to be there, I would make myself unnoticeable, invisible.

I do not know how long this went on. As I remember it, it never really ended (but that now seems to me unlikely). Gradually the look of pain that came over her face—or that perhaps she put on—when she saw me became less and less marked and eventually, no doubt, vanished altogether, and gradually I slunk away less and less, but there was no moment ever (at least that's how I would come to tell myself this story) when she took me back and let me know that I was good and that she cared about me again. And gradually, making myself unobtrusive, invisible, became a habit and I forgot, perhaps, why it was so.

Later, within two or three or maybe four years, I judged her to be stupid and unjust and governed by meaningless beliefs if she really thought she would have had to kill me and then herself. She was just plain stupid, I decided. I began reading Somerset Maugham at about twelve and immediately took to him and began at once, too, to believe in the follies of human beings in their rules about sex. And I also thought that it had been a lie, what she had said about my father, that if he had been there he would have killed me.

Looking back, of course, I understand all of this, and the earlier

scene between us, quite differently. I do not see someone blindly and
stupidly obeying the laws of her society. Rather, I see a mother terrified for her daughter and probably also feeling guilty that, out of her
own neglect in allowing me to play with boys, she had failed to protect
me and that I had in consequence perhaps been harmed in a way
that could be very costly to me in this society. For this *was* the reality
in that society—loss of virginity or any other consequence of forbidden sex could indeed be enormously costly. And I see someone determined to instill a proper terror in her daughter so that she would
never again be in danger of being harmed in that way. That was
why—as I see it now—I had such a peculiar, confusing feeling of
unreality as the scene played itself out, the feeling that my mother
was somehow not present in what she was doing, that she was enacting anger rather than actually angry and hitting me as if it were
some formal, obligatory thing she was doing. I am sure that she had
to steel herself to hit me and did it with the object of thoroughly
terrifying me so that I would never again engage in prohibited sexual
games. And I see in this scene both a mother uncertain and fearful
of what harm had been done her daughter and a woman who, at the
best of times, did not know how to deal with children. I see her trying
to deal, too, with a subject that was excruciatingly hard for her to
handle—sexuality.

It is not in fact true that I had never been hit by either parent.
My father had hit me once, when I was about six. I had been running
back and forth on top of a structure we had in the garden that we
had been forbidden to climb onto. It was a long, high structure like
a room made of lattice woodwork whose function was to provide shade
for young plants and seedlings until they were ready for transplanting
to the open garden. It was not a sturdy structure and, besides sagging
slightly under one's feet with each step, it swayed wonderfully from
side to side as we ran across it. (That was a game all of us sometimes
played.) My father, coming out into the garden, saw me running
across it and ordered me down at once. Then he told me to hold out
my hands and he hit me on them—not hard, but because we were
not supposed to be hit, it upset and hurt me enormously. I also re-

member looking into his eyes and seeing in them how stricken and miserable he was to be hitting me. So why, why was he doing it?

I remember only how hurt I was, but my sister has told me that I refused to speak to Father for days and perhaps weeks afterward and that he sent her on many missions to ask me to forgive him and please speak to him again.

~

This event with my mother, and everything that followed from it —the end of playing in the garden, of having playmates at home, of feeling that I belonged and was wanted in that home—was the great fracture line dividing my life: it marked the end, in my mind, of my childhood. Everything thereafter, in my thoughts, was marked Before and After. Joyousness belonged to before, only to before, to the past, and the past was over. It would never again be possible, I would say to myself, for me to feel joy the way I used to, nor would I ever laugh again the way I used to. All this was in the past now because now I knew. I do not know what exactly it was that I thought I knew, but I do know that that was how I put it to myself, that I now knew, and what I knew would make it impossible, from now on, to feel a joy that was untainted, that did not have running through it, even if almost invisibly, the taint of that knowledge, and would make it impossible henceforth to laugh fully, with the whole of one's being, with a laughter that did not have in it a memory of darkness.

I moped about the house thinking these thoughts, thinking of the garden into which I no longer ventured, thinking of all I had lost. I do not recall how long it was before I began to revive—a long time. And the rupture begun by this event was soon completed by the departure for university in England of my sister and my remaining brother, my eldest brother having been in England for some years. This second rift ushered in fully my years of intense loneliness, but it was preceded by a magical voyage. The entire family, it was decided, my parents and I as well as my sister and brother, would go to England for the summer, to see them established in their colleges in Cambridge and to look into perhaps placing me as a boarder at the Perse School, a girls' school also in Cambridge.

Everything about that voyage delighted me—the grace of our ship at the pier, an elegant white Italian ship called *Esperia*, the drawing up of its gangplank and then of its anchor, its slow towing through the harbor by a barge toward the great stone breakwater and the lighthouse, and its roll and creak as it emerged into the open sea.

Night was falling as we left Alexandria. The harbor and breakers fell away behind us into darkness, and as the ship rose and fell with the swells we saw briefly the lights of the low Alexandrian coastline, and then it too fell away. And the sea was magical, with dolphins and flying fish by day and in the night phosphorescent fish like stars in the ship's churning wake. And, on the first day out, distant, a blue shape on the horizon—Cyprus. Even being seasick was interesting. I remember thinking—as I staggered with the roll of the ship and later lay in my bunk and looked out the porthole at the stars and sat up to vomit in the bags they had given us—that now, anyway, I knew what it was to be seasick. There was nothing that was not worthy of passionate attention. My sister, who shared my cabin, was much sicker than I; by morning of our second day I had my sea legs and was out rushing about on deck or hanging over the ship's rails watching for dolphins and flying fish and islands and sweeping the sea with Father's binoculars.

And the color of the sea, a midnight blue as you looked down into it in the brightness of day.

The second night out I awoke smelling land. We were passing the first Greek islands, islands aromatic with thyme and the scent of earth and grasses and dry land. We passed close, so that their hillsides reared up above us against the stars.

And then Athens and Naples and Capri and Marseilles. And from there the crossing of France: villages and towns and rivers and snow on the mountain peaks and waking in the upper bunk in the wagon-lit, the train whistling and pulling in at dawn to a small station where there were carts selling milk and coffee and bread. And then Calais, and the blustery English Channel, and the white cliffs of Dover—there they really were, white cliffs, just as it said in our books—drawing closer and closer.

And then Cambridge. But of that I remember little. I remember the crabapple trees that lined some streets, and the strange, tart taste of their fruit. And I remember the woods and trees of Girton College, where we took my sister. All those wonderful trees to climb, I thought, except that now my sister was all silly and grown up and did not even care anymore about climbing trees. That would never, I thought, happen to me. I was nearly twelve.

They would not leave me at the Perse School: my mother refused. I was too young, she said.

It broke my heart. I wanted more than anything to stay.

I cried all the way back. On the train from London to Dover, on the boat crossing the Channel, on the train through France, and on the boat back, I cried and cried and cried.

Back home I stopped crying, and then, as life settled into its new routine, I disappeared entirely into books. I scarcely saw my parents. I would go in to greet them in the morning, after dressing for school, and I would get my pocket money for the day to spend at the school's snack store, a crisp new five-piastre note (which would just pay for a sandwich and a soda at break) from my father. That was the sum of the time that I spent with them. I had my meals on my own, Nanny sometimes sitting watching me, sometimes eating with me.

That is how I remember it, and yet again this cannot quite have been how it was. Because I remember my mother during that period looking at me and saying, "I used to ask myself why God gave you to us so long after your brothers and sister and now I understand. It was so that you could be here to console us. The house would have been so empty now that they're gone and we would have been so unhappy without you." And sometimes she would say also, contemplating me, "You know how they say, '*Akhir al-ʿanud ahlahum*'? The last grape in the bunch is always the sweetest? That's what you are to us." For her to have sat contemplating me and saying these things, we must sometimes have sat in the same room, but I do not remember it. And now her words say to me that she must have been aware of my sadness and was trying to offer some consolation, whereas in my memory she simply did not bother with me at all, had made a scene about not leaving me in England because I was too young and had brought me home just to ignore me, to not give me another thought. I felt uneasy when she said that she used to wonder why God had given me to them and that it was to keep them company. I sensed that she meant well, but something about her words was troubling to me. Why should my existence have meaning only in the scheme of someone else's life? Why did it need that justification? Why did I not exist just because I existed, the way she did or any of my siblings did? I remember trying to understand what it was that I felt to be wrong and not quite identifying it, other than to wonder why it was that God cared—or why she thought God cared—about how they felt but not about how I felt. And I think I was troubled, too, by her wondering why I was born.

I was to learn years later that there was more substance to those musings of hers about my existence and why I was born than I could then have imagined.

I have two other memories from the months following our return. One is of stumbling to the bathroom, half asleep. The bathroom window was wide open and dawn was breaking. I remember that I stopped, sleepy though I was, because it was so arrestingly beautiful, and that I stayed there, leaning on the windowsill watching the colors change in the sky and feeling a light, sweet breeze on my skin, and that as I stood there the call to prayer began from a minaret that I could see on the horizon. Everything, the chant, the dawn, seemed that moment to be exquisitely, achingly beautiful.

No other room, except for Father's, had the clear view to the horizon that the bathroom had, and I particularly liked that view. I first saw this world and the light of day in one of those two rooms, and I have always remembered and liked the memory of the light and the look of the sky from those windows, perhaps because of having witnessed that spectacular dawn there or perhaps—who knows—because they were my first glimpse of this world, and it was dawn then, too. My mother gave birth to me, attended (my sister told me) by Cairo's leading obstetrician, at home, in Father's room, on his bed, and it was my father who on my arrival took me into the bathroom and washed me in the hand basin. He would tell me about it when I came in sometimes as a small child and stood watching him shave, loving the foam he lathered on his face with his shaving brush—he would sometimes let me run a finger through it. You washed me in this basin? I would ask, always intrigued anew that I could fit into a hand basin. Yes, he would say. And then? I would ask. And he would tell me again how he had taken me to the hall and held me up to show to my brothers, who were quarantined in their room because they had measles. The upper half of the door to their room was made of glass with fitted curtains that they pushed aside in order to see me. Then he took me back to my mother. My sister remembers how my mother kept exclaiming at how lovely I was, as if surprised.

My other memory from those first months after our return is of my falling ill with pneumonia. I remember being very ill and that my aunts would come every day to be with my mother and they would all sit in the hall outside my room talking. My head hurt and their talking disturbed me and I called my mother and asked her to ask them to please stop talking because my head hurt and I wanted to sleep, and she said something like, I can't tell them not to talk, that would be very rude, but in fact their voices dropped for a while.

But I remember sensing, in the way that my mother was, that in some way she wanted me to die. I sensed that she was enjoying being the center of attention, my aunts all being there, and that my illness, which had brought them there, was something she somehow enjoyed. I do not know what words I used to put this to myself then, but I know that something of this feeling about her and my illness and her wanting my death was there in me then. And I know that it connected with another feeling I had had about her and her imagining and even wanting my death. It was in connection with what she used to say about Grandmother, that no fate was more terrible than that of losing a child and that that was the worst thing a mother could endure. But I felt that there was something in the way she said it, in the way she looked perhaps as she said it, that made me feel that she was in some sense hankering for this to happen to her, for the importance such a fate would give her, making her someone singled out, the center of attention, as it had made Grandmother. And I felt that the child she

had in mind for this loss that would give her life drama and importance was me.

Of course it is entirely possible that these feelings I thought I
sensed in her represented only the imaginings of a child. And it is
entirely possible that this whole reverie was simply a child's attempt
to grasp how it could be that the reason that my aunts and mother
were all gathered outside my room was concern for me and the wish
to see me better—and yet my mother was apparently more concerned
about not being rude to them than she was about allowing me to
sleep. But it is possible, too, that these feelings represent a child's
divining of the unacknowledged, unwanted desires that cross the human heart, for I believe that children can divine the inner projects
and secret emotions of the adults they are close to and that they can
know them as well and perhaps sometimes better than the adults
themselves do.

And I believe now that I was right, at least to this extent: that the
thought of my death and the enigma of my life and my living despite,
at one time, her intentions for me were matters that my mother ac-
tively pondered. And perhaps it was this that I was picking up on, the
presence of the thought of my death in my mother's meditations.

I learned of something that would make her musings about my
existence intelligible to me the summer before my final year at university. My parents were in England that summer and had rented a
house in Finchley, which they shared with my sister and her husband
and infant daughter. I was visiting. My parents and I were sitting at
the kitchen table and my father said, I cannot now recall à propos of
what, "Do you remember, Bella, what you tried to do when you were
carrying her, how you asked me to drive you to Alexandria? How you
said to me, 'I feel like going to Alexandria right now, drive me to
Alexandria,' and I understood at once what you were thinking. That
you wanted to drive to Alexandria because you thought the desert road
and the bumps and its ups and downs would bring about her birth
prematurely. I said '*Ha-adir!*'—At your service!—and we got into the
car and I drove you to the hospital instead, in case you had said that

because you felt that she might be about to come. If I had done what you wanted, she wouldn't be here now."

My mother flushed and seemed stricken as she looked at me. "Why did you tell her that!" she said, turning to him, clearly distressed.

It was a shock and a difficult and oddly hurtful thing to think about, even though I knew that what she said to me a few moments later, when she had recovered a little, was obviously quite true. "I did not know you then," she said, making a gesture with her hands of unknowing and helplessness, "I didn't know you!"

I have no idea why, at least by her later pregnancies, Mother apparently so definitively did not want any more children. And I do not know to this day why my father told me. He was not a malicious man or someone who wanted to show himself to us in a better light at the expense of my mother. Quite the contrary usually. Perhaps he told me out of a regard for the truth, perhaps it was something about my own existence that he felt I ought to know.

And perhaps too, for this also is altogether possible, I misunderstood the entire exchange between us that day in the kitchen. For of course I have no solid evidence one way or another in the matter. Only those few words and the insubstantial evidence of a look, a gesture, from which I drew my own and perhaps erroneous conclusions. And yet I'd come to feel certain that that exchange had meant what I had taken it to mean, and to feel glad that I had had this information: it felt like a missing piece, without which I would never have unraveled the raveled and at certain moments centrally somber connection there was between me and my mother. For I'd come to believe that watching me grow my mother had remembered and inconsolably mourned the sister who'd survived just moments and that (rightly or wrongly) she had blamed herself for her premature birth. And understanding this I'd feel that I now understood too how it was that my mother had arrived at the belief that the most important thing one could do in life was to harm no one and why it was that she placed on her sons a prohibition against ever engaging in war. But I came to this understanding through an extraordinary experience, the experience of feeling that I had actually been visited by my mother's spirit.

It happened when I was living in western Massachusetts shortly after I moved to America. It was at a time when having to start life all over again in a new country, in a new job in a new field, had come to seem insuperably difficult. The work was hard and the cold bitter, my students were demanding in ways that I was not used to, and my colleagues were absorbed in their own lives. Besides finding America unfamiliar, I felt altogether at sea in women's studies and had no one to talk to about it.

I lived in an apartment with stupendous views of meadows and hills, views that were always present to me because one entire side of the living room consisted of glass and sliding glass doors. I remember sitting in that living room, weary with cold and exhaustion, looking out onto the deep, snowy fields and distant hillsides on which the snow-covered firs were mere lines and brush strokes, feeling overwhelmed by the scene's blank desolation. This sense of an unrelenting despair lingered for weeks. At first I thought what I had always thought in the past at moments of acute depression, that this was simply the heritage that it was given me to struggle with, a capacity for intense depression that I had from my mother's family and that had taken my aunt Aida and her brother Fuad before her all the way into the abyss of suicide. Then I suddenly remembered—its significance coming home to me only then, abruptly, like a revelation—what I had learned that summer: perhaps it was not, after all, the family legacy I was struggling with but my own mother's wish for my death while she was carrying me, her thoughts and desires translating into chemicals of rejection. They had remained circulating in my blood ever since, ready when the circumstances came, to pervade all my cells again and stain my mind with bleakest gloom.

I thought these thoughts having stayed up all night, miserable, unable to sleep, falling asleep at last briefly not in my bedroom but on the living room sofa, the curtains still undrawn. I awoke to the dawn and lay watching gradations of light and color suffuse the sky.

Then I made myself coffee and sat at the table, looking out onto the delicate morning—it was by now late spring—and I wrote in my notebook, "I will not let my mother's old wish for my death kill me. I vow right now that this will be the end of it. I will never, no matter what, take my own life."

It was then that I felt her presence. I felt that she was there in the room and that my father was with her, and that he was with her because he was there to help her.

I felt them both convey to me they had waited for this moment in order to be able to leave. But I felt in her a great grief, grief or anger—I could not tell. There was something she wanted from me, I did not know what. I felt it so intensely, her grief or anger—it was still not clear which—that I cried. And then I felt what it was begin to clarify, and it resolved into her conveying to me that she had not been able to rest and wanted forgiveness. "But that's not in my power," I said. I said it out loud, so real was her presence to me. "You must turn elsewhere for that, but what is in my power I will give you, and so I release you," I said, still speaking out loud. "I release you from any harm you might have done me," and I opened my hand as I spoke, releasing her. And I instantly felt, as I opened my hand, the surge and outpouring of her relief. They would go away now, they said, and never again be back; the business for which they were here was over. And they left.

When I said that I did not have the power of forgiveness and that she must seek it elsewhere, I was probably thinking of God but also of the infant sister who had lived only a few hours and was buried, in my mind, by the Seville orange tree.

And then I went out for a long walk and I thought, as the shadows of the delicate spring leaves played on the path and I smelled the scent of the earth and the scent of the first flowers, of this extraordinary exchange, and I wondered whether it had in any way been real. And then it came to me as I thought over my own words, "I release you from any harm you might have done me," stopping this time at the word "harm." I stopped walking. Harm. Her own word when she had said, Harm no one, this above all, harm no one, choose even to harm yourself rather than someone else, because it is easier to live with anything that happens to oneself than it is to live with the knowledge that you have harmed someone.

And I understood now how she had known that, understood the harm that she thought she had done to another and that she had lived to know was the greatest burden of all. My infant sister and I, I saw, in this new understanding that came to me, had been key to what my mother would come to believe was the most important thing of all in life, the most important thing of all to live by. It was thanks to us, in a way, that my brothers would be made to promise never to go to war.

5

AREM

Looking out onto the garden, the trees that I had loved now gone, felled to make way for the marquees put up for the night's celebrations, I cried and cried. I cried for my trees, I cried for my childhood, I saw in the barren garden before me a picture of the life I must now live, bereft of everything I had loved and of everything companionable to me.

Huda Shaarawi (1889–1945),
Memoirs of an Egyptian Feminist

I KNOW MY father's date of birth, November 13, 1889, but not my mother's. Hers fell in early May, perhaps the fifth. The year was 1909. My mother sometimes said it was the fifth when I pressed her as a child, but usually she just said May, early May. Why didn't she know? I've sometimes wondered. Could it be that they recorded the date according to the Islamic calendar and nobody got around to figuring it out in this other calendar? They must have had birth certificates in those days; otherwise, how was it Father knew his birth date? Or could it be that they kept records in Alexandria, where he was born, but not in the small country town where she came into the world?

At any rate, it was at Benisweif, on her grandfather's estate, that my mother first saw the light of day. She grew up partly in Cairo, in the house that I knew, and partly on her father's estate in al-Fayyum, the rich, fertile oasis a hundred miles or so southwest of Cairo. A place of fruit trees and orange-blossom scents and a veranda and roof garden that I also remember. Nearby was Birket Qarun, a vast gray lake, its edges dense with reeds, reeds that were alive with the shuffle and stir of birds—ducks and waterfowl.

By the time my mother was a child, change for women was well under way in Egypt. Women's magazines were flourishing, feminists were writing newspaper columns, and French, British, and American schools for girls had opened and were attended by the daughters of the well-to-do. When she was an adolescent, Egypt won partial independence from the British, and in 1924 a new government, made up of the country's modernizing intellectuals, came into office, Egypt's first elected government. Although still locked in battle with the British for full independence, the new government began at once to effect changes in the areas under its control. Immediately it opened more schools, and soon also a modern university named after King Fuad. Almost from the start, it admitted women.

The women leading the way in education were from the ambitious, progressive, broad middle class, my father's class. My mother did not belong to this class. Among people of her class, formal education, whether for men or women, was not a matter of importance. They were not, though, wholly isolated from the changes afoot; my mother and her sisters were all sent to the Mère de Dieu, a school run by French nuns. But Mother, the eldest, was withdrawn from the school at the age of twelve and thereafter had private tutors at home. In that fast-changing world, by the time the sister next to her in age, just three years younger, reached that age, Grandfather had decided that there was no harm, after all, in allowing girls to complete their education at school.

It was about then, the mid-twenties, that Huda Shaarawi, returning from an international women's conference in Rome, would formally set aside her veil as she stepped off the boat in Alexandria. Photos of her unveiled face—this leader of the Egyptian feminist movement, whose husband was a prominent figure in the government—appeared on the front pages of the national papers. In the ensuing years European dress and no veil would increasingly become the norm among the middle and upper classes, and soon it would be the ordinary dress of the women of modern Cairo. Old Cairo and the towns and villages of the countryside were, of course, a different matter. But before long, if you saw outside the apartment blocks or mansions of modern Cairo a woman wrapped in the black *milayya* of traditional dress, you would automatically know that she must be the maid or a nanny or the washerwoman.

Still, the veil might go, but not necessarily the attitudes that accompanied it—the habits of seclusion and the cultural conditioning about the meaning of seeing and not seeing, of being visible and invisible. My own parents did not see each other before marriage (in the late 1920s). Not only that, my father had proposed to another woman before proposing to my mother, but he had withdrawn his offer. He called at the woman's home after the marriage broker, Amina al-Turkiyya (Amina the Turk), had conveyed his offer and the family had agreed to receive him. On his way out he saw her trying to catch a glimpse of him from behind the *mashrabiyya*, the elaborate woodwork lattice that, in those days, shielded the windows of the women's quarters. Or perhaps someone told him that she had tried to get a glimpse of him, for how could he possibly have been sure it was she behind the lattice? In any case, he was shocked: if he was content to marry on the basis of a description and a photograph, she too should have been. Or possibly he decided that she was too interested in men and how they looked, and that seemed not to augur well.

Who would have thought, though, that a man who would one day send his daughters to college in England and who throughout his life would give his wholehearted support to women's rights would think a woman improper for wanting to sneak a glimpse of her future husband—so improper that he would withdraw an offer of marriage? Whatever he thought about women's rights clearly did not, in that moment of decision, weigh as much with him as some other understanding that he had, an understanding of life and its meanings and the significance of actions rooted not in intellect and the ideas to which he adhered but in some quite other order of things—feelings, intuitions, responses, potent and "irrational," that now swept right out of the way whatever it was he thought he believed in.

Thinking about my mother's life, reading the memoirs of women of her era, I cannot find a life that seems parallel to hers. This is not to say that I find nothing in what I read that is evocative of her. On the contrary, the reminiscences of Huda Shaarawi are so evocative that sometimes I hear my mother's voice in the words, particularly when Shaarawi allows her personal voice to break through her otherwise formal voice. In those moments Shaarawi is often speaking of gardens, remembering their loveliness and how she found solace in them, taking refuge there from some wound inflicted by the human world.

Shaarawi was from the same broad class background as my mother, though from a much wealthier family. For Shaarawi the wounds inflicted by the world were above all the wounds of being female. All her material needs were lavishly seen to, but she felt uncared for and unworthy of being loved, chiefly because her mother focused all her attention on Shaarawi's brother. Only her father's senior widow, whom Shaarawi called Mama al-Kebira, Great (Senior) Mother, was consistently kind to her. On one occasion, anguished at being yet again rebuffed by her mother, she asked Mama al-Kebira why it was that, though she was the eldest, her brother was always preferred over her.

"Haven't you understood yet," Mama al-Kebira gently replied, "the difference between you?"

This passage always brings to mind my mother, in particular the way she is in that photo I have of her standing under the trellis in her father's house. Something about her air, the way she stands, tells me that that question, "Haven't you understood yet?" would have been, for her, unnecessary. There's a photo of me too as a child, at a younger age, maybe only five or six, with exactly that same solitary, uncertain air. And also one of my eldest brother, a child in this photo of no more than three or four, and yet he too already looks profoundly uncertain of his place in the world.

My mother did not show any preference for her sons over her daughters. She passed on to us all equally her own deep uncertainty as to her welcome, her own childhood anguish at existence.

In the passage from Shaarawi's memoir with which I began this chapter, Shaarawi is recalling the morning after her wedding, when she stood at the window looking out onto the barren garden below, the trees she had loved cut down to make way for the tents put up for her magnificent wedding.

She was twelve and had been forced into marriage to her guardian, a much older man who already had one wife.

These were not, of course, my mother's circumstances. Shaarawi was of an older generation and came from a somewhat different cultural tradition. For Shaarawi was half Egyptian, whereas my mother's family was entirely Turkish or Turco-Circassian (though this was the term used for this group of people, they were drawn from all over the Balkans and the regions around Turkey). And ethnic traditions differed in their customs regarding women.

I remember this, for instance. Someone, a visitor, mentioned to my mother that some other family had just had their daughter circumcised—that is, that she had just had a clitoridectomy. Could the visitor have been a midwife, someone who performed clitoridectomies? Somehow I do not think so: she was dressed as we were, and a midwife would probably have been dressed in a *milayya*. I remember the grimace that crossed my mother's face and her perceptible air of withdrawal. Still, it was a polite, restrained withdrawal.

"That is not something that we do," was all that Mother said.

I did not know what circumcision was. The word in Arabic, *tuhur*, meaning "purification," sounded quite nice. I probably thought that because of Mother's strictness and her very clear sense of what it was that "we" did or did not do, my sister and I were yet again missing out on something special. In any case, clitoridectomy is not a common practice among the urban middle and upper classes.

There was another difference between Shaarawi and my mother. Shaarawi's mother, a Circassian, was her father's concubine, not his wife. Her financial insecurity (a slave woman who had borne her master children was free on his death but not entitled to an inheritance) probably made her more willing to force her daughter into marriage with the girl's powerful guardian.

Before slavery was outlawed in 1885, slave women were not at all uncommon in Egypt's Turkish upper classes. Often they were Circassian women who, renowned for their beauty, were especially prized as concubines. Slave women are there in my mother's family, too. My mother's grandmother, for instance, who was not Circassian but from Russian Georgia, had been "given as a gift" by the khedive to my great-grandfather. No one ever said openly when I was a child that she had been a slave, for by then having been a slave had come to carry a stigma. They just said that she'd been "given as a gift," without further explanation. Free women cannot be gifted away.

Several centuries back, in the Mamluk era, a good proportion of the upper classes in Egypt were slaves or the descendants of slaves. The Mamluks, a Turkish people who conquered Egypt in the thirteenth century, based their society and military system entirely on slavery (*mamluk* means "owned"). The ruling class was made up of men and women (and their descendants) originally captured as children, mainly from the Slav and Balkan regions, and brought to Egypt. The males were trained for the military; the theory was that young boys raised together with no family other than one another and the officers training them would feel utter loyalty to this group and consequently make the best soldiers. As they grew up, they were freed and married into the local Turkish aristocracy. Women were incorporated into this class as concubines or wives. Once a woman bore a free man a child, even if the father did not free or marry her, she became legally free on his death.

To us, with our notions of slavery grounded in the history of American society, the very idea that slaves constituted the upper classes is so counterintuitive as to seem almost nonsensical. But in the Middle East, slaves and slave origins were so fundamentally part of aristocratic and royal life that for over a thousand years nearly all caliphs, kings, and sultans in the region were the sons of slave mothers.

By the end of the nineteenth century, as slavery was slipping into the past, slave origin began to seem shameful. Shaarawi's mother, Ikbal (she had the same name as my mother), never admitted her status to her daughter, maintaining a complete silence about her past. For the same reasons, I expect, I do not know how many of my mother's foremothers had been brought to Egypt as slaves. But no doubt a number of them were, for the family retained the memory that several of them had been Circassians, and slavery was the ordinary route by which Circassians came to be in Egypt.

In this era of change, the knowledge that their mothers had been slaves seemed to spark in some daughters a sense of outrage and a passionate desire to take a stand in their mothers' defense. Those daughters would grow up to take that same stand on behalf of all women. In a work of autobiographical fiction, Oot el Kouloub, an Egyptian feminist of Shaarawi's era and background, attributes the feminism of her heroine, Ramza, to the tales of slavery that Ramza heard as a child from her mother and aunt. It was these tales that "watered the seeds of revolt in my young heart," Ramza declares, even though her aunt and mother themselves expressed neither protest nor dissatisfaction with their former enslavement and even defended slavery (which had rescued the aunt from poverty), speaking of it as an entirely ordinary and acceptable part of their world.

In any case, by the time my mother was a child, the practices of concubinage ceased to be. But the attitudes underlying those bygone customs were not quite gone.

Even in my own childhood, Zatoun, my mother's paternal home, was a place palpably apart, imbued with some unnamably different order and way of being. The aura and aroma of those other times and other ways pervaded it still, in the rustle and shuffle of silks and the soft fall of slippers along hallways and corridors, in the talk and the gestures and in the momentary tremor of terror precipitated by the boom of Grandfather's voice, and then the quiet, suppressed, chortling laughter of the women as its boom faded and he passed into the recesses of the inner hall. The odor and aroma of another time, other ways, another order.

As a child, I found Zatoun at one and the same moment enticing, pleasurable, engulfing, and perilous—obscurely perilous. I could sense, in the way that children can sense such things, that once we had entered its portals, the doorkeeper slowly bringing together behind us the huge iron leaves of the gate he had opened to let in our car, we had crossed into some other world. It was a world whose underlying rules and rhythms, profoundly inscrutable to me, were, as I also naturally sensed, quite known and familiar to my mother. This was the world in which, even more than in our own home, she was completely at home. This was Mother's true home, her true and native land.

Nor was my mother in any sense a rebel in this world. Its ways seemed to her to be completely natural and even deeply moral. Of course, those features that had sparked Ramza's and Shaarawi's rebellion—slavery and concubinage—were not in any direct sense part of my mother's reality. They were there only as distant facts, probably not quite understood, about a grandmother—instances of the strange things they did back then, in olden times.

Looking back now with the assumptions of my own time, I could well conclude that the ethos of the world whose attitudes survived into my own childhood must have been an ethos in which women were regarded as inferior creatures, essentially sex objects and breeders, to be bought and disposed of for a man's pleasure. But my memories do not fit with such a picture. I simply do not think that the message I got from the women of Zatoun was that we, the girls, and they, the women, were inferior. But what, then, was the message of Zatoun? I don't think it was a simple one. I can only set down what I remember of Zatoun and of Siouf in Alexandria, my mother's family's summer home.

It is quite possible that, while the women of Zatoun did not think of themselves and of us as inferior, the men did, although—given how powerful the cultural imperative of respect for parents, particularly the mother, was among those people—even for men such a view could not have been altogether uncomplicated. But men and women certainly did live essentially separate, almost unconnected lives. Men spent almost all their time with other men, and women with other women. It is entirely likely that women and men had completely different views of their society and of the system in which they lived, and of themselves and of the natures of men and women. Living differently and separately and coming together only momentarily, the two sexes inhabited different if sometimes overlapping cultures, a men's and a women's culture, each sex seeing and understanding and representing the world to itself quite differently.

I spent a great deal of my childhood and adolescence among the women of Zatoun, whether at Zatoun itself or at the family home in Alexandria. My view of that world, and of the nature and meaning of life, I learned from the women, not the men. The men figured as dominant beings, naturally, but they were more like meteors, cutting a trail across our sky, causing havoc possibly, but present only briefly. It is for this reason, no doubt, that the novelist and Nobel laureate Naguib Mahfouz's *Palace Walk*, depicting a family similar to that of Zatoun, is to me both familiar and profoundly alien. For it is a portrait of that same world—but through the eyes and ethos of its men.

There was indeed, for a child anyway, as I have said, a distinctly perilous feel to Zatoun. I invariably felt a twinge of fear, along with feelings of pleasure and anticipation, when the car rounded the slight bend in the road and Zatoun's high ochre walls loomed into view.

Zatoun, which means "olives," took its name from the surrounding district. It was three miles from our house, down the straight road along the railway line toward Cairo. If you took the back route you would pass first through the heart of Matariyya, then through the center of Zatoun, both of them *shaabi* (popular) districts that gradually became, over the course of my childhood, more and more densely crowded.

Our car would draw up to the great iron gate of Zatoun as Amm Hasan the *bawab* (doorkeeper), an aged man whose white beard matched his white turban, first peered out from a smaller side door then slowly drew back the gate, one heavy leaf, then the other. Zatoun's garden, unlike ours at Ain Shams, was a formal garden of clipped hedges and precisely cubed shrubs and ordered flower beds. Perhaps the only touch or evocation of wildness in the entire front garden was the trellis with its clambering bougainvillea and loofah plant, where my mother had stood in that photograph and under which I remember playing. On the opposite side, over the garage, was the *salamlek*, an apartment set aside exclusively for male guests. I remember hearing on rare occasions that some friend of my uncle's was staying there, but most of the time it stood empty. (I never even saw inside the *salamlek*, and I don't remember any male guests ever coming into the main house of Zatoun.) Then, along the garden wall on the right of the house (and opposite the kitchen), were the servants' quarters, a hedge screening them off from the rest of the garden. The back garden wall was as high as the house, protecting it from the eyes of the neighbors in the adjoining but quite invisible house.

Past the gate was a circular driveway of pressed red sand, which rose in a paved slope to the front door of the house, a large, heavy door of wrought iron and dense opaque glass. Over it was a high stone archway whose fluted recesses were stained with the excrement of bats. House and archway, like the garden walls, were a deep ochre.

Strangely, the birds at Zatoun were different from those of Ain Shams, perhaps because of the different kinds of gardens. At Ain Shams we had hoopoes and woodpeckers; at midday and particularly in the siesta hour, the soft cooing of mourning doves; then, at dusk, the call of the karawan carrying to us from the fields. At Zatoun, besides the circling and swooping of bats at twilight (we had them at Ain Shams, too, but perhaps not in such great numbers), the characteristic sight and cry over the garden was that of kites, their high, slow circling and their sharp, distinctive cry contributing to the particular quality of specialness and eeriness that seemed of the essence of Zatoun.

Now, in retrospect, it is the pleasures of Zatoun and in particular the warmth of the women's gatherings in Grandmother's room that stand out in my mind, but when I was a child the terrors of Zatoun were also intensely real. The main focus of my childhood terror was the Locked Room, but there was also the *badraun*, the basement, an entire empty replica of the house upstairs, with its two grand halls and its various rooms going off them. Here, downstairs, was the *offees*, the pantry, with its sacks of rice and tall jars of oil, and in the cupboards sugar, coffee, and other things, the keys held by Grandmother and given daily to Umm Said, Grandmother's personal maid, with instructions as to what she was to dispense to the cook. There was another pantry upstairs, off the dining room, whose keys also were held by Grandmother. I don't recall what was in it, but this Grandmother would open herself, dispensing things to Umm Said.

The basement was identical to the upper floor except that, while the upstairs halls and rooms were carpeted, the halls downstairs and some of the rooms were tiled with diamond-shaped dark-red and white tiles. Down here, too, the rooms were furnished differently. Upstairs, except for Grandmother's visiting room, the furniture was "ordinary" European-style furniture. Austerely simple, the overall impression at Zatoun was of dark, polished wood and white walls, bare of decoration, the only color imparted by the glow of the carpets. Downstairs, the rooms, other than the pantry and kitchen, were lined with sofas along the three walls, with varieties of rectangular and elongated circular cushions—some of which were ideal for building "shelters" while others made excellent "torpedoes" in the battles we children staged down there. It was always dim; upstairs, a dome of thick opaque glass in the ceiling meant that in the daytime the inner hall was always suffused with a gentle, watery light, but in the basement daylight only penetrated in distant glimmerings. Downstairs, I would frighten myself with the echo of my footsteps and with what I imagined might be coming at me from the dark edges of the diagonally receding tiles.

My mother went to Zatoun daily or almost daily, setting off every morning almost as regularly as Father set off for work; on days when we were not at school, she sometimes brought us with her. Father would occasionally drop Mother off on his way to work, but this was usually too frantic. Father would send us in from where he sat in the car, clicking his tongue, to tell Mother to hurry up. She would be having a last-minute conference with the cook. "*Tayeb! Tayeb!*—Okay! Okay!—Tell him I'm coming!" Usually, though, Grandfather's car would come for her about midmorning and bring her back a couple of hours later, well in time for when Father arrived for lunch. If we were not at school, we would have had our lunch, but we would sit with them, listening to their talk, taking an interest, too, in the contents of the brown bags of fruit—bananas, guavas, melons—that Father purchased from the fruiterers of the city on his way home. These were unpacked, washed, and brought to the side table.

All the aunts came nearly daily to Zatoun, sometimes with their children. Going to Zatoun and spending a couple of hours with Grandmother and with other women relatives was no doubt an enormous source of emotional and psychological support and pleasure. It was a way of sharing and renewing connection, of figuring out how to deal with whatever was going on in their lives with husbands, children, and the people who worked in their homes. All five sisters had married men they had never met, and no doubt these daily sessions in which they shared and analyzed their lives were vital to adjusting to what must have been at times enormously trying circumstances. Their meetings surely must have helped them keep their homes and marriages running reasonably smoothly; three of the five, including my mother, managed to have tranquil, happy marriages. But there were many other lives to be overseen. There were the other people of their community, as well as the women relatives who gathered here with them occasionally and those women's menfolk; everyone's issues and problems had to be analyzed, discussed, and resolved. And there were, too, the lives of the workers, the servants, who were in some sense under their jurisdiction. Generally speaking, the women of Zatoun knew intimately the personal details of the lives of those who worked for them, particularly their women servants, all of whom had been with the family, in one household or the other, for many years and many of whose mothers also had. Discussing and resolving these people's problems when they could, delegating this sister or that relative to talk to her lawyer husband or doctor husband were intrinsic parts not only of their conversations but, to them, of their responsibilities.

The atmosphere in Grandmother's receiving room was always wonderful. I do not remember a single occasion when it was not a pleasure to be there with the women. Relaxed, intimate, affectionate, rarely solemn, their conversations and exchanges were often extremely witty and sharp and funny. My aunt Aisha in particular, the youngest and the most irreverent, would reduce us all to helpless laughter. She and Farida were particularly good at imitations and could do hilarious renderings—exaggeratedly grand, authoritarian, and pompous—of Grandfather.

The room was furnished with deep, wide sofas all the way round. Grandmother, always on her particular sofa, always in the same corner, would sit cross-legged or with her legs tucked up beside her under her black robe. On the carpeted floor beside her sat Umm Said, joining in the conversation when moved to do so or when invited to comment. Generally, though, she sat quietly listening, gently massaging Grandmother's feet and lower legs. This kind of massage, called *takbees*, was much valued in that part of the world. Umm Said, about the same age as Grandmother, had been with her since girlhood and had come with her to her new home when Grandmother married. Her own marriage had been arranged by Grandmother's family: her husband, once a worker on Grandmother's family estate and now a butcher, after a few years of marriage—and two sons by Umm Said —had taken another and younger wife. He had not divorced Umm Said and she did not press for divorce—although he sometimes came back and harassed her for money—because, ambivalent and at times deeply scornful of him though she often was, occasionally she would also wonder, somewhat wistfully, whether he might not yet see sense one day and come back to her. Being permitted to sit with the women, privy to their conversations and intimate revelations, was a privilege granted only, among the servants, to Umm Said. Other women working in the household came to bring in or take away, for instance, coffee cups, but they did not remain or share in the conversation.

The rest of the company sat, cross-legged or legs drawn up beside them, on the sofas all around. They would drink Turkish coffee, smoke (although not all of them, and never Grandmother), and munch on *lib* (a salted, roasted seed that has to be cracked open) as they talked. Grandmother's receiving room was the first room on the left at the top of the stairs as one came in at the front door; on the other side of the stairs, on the right, was Grandfather's "study" (although he never studied and was rarely there anyway), which smelled faintly and deliciously of cigars, the handsome empty boxes of which we children sporadically collected.

Sometimes Umm Said would read the women's coffee cups after the coffee dregs had been duly swirled and the cups overturned in the requisite manner, but she did not have the reputation of being a particularly gifted coffee-cup reader. Occasionally one of the visitors who knew how to read cups would read them or someone visiting downstairs (a relative of one of the servants) who was thought to be gifted would come and read them, but it was not something that people took seriously. If, for example, the coffee-cup reader said, "I see you coming to a road that forks, and down one of the forks I see a stranger," someone would usually jump in with a bit of jocular speculation.

I used to love running in to Grandmother and, after greeting her, resting my head in her lap as she gently stroked my hair. Her eyes, a kind of green-gold that we call *ʿasali*, honey-colored, looked down from under wide, unplucked eyebrows with love and without artifice. I was often told as a child that I looked like her and that I was in fact just like her, and so I would lie looking up at her, studying intently, upside down, the planes and curves of her face, searching it to see who I was and what exactly I was like.

But we children could only stay with them a short while. We were soon told to go out and play or, on the rare occasions when it was raining, to go down into the *badraun*. Obviously our presence would have inhibited the freedom with which they could talk.

Grandfather was only occasionally at Zatoun. He spent four or five days a week, sometimes longer, on his farm at al-Fayyum. His land was given over to the farming of fruit, grapes especially but also oranges, lemons, bananas, and tangerines. Sometimes, though less as I got older, we would visit al-Fayyum for a few days. He had a lovely house there, with orange and lemon trees planted all around, their blossoms scenting the air in the spring.

Grandfather was an astute and dedicated farmer who devoted much of his time to attending to the land. But he also had other pastimes at al-Fayyum as well, like playing cards with other landowners at a club on Lake Qarun near his farm.

When Grandfather returned to Zatoun from one of his sojourns at Fayyum, a message would somehow run through the household, a whisper like a breath of wind through wheat, that he had arrived: *"El-bey el-kebir! El-bey el-kebir geh!"* ("The senior master! The senior master is here!") or "Baba!" ("Father!") or "Grandpapa!" depending on who was speaking. Servants would scurry off to do whatever they were supposed to be doing, and everyone—my aunts and mother and whoever was there visiting with Grandmother—would rearrange how they sat, adjust themselves, stifle their laughter. Not that Grandfather ever entered Grandmother's receiving room. No man, not even Grandfather, ever set foot there, to my knowledge: his presence would have been a violation of the seclusion rights of any woman present who was not his wife or daughter or close relative. (My brothers and cousins, so long as they were mere boys, were of course a different matter.)

My aunts and mother and uncle were very formal and deferential in Grandfather's presence. If he came into a room where they were sitting, they would scramble to their feet, the very hurriedness of their motion probably being part of the appearance of respect that was due him. They would then present themselves to him and make to kiss his hand in greeting, whereupon at almost the same instant and before his hand touched their lips, he would draw them to him instead and plant a kiss on their heads. The sight of my mother, herself such an august figure, standing before Grandfather, head bowed, eyes lowered until he invited her to sit down, was always astonishing to me. We grandchildren were not obliged to observe this code, although we were required to troop in to greet Grandfather when he arrived. He would take the small ones on his knees and give them loud, smacking kisses, often on the lips, then put them down. Even the older grandchildren got those loud kisses. I remember still how big and blubbery his lips seemed to me, and his nose and his entire face, and his domed, knobbly, clean-shaven head. He was very big and tall but also svelte, with a hawk nose and piercing blue eyes. An athlete once, he had regularly swum the length of the Alexandria coastline as a young man. He had a loud, resonant, and naturally booming voice. I never heard him shout at anyone, except (rarely) at his valet, who went everywhere with him. This man, Abdel Athim, held himself aloof from the rest of the servants, considering himself a rank apart. He dressed differently from the other servants, in particularly fine brocaded caftans, cummerbunds, and turbans.

Grandfather himself dressed, always very elegantly, in European-style suits; outdoors, he wore his red felt tarboosh. Grandmother invariably wore a long black robe and a black head veil that closely framed her face. On occasion, when she was at prayer, she might wear a softer-shaped white head veil. She never left the house, as far as I know, except to travel in the summer to Alexandria and, in her younger days, to Fayyum and, once that I remember, to attend a funeral. (I remember noticing her stern, handsome, buckled black shoes—I was used to seeing Grandmother only in slippers and stockinged feet.) I don't believe that she ever even went to the cinema. On those rare occasions when she stepped outdoors, she traveled always in Grandfather's main car, its curtains drawn.

Observing this strict etiquette of deference, Grandfather's children nevertheless made him the butt of their humor in private. But they were also quite fond of him. My two surviving aunts, Aisha and Nazli, speak lovingly of Grandmother and of my mother and their other siblings and of how they look forward to meeting up with them soon. And they even look forward to seeing Grandfather again. When I visited recently, Nazli said, "I always mention him in my prayers, along with everyone else." "Me too," said Aisha. Then Aisha said that she had been wondering recently whether it was a sin to ask at the end of salat (formal prayer) for God to take one. "It's enough now," she said, "enough." Nazli thought it was a sin; it was up to God to decide when one's time was up. Aisha was depressed—things had been hard the last few years. Her husband, in his eighties, had been suffering for several years from what was probably Alzheimer's, and she alone had been looking after him, although someone came in two days a week to cook and clean. Then, the subject of death still on our minds, Aisha said that Amm Saleh, the Nubian head servant at Zatoun and Alexandria, whom everyone had been very fond of and who had retired to a small plot on Aisha's land, had been to see her a few days before he died and had told her that he knew for certain that he was going to die very soon, although he was in good health. "How do you know?" she had asked him, and Saleh had replied that for several nights in a row he had dreamed that Grandfather was calling out to him in his great booming voice, "Saleh! Saleh! Come here! Saleh, come here!"

"Are there going to be servants up in heaven, too?" I asked. "Is Saleh doomed forever to be a servant?"

"How do we know?" said Aisha. "I am just telling you what happened."

"Did Grandmother ever hit you when you were children?" I had been asking my aunts to tell me about their childhoods and I returned now to the subject.

"Never! Don't you remember her? How gentle and loving she was?"

"What about Grandfather, did he ever hit you?"

"Hit us! He had a doctorate in hitting! His brother Halim—do you remember him?—he was a gentle, sensitive man. He would call your grandfather whenever his children misbehaved and needed a beating."

"But," said Nazli, "we always deserved it—we were very mischievous children."

"What did you do?" I wanted to know. But I got no answer.

Only Grandmother was exempt from making the show of deference and obedience with which everyone treated Grandfather, at least to his face. The relationship between the two of them was extremely courteous and formal, but it was a relationship—at least in outward conduct and manners—of equals. If anything, it was Grandfather who deferred to Grandmother, treating her with a more humble courtesy than she him. Grandmother, for her part, although always utterly civil and courteous, held herself aloof. And he, in the way that he looked at her sometimes, seemed contrite, as if imploring her forgiveness.

As a child, I did not know the story behind this. I did not know that their son Fuad had committed suicide and that Grandmother believed, and in retrospect Grandfather perhaps concurred, that it had been Grandfather's stubborn hardness of heart that had driven his son to it. I was told that the young man had died of typhus when he was a student in Vienna. Grandmother had seen him in a dream, I was also told, the night of his death. He had come on a white horse to bid her adieu. The telegram bringing news of his death arrived the next day, and then his coffin was brought home.

I finally learned the truth sometime in my teenage years. Fuad, who was the next child after my mother, had been a student in Vienna and had fallen in love with an Austrian girl and wanted to marry her. Grandfather was adamantly set against the marriage and steadfastly refused to permit it.

It was this tragedy that lay behind the mysterious and terrifying Locked Room of Zatoun. This was Fuad's room, kept exactly the way it was when he was alive. Grandmother kept the key with her always and entered it at regular intervals with Umm Said to dust. I never caught even a glimpse of the inside, and if I happened to pass the sealed white door, I would run by as fast as I could.

Grandmother was in perpetual mourning. That was why Mother and my aunts needed to spend so much time at Zatoun with her, because without them her grief would be unendurable. Although she had always been pious, Fuad's death had transformed her, they said, from a cheery person who had laughed easily to a quiet, often sad person, who performed many extra prayers besides the required five and always dressed in black. Her voice was soft now (in the old days she could be as sharp as anyone, they said) and her laughter, in the rare moments when she laughed outright, was also quiet and gentle.

No one seemed to think that Grandmother's unending mourning was strange. (I found myself thinking about this just the other day, watching a program on American television in which a woman was consulting a psychiatrist because her daughter had been dead six months and she was still grieving.) It seemed, on the contrary, to be accepted as a terrible but appropriate grief, a grief that did honor to the depths of her feelings as a mother. And it was dogma that nothing, no loss or suffering, equaled the suffering of a mother who had lost a child. I seem to remember that my father once or twice cautiously broached the idea that perhaps it was time that Grandmother put the past behind her just a little. My mother would agree that it was hard that she still suffered so much, but how could my father say such a thing? What did he know of a mother's heart?

Motherhood was mysterious. It was sacred, but it had little to do, apparently, with actually looking after or tending to one's children. It was, I suppose, about having one's children around one, under one's broad physical and moral guardianship and protection—even if, in the routines and practicalities of daily life, it was someone else who actually looked after them. And it connoted also some powerful, un-severable connection of the heart. Everything my mother did seemed to be an expression of this notion of motherhood, from her apparent lack of interest in the dailiness of our lives to the scenes she made at the quayside in Alexandria, waving her large white handkerchief in a tear-drenched goodbye as one or another of us and sometimes several of us left for England.

I remember now, recalling her there at the quayside, a song my mother sang. It was one of Asmahan's. *"Adi'l habayib ʿal gambein,"* the song went. "With my loved ones all around me, what sweeter joy has heaven to offer?" My mother would croon it to herself on those increasingly rare occasions when all of us—all her children—were back in Egypt at the same time.

For my mother, these were some of the hidden, uncounted costs of colonialism: her children's growing up speaking a language she did not understand and going off in their teens to college in a faraway land and a culture that would eventually steal them away. Among other things, there were hard, practical consequences. The children would not be there in the way that children traditionally (and according to both the Bible and the Quran) were supposed to be there when parents grew old and frail.

~

The Alexandria house at Siouf, where all of us—my mother and her sisters and their children and Grandmother—summered together, had all the pleasures of Zatoun and nothing of its atmosphere of somberness and sorrow or its sense of hidden impending danger. At Siouf, even Grandmother's constant prayerfulness was mysteriously transformed. The sight of her at prayer, standing, hands folded, her white veil draped over her head and lightly across one shoulder, then kneeling and bowing in the ritual motions, touching her head to the ground and rising again—all this, instead of reminding one of death and mourning, as it did at Zatoun, was profoundly reassuring. Perhaps because here we lived with her and so observed the regularity with which these moments of prayer occurred and their harmony with the rhythms of the day and of life, we were less inclined to imagine them, as perhaps we did at Zatoun, as merely marking an overflow of sorrow. At Zatoun, the sight of Grandmother at prayer accentuated her connectedness with the realm of spirits, a realm that seemed to hover so dangerously close as to always be on the verge of breaking through. At Alexandria, Grandmother seemed instead to have connections and influence among another set of unseen powers, powers that had the capacity to bless, and so living in this house over which she presided, I felt safe, reassured, as if we were all there under her—and consequently under their—protection. My memory of the night she took me up on the roof to watch for angels was just one instance of the feelings of wellbeing and safety, and the sense I had of the imminent nearness of the marvelous, that being at her side could engender.

The Alexandria house itself was also different from Zatoun. It was lighter, more open to the world, to the garden around it. Certainly there was no Locked Room in Alexandria. It may even be that my grandparents did not own the house during Fuad's lifetime, for I believe that Grandfather bought it specifically so that his daughters and their growing numbers of children could spend their summers together. Grandfather himself rarely came there, perhaps no more than twice in an entire summer, each time for just a few days. Similarly, the husbands, including my father, came only intermittently, for weekends usually, though sometimes for longer. Even when they were there, though, they were marginal figures. The moods of the Alexandria house and the rhythms and currents of its life were ours, those of my aunts and mother and grandmother and us children.

An essential element of the pleasure of being in Alexandria was that of being part of that large household and above all of being with the aunts. Those we were closest to were Aisha and Nazli, though we loved them all. The five sisters were extraordinarily different in both looks and personality, except that all were tall and two, Aisha and Aida, very tall. Aisha was a tawny redhead with brown eyes and Aida, considered, along with Farida, the beauty of the family, had liquid black eyes and black hair. Farida was a dark blond with blue eyes, and my mother and Nazli, who looked alike, had black hair and gray-blue eyes. All were exceedingly handsome.

Aisha, the youngest, was a wonderful athlete and swimmer, and always fun and funny and full of life. She was my favorite. She was everyone's favorite.

Grandfather had decreed that all the sisters were to marry at twenty, a fairly late age. And all except for Aisha were married to native Egyptian men like my father, self-made professionals. Grandfather had taken a dislike to the "wastrels" of his own well-to-do class and had vowed not to marry his daughters to them or to anyone who had inherited wealth. But by the time Aisha's marriage came along he had relented a little as to the last condition. Aisha's husband was a professional man of Egyptian, not Turkish, background, but he was from a landed family. He was about twelve years older than she and doted on her, his face lighting up whenever he set eyes on her. She, in turn, was clearly fond of him. They had three children.

Nazli, too, had a happy marriage. She had wanted at least one daughter but kept producing boys, so she continued trying till, the fifth time around, she got a girl. Nazli was the unofficial family medic, "specializing" in children's illness, appearing at our bedsides the moment any of us was sick, prescribing what should be done. She was also the most tenderhearted of all the sisters. It was she who, if any of us was crying, would be the first to gather us up in her arms to soothe us. Even if she was punishing her children or one of the rest of us, she would melt the moment we looked woeful and would immediately give up and kiss us. She involved herself in every detail of her children's lives, from supervising what they ate, to sitting with them through their homework, to insisting that they retire for a siesta in the middle of the day, a matter they resisted daily. Aisha was equally involved in her children's lives. Both sets of children, as the rest of us witnessed in our shared life in Alexandria, bawled loudly and cried real tears every time their mothers went out. We found this astonishing.

Farida's husband, after a few years and five children, secretly took a second wife. When Farida learned of it she was distraught and resorted to all sorts of methods—including consulting sorceresses and performing odd practices on their instruction (brewing certain teas and putting potions in his drink)—to cause him to divorce his new wife. All this earned her the reputation in the family of being a rather silly, credulous person. Eventually, as her husband tired of her various schemes and machinations, he divorced her, which Farida had not wanted either. Their last child, a daughter named Nair, arrived when her mother was in the throes of these troubles, and I spent many summer hours as a young teenager playing on the veranda with this excruciatingly shy and lovely child and teaching her to walk and talk.

Farida married twice afterward, both times briefly and, obviously, unhappily. She was destined, like her mother, to suffer the "worst of all fates," the loss of a child. One of her sons, a lovely, dreamy-eyed boy, Ali, became a sailor in the navy and drowned in his twenties when his ship went down in a freak accident in the Strait of Messina. I never saw her again, but people told me that, like Grandmother, she became a prayerful, religious woman, making many pilgrimages to Mecca. Unlike Grandmother, though, she always dressed in white. In fact, all my aunts became more pious as they grew older—the ones who survived to late middle age, that is. This was, I believe, a cultur-

ally sanctioned progression in that society: as people fulfilled and left
behind the duties of their younger years they gradually gave themselves more fully to piety and to the rhythms and preoccupations of
religious life.

⁓

In Alexandria, we spent the mornings on the beach, each group
of children with its "dada," or nanny, setting off at its own pace,
arriving at the beach, where we had cabins, at different times. (My
siblings and I were the only cousins with a foreign nanny.) The aunts
and my mother, if they came to the beach, would arrive together in
midmorning and would sit on the main family cabin deck, chatting,
the sea wind snapping the canvas drapes around the cabin. We would
be out swimming or playing on the beach. Only Aisha, among the
adults, swam, but she did so only in the afternoon, at about sunset,
when some of us (having gone home for lunch) would return with her
to the beach. Aisha would wear a burnoose—a terry-cloth bathrobe
—down to the edge of the sea. Handing it to her maid, who had
accompanied her down specifically for that purpose, she would run
into the sea and dive into the waves. The maid, remaining on the
beach, would keep a lookout for when Aisha was ready to emerge,
whereupon she would meet her at the water's edge holding up the
burnoose. My sister, too, had to adopt the burnoose on reaching pu-
berty, going down to the sea's edge in it and then tossing it on the
beach and running in. We were not supposed to be seen in bathing
suits by strange men. When I reached that age there was a discussion
as to whether I needed to take on the burnoose, and I wore it for one
summer or perhaps half a summer and then it was decided that these
things were too old-fashioned.

Often I would go in the water with Aisha, but she was a powerful
swimmer and I could not keep up with her. After our swim we would
shower and dress and Aisha would set off on her walk, sometimes
joined by a band of us—her daughter, my sister, and me. A five- or
six-mile walk along the Corniche was for her just an ordinary walk,
but when we were with her we did not walk that far. Sometimes we

would buy the corn that was roasted on embers and sold all along the Corniche and would sit for a while looking out to sea, talking and eating.

Sometimes we went on day trips and picnics, organized usually by Aisha. We would take boat trips to Agami, for instance, down the coast from Alexandria, in those days an almost empty shore where the sands were white and the sea an azure blue and where fig trees grew almost up to the beach. We would anchor at sea and go over the side of the boat into the turquoise water and swim to shore, Aisha joining us. Then we would swim back to the boat for a wonderful picnic lunch of stuffed vine leaves and stuffed peppers and tomatoes and cold chicken and salads. Aisha took us on such outings in Cairo also, to the Barrages gardens along the Nile, for instance, where she would play tag with us, running as fast as we did. I remember in particular her taking us to Alexandria one spring and our stopping at the rest house in the desert halfway there; the desert silence was so profound that our words seemed scarcely to disturb it, as if they were mere ripples in an ocean of stillness. I remember this outing because I had never until then seen the desert in spring and never witnessed how its usually harsh, barren surface could become covered in tiny delicate flowers, flowers that formed slashes of vivid color on the dunes in the distance and even more vivid pools of color, purple and gold, in their dips and hollows. It was astonishing and marvelous to see that the desert was capable of nurturing such a fragility of life. And even now, whenever I hear inhabitants of lush, green lands speak dismissively of a place as "just desert, nothing but barren desert," I think of this—and of how little they know of the miraculous loveliness of the desert.

It was Aisha, too, who would take us in the evening to the amusement park, riding with us on the Ferris wheels and the bumper cars and the Ghost Train, screaming as much as any of us at the luminous skeletons, scaring us even more. And buying us cotton candy.

Some evenings the aunts went out, occasionally taking the older children with them and sometimes going on their own, to see a play perhaps or visit friends. And sometimes they took some of us younger ones on rides along the Corniche, in open carriages drawn by horses, to Délices in the main square by the Cecil Hotel, where we would buy ice cream. Usually, though, they would stay home. Joined on occasion by various women friends and relatives, they would sit together with Grandmother out on the upstairs veranda, a veranda onto which all the rooms at the front of the house opened. The front of the house was rounded, like the prow or bow of a ship. We would sit with them, those of us who felt like it, listening to their talk, joining in their laughter, on nights that were always bright with starlight and sometimes brilliant with the light of a moon that cast shadows sharper and blacker than the sun's.

I must sometimes have slept in one of those upstairs rooms, because I remember the pleasure, the veranda door open, of relinquishing myself to sleep to the murmur of their voices drifting in to me from where they sat chatting under the stars, smoking, drinking lemonade, the ice in their glasses clinking faintly.

Of course, too, my mother's family had its share of tragedies.

Grandmother, fortunately, did not live to see the early death of Yusef, her only surviving son. She died when I was ten, quietly, gently, as she did everything, after an illness of just a few weeks. When it was clear that the end was near, we were taken to say goodbye. She was half sitting up, resting on a bank of pillows, wearing an oxygen mask, and was as sweet and loving as ever, more concerned about our frightened faces than she was about herself.

Within about a year we were taken to Zatoun once more to say a last goodbye, this time to her son, who had moved back there for his last illness. I remember his agonized cries coming to us muffled from behind the heavy white door to where we waited in the hall. We were sent out into the garden to wait for a quieter moment, when the morphine had taken effect and he was more able to receive children and presumably also so that our last glimpse of him would not be so dreadful.

He was only thirty-six and was dying of lung cancer. But the last year of his life was packed with heart-wrenching tragedy over and

above his illness. Yusef was the last male of the line, the last bearing
the Ramzi name, and he was childless. His wife, Colette, was infertile.
Colette was French, and they had been married for twelve years and
loved each other enormously. They had met and fallen in love in
France and Colette, who they said was from a "good" French family,
surprised and moved everyone by converting to Islam. (While it is
legally required that men convert to Islam if they marry Muslim
women, women are not legally required to convert to marry Muslim
men.) She learned Arabic and came to speak it beautifully, with just
a slight accent. She was very much loved in the family, and everyone,
Grandmother in particular, was moved by the sincerity of her devotion
to Islam, which she spoke of as being (as in fact Muslims believe)
what Christianity ought to be, what it was meant to be. But everyone
was touched more than anything else by her love for and loyalty to
Yusef, who, though a handsome and engaging man (in looks he and
Colette were well-matched), distinctly had his problems. He was an
alcoholic and a compulsive gambler, repeatedly losing at the tables
large sums of money. But he had periods, months at a time and once
a stretch of years, of sobriety, and in those times he and Colette would
briefly appear in our lives, at Zatoun or Alexandria, laughing a lot,
talking about their travels and parties and their glamorous lives.

When he was diagnosed with cancer the issue of his having no
offspring, and specifically no son to carry forward the family name,
became something of major importance, apparently for him and Colette as well as for Grandfather. I can only assume that to have been
the case, because I cannot otherwise understand or explain what then
happened. It was decided that Yusef must have a son immediately,
and since Colette was infertile (they had determined this medically),
he had to take another wife and divorce Colette. Both were bereft at
the idea, but they went through with it. I do not know why Yusef's
taking an additional wife, without divorcing Colette—as of course
Islam permits men to do—was not an option, but apparently it was
not.

Yusef's health immediately deteriorated and he moved back to
Zatoun. Colette came daily to be with him, then simply moved to

Zatoun herself, though she did not share Yusef's suite and did not, as she made clear, live with him as his wife. She cried a lot. Meanwhile arrangements for his remarriage went ahead. Finally a woman thought to be suitable was found, although it was clear too that for both the bride and her family this was a practical, financial transaction, since it was plain now that Yusef was dying. The marriage obviously would not last, but Yusef might have a child, hopefully a son, and she would be his widow and heir. The marriage went forward and then was immediately terminated. The young woman, who was twenty, apparently was not a virgin, and Yusef at once divorced or anyway separated from her, presumably thinking that any child that came would not necessarily be his.

Colette stayed with him through the remaining time that he had and was at his side when he died.

~

And then there was the tragedy of my aunt Aida. She had, I know, an unhappy marriage. The details were kept from us. I saw her arrive at Zatoun once in tears, looking as if she had thrown on her clothes and fled there. We children were instantly shooed out, the way we had been on one occasion when my uncle Yusef had come home openly drunk. I know that Aida wanted a divorce and that her husband refused to give her one and that when she appealed to Grandfather he said categorically that divorce was not a thing he permitted in their family. Farida, her sister, had been divorced but that had been entirely her husband's decision and Grandfather could not have prevented it. I know that at one time Aida's marriage had seemed totally unendurable to her and that she had become deeply depressed and that her husband, who was in the medical profession, arranged for her to see a psychiatrist, who gave her electric-shock treatment. For a time after that she was strange and developed a facial twitch. But then she returned to herself. She was most like Aisha among her sisters, often funny and witty like her, but quicker and more mercurial. She took a lot of pills and was seeing a psychiatrist at the time she took her life.

She jumped from the bathroom window of their fifth-floor apartment one day when she and her husband were at lunch. They were having an argument. She had said again that she wanted a divorce and he had refused. That is all I know. She ran from the table and locked herself in the bathroom. He had had no idea, he said later, weeping out loud, that what she was doing was climbing out the window.

I remember going to their apartment the day after her death for 'aza (condolence). She had survived for only a few moments on the pavement, a crowd forming round her as she moaned in great pain, and then had died, no one she knew at her side. She was buried the same day. She was forty-two.

I almost could not bear to offer my sympathies to her husband, as I was required to do, going into the room where he sat with the men, receiving condolences, his face looking stricken and shriveled.

And I found myself angry also at her sisters, my mother and aunts, their eyes swollen and red, receiving condolences in the rooms for women. Why are you crying now? I thought. What's the point of that? Why did you do nothing to help her all this time, why didn't you get her out of that marriage? I thought it was their fault, that they could have done something. If they had cared enough they could have done something.

That is what I thought then. Now I am less categorical.

Grandfather lived into his nineties, dying just as the new revolutionary government enacted the Land Reform Laws, redistributing the land once owned by the "feudalists" to its legitimate owners, the Egyptian peasantry.

By some process the details of which I do not know, Zatoun was taken over ("rented" for a nominal sum) by the government and put to use as a school. That is what Zatoun is today.

⁓

It is easy to see now that our lives in the Alexandria house, and even at Zatoun, were lived in women's time, women's space. And in women's culture.

And the women had, too, I now believe, their own understanding of Islam, an understanding that was different from men's Islam, "official" Islam. For although in those days it was only Grandmother who performed all the regular formal prayers, for all the women of the house, religion was an essential part of how they made sense of and understood their own lives. It was through religion that one pondered the things that happened, why they had happened, and what one should make of them, how one should take them.

Islam, as I got it from them, was gentle, generous, pacifist, inclusive, somewhat mystical—just as they themselves were. Mother's pacifism was entirely of a piece with their sense of the religion. Being Muslim was about believing in a world in which life was meaningful and in which all events and happenings were permeated (although not always transparently to us) with meaning. Religion was above all about inner things. The outward signs of religiousness, such as prayer and fasting, might be signs of a true religiousness but equally well might not. They were certainly not what was important about being Muslim. What was important was how you conducted yourself and how you were in yourself and in your attitude toward others and in your heart.

What it was to be Muslim was passed on not, of course, wordlessly but without elaborate sets of injunctions or threats or decrees or dictates as to what we should do and be and believe. What was passed on, besides the very general basic beliefs and moral ethos of Islam, which are also those of its sister monotheisms, was a way of being in the world. A way of holding oneself in the world—in relation to God, to existence, to other human beings. This the women passed on to us most of all through how they were and by their being and presence, by the way *they* were in the world, conveying their beliefs, ways, thoughts, and how we should be in the world by a touch, a glance, a word—prohibiting, for instance, or approving. Their mere responses in this or that situation—a word, a shrug, even just their postures—passed on to us, in the way that women (and also men) have forever passed on to their young, how we should be. And all of these ways of passing on attitudes, morals, beliefs, knowledge—through touch and the body and in words spoken in the living moment—are by their very nature subtle and evanescent. They profoundly shape the next generation, but they do not leave a record in the way that someone writing a text about how to live or what to believe leaves a record. Nevertheless, they leave a far more important and, literally, more vital, living record. Beliefs, morals, attitudes passed on to and impressed on us through those fleeting words and gestures are written into our very lives, our bodies, our selves, even into our physical cells and into how we live out the script of our lives.

It was Grandmother who taught me the *fat-ha* (the opening verse of the Quran and the equivalent of the Christian Lord's Prayer) and who taught me two or three other short suras (Quranic verses). When she took me up onto the roof of the Alexandria house to watch for angels on the night of the twenty-seventh of Ramadan, she recited the sura about that special night, a sura that was also by implication about the miraculousness of night itself. Even now I remember its loveliness. It is still my favorite sura.

I remember receiving little other direct religious instruction, either from Grandmother or from anyone else. I have already described the most memorable exchange with my mother on the subject of religion—when, sitting in her room, the windows open behind her onto the garden, the curtain billowing, she quoted to me the verse in the Quran that she believed summed up the essence of Islam: "He who kills one being [*nafs*, self, from the root *nafas*, breath] kills all of humanity, and he who revives, or gives life to, one being revives all of humanity." It was a verse that she quoted often, that came up in any important conversation about God, religion, those sorts of things. It represented for her the essence of Islam.

I happened to be reading, when I was thinking about all this, the autobiography of Zeinab al-Ghazali, one of the most prominent Muslim women leaders of our day. Al-Ghazali founded a Muslim Women's Society that she eventually merged with the Muslim Brotherhood, the "fundamentalist" association that was particularly active in the forties and fifties. Throughout her life she openly espoused a belief in the legitimacy of using violence in the cause of Islam. In her memoir, she writes of how in her childhood her father told her stories of the heroic women of early Islam who had written poetry eulogizing Muslim war-riors and who themselves had gone to war on the battlefields of Islam and gained renown as fearless fighters. Musing about all this and about the difference between al-Ghazali's Islam and my mother's pac-ifist understanding of it, I found myself falling into a meditation on the seemingly trivial detail that I, unlike al-Ghazali, had never heard as a child or a young girl stories about the women of early Islam, heroic or otherwise. And it was then that I suddenly realized the dif-ference between al-Ghazali and my mother and between al-Ghazali's Islam and my mother's.

The reason I had not heard such stories as a child was quite simply that those sorts of stories (when I was young, anyway) were to be found only in the ancient classical texts of Islam, texts that only men who had studied the classical Islamic literary heritage could un-derstand and decipher. The entire training at Islamic universities—the training, for example, that al-Ghazali's father, who had attended al-Azhar University, had received—consisted precisely in studying those texts. Al-Ghazali had been initiated into Islam and had got her notions as to what a Muslim was from her father, whereas I had received my Islam from the mothers, as had my mother. So there are two quite different Islams, an Islam that is in some sense a women's Islam and an official, textual Islam, a "men's" Islam.

And indeed it is obvious that a far greater gulf must separate men's and women's ways of knowing, and the different ways in which men and women understand religion, in the segregated societies of the Middle East than in other societies—and we know that there are differences between women's and men's ways of knowing even in non-segregated societies such as America. For, beside the fact that women often could not read (or, if they were literate, could not decipher the Islamic texts, which require years of specialist training), women in Muslim societies did not attend mosques. Mosque going was not part of the tradition for women at any class level (that is, attending mosque for congregational prayers was not part of the tradition, as distinct from visiting mosques privately and informally to offer personal prayers, which women have always done). Women therefore did not hear the sermons that men heard. And they did not get the official (male, of course) orthodox interpretations of religion that men (or some men) got every Friday. They did not have a man trained in the orthodox (male) literary heritage of Islam telling them week by week and month by month what it meant to be a Muslim, what the correct interpretation of this or that was, and what was or was not the essential message of Islam.

Rather they figured these things out among themselves and in two ways. They figured them out as they tried to understand their own lives and how to behave and how to live, talking them over together among themselves, interacting with their men, and returning to talk them over in their communities of women. And they figured them out as they listened to the Quran and talked among themselves about what they heard. For this was a culture, at all levels of society and throughout most of the history of Islamic civilization, not of reading but of the common recitation of the Quran. It was recited by professional reciters, women as well as men, and listened to on all kinds of occasions—at funerals and births and celebratory events, in illness, and in ordinary life. There was merit in having the Quran chanted in your house and in listening to it being chanted wherever it was chanted, whereas for women there was no merit attached to attending mosque, an activity indeed prohibited to women for most of history. It was from these together, their own lives and from hearing the words of the Quran, that they formed their sense of the essence of Islam.

Nor did they feel, the women I knew, that they were missing anything by not hearing the exhortations of sheikhs, nor did they believe that the sheikhs had an understanding of Islam superior to theirs. On the contrary. They had little regard, the women I knew, for the reported views and opinions of most sheikhs. Although occasionally there might be a sheikh who was regarded as a man of genuine insight and wisdom, the women I knew ordinarily dismissed the views and opinions of the common run of sheikhs as mere superstition and bigotry. And these, I emphasize, were not Westernized women. Grandmother, who spoke only Arabic and Turkish, almost never set foot outside her home and never even listened to the radio. The dictum that "there is no priesthood in Islam"—meaning that there is no intermediary or interpreter, and no need for an intermediary or interpreter, between God and each individual Muslim and how that Muslim understands his or her religion—was something these women and many other Muslims took seriously and held on to as a declaration of their right to their own understanding of Islam.

No doubt particular backgrounds and subcultures give their own specific flavors and inflections and ways of seeing to their understanding of religion, and I expect that the Islam I received from the women among whom I lived was therefore part of their particular subculture. In this sense, then, there are not just two or three different kinds of Islam but many, many different ways of understanding and of being Muslim. But what is striking to me now is not how different or rare the Islam in which I was raised is but how ordinary and typical it seems to be in its base and fundamentals. Now, after a lifetime of meeting and talking with Muslims from all over the world, I find that this Islam is one of the common varieties—perhaps even *the* common or garden variety—of the religion. It is the Islam not only of women but of ordinary folk generally, as opposed to the Islam of sheikhs, ayatollahs, mullahs, and clerics. It is an Islam that may or may not place emphasis on ritual and formal religious practice but that certainly pays little or no attention to the utterances and exhortations of sheikhs or any sort of official figures. Rather it is an Islam that stresses moral conduct and emphasizes Islam as a broad ethos and ethical code and as a way of understanding and reflecting on the meaning of one's life and of human life more generally.

This variety of Islam (or, more exactly perhaps, these familial varieties of Islam, existing in a continuum across the Muslim world) consists above all of Islam as essentially an aural and oral heritage and a way of living and being—and not a textual, written heritage, not something studied in books or learned from men who studied books. This latter Islam, the Islam of the texts, is a quite different, quite other Islam: it is the Islam of the arcane, mostly medieval written heritage in which sheikhs are trained, and it is "men's" Islam.

More specifically still, it is the Islam erected by that minority of men who over the centuries have created and passed on to one another this particular textual heritage: men who, although they have always been a minority in society as a whole, have always been those who made the laws and wielded (like the ayatollahs of Iran today) enormous power in their societies. The Islam they developed in this textual heritage is very like the medieval Latinate textual heritage of Christianity. It is as abstruse and obscure and as dominated by medieval and exclusively male views of the world as are those Latin texts. Imagine believing that those medieval texts on Christianity represent today the only true and acceptable interpretation of Christianity. But that is exactly what the sheikhs and ayatollahs propound and this is where things stand now in much of the Muslim world: most of the classic Islamic texts that still determine Muslim law in our day date from medieval times.

Aurally what remains when you listen to the Quran over a lifetime are its most recurring themes, ideas, words, and permeating spirit, reappearing now in this passage, now in that: mercy, justice, peace, compassion, humanity, fairness, kindness, truthfulness, charity, mercy, justice. And yet it is exactly these recurring themes and this permeating spirit that are for the most part left out of the medieval texts or smothered and buried under a welter of obscure and abstruse "learning." One would scarcely believe, reading or hearing the laws these texts have yielded, particularly when it comes to women, that the words "justice," "fairness," "compassion," "truth," ever even occur in the Quran. No wonder non-Muslims think Islam is such a backward and oppressive religion: what these men made of it *is* largely oppressive. Still—to speak less judgmentally and, in fact, more accurately—the men who wrote the foundational texts of official Islam were living in societies and eras rife with chauvinism, eras when men believed as a matter of categorical certainty that God created them superior to women and fully intended them to have complete dominion over women. And yet, despite such beliefs and prejudices, here and there in the texts they created, in the details of this or that law, they wrote in some provision or condition that, astonishingly, does give justice to women. So, even in those bleak days, the Quran's recurring themes filtered through. They did so, however, only now and then in a body of law otherwise overwhelmingly skewed in favor of men.

I am sure, then, that my foremothers' lack of respect for the authority of sheikhs was not coincidental. Rather, I believe that this way of seeing and understanding was quite common among ordinary Muslims and that it was an understanding passed on from mothers and grandmothers to daughters and granddaughters. Generations of astute, thoughtful women, listening to the Quran, understood perfectly well its essential themes and its faith. And looking around them, they understood perfectly well, too, what a travesty men had made of it. This ingrained low opinion that they had of sheikhs, clerics, and ayatollahs stemmed from a perfectly just and astute understanding of their world, an understanding that they passed on to their daughters and indeed their sons.

Leaving no written legacy, written only on the body and into the scripts of our lives, this oral and aural tradition of Islam no doubt stretches back through generations and is as ancient as any written tradition.

One could even argue that an emphasis on an oral and aural Islam is intrinsic to Islam and to the Quran itself, and intrinsic even to the Arabic language. Originally the Quran was an aural, and only an aural, text recited to the community by the Prophet Muhammad. And it remained throughout his life, and indeed for several years after his death, only an aural text. Moreover, a bias in favor of the heard word, the word given life and meaning by the human voice, the human breath (*nafas*) is there, one might say, in the very language itself. In Arabic (and also Hebrew) script, no vowels are set down, only consonants. A set of consonants can have several meanings and only acquires final, specific, fixed meaning when given vocalized or silent utterance (unlike words in European script, which have the appearance, anyway, of being fixed in meaning). Until life is literally breathed into them, Arabic and Hebrew words on the page have no particular meaning. Indeed, until then they are not words but only potential words, a chaotic babble and possibility of meanings. It is as if they hold within them the scripts of those languages, marshaling their sets of bare consonants across the page, vast spaces in which meanings exist in a condition of whirling potentiality until the very moment that one is singled out and uttered. And so by their very scripts these two languages seem to announce the primacy of the spoken, literally living word, and to announce that meaning can only be here and now. Here and now in this body, this breath *(nafas)* this self *(nafs)* encountering the word, giving it life. Word that, without that encounter, has no life, no meaning. Meaning always only here and now, in this body, for this person. Truth only here and now, for this body, this person. Not something transcendent, overarching, larger, bigger, more important than life—but here and now and in this body and in this small and ordinary life.

We seem to be living through an era of the progressive, seemingly inexorable erasure of the oral and ethical traditions of lived Islam and, simultaneously, of the ever-greater dissemination of written Islam, textual, "men's" Islam (an Islam essentially not of the Book but of the Texts, the medieval texts) as *the* authoritative Islam. Worse still, this seems to be an era of the unstoppable spread of fundamentalist Islam, textual Islam's more narrow and more poorly informed modern descendant. It is a more ill-informed version of old-style official Islam in that the practitioners of that older Islam usually studied many texts and thus at least knew that even in these medieval texts there were disagreements among scholars and many possible interpretations of this or that verse. But today's fundamentalists, literate but often having read just a single text, take it to be definitive and the one and only "truth."

Ironically, therefore, literacy has played a baneful part both in spreading a particular form of Islam and in working to erase oral and living forms of the religion. For one thing, we all automatically assume that those who write and who put their knowledge down in texts have something more valuable to offer than those who simply live their knowledge and use it to inform their lives. And we assume that those

who write and interpret texts in writing—in the Muslim context, the
sheikhs and ayatollahs, who are the guardians and perpetuators (per-
petrators) of this written version of Islam—must have a better, truer,
deeper understanding of Islam than the non–specially trained Muslim. Whereas the fact is that the only Islam that they have a deeper
understanding of is their own gloomy, medieval version of it.

Even the Western academic world is contributing to the greater
visibility and legitimacy of textual Islam and to the gradual silencing
and erasure of alternative oral forms of lived Islam. For we too in the
West, and particularly in universities, honor, and give pride of place
to, texts. Academic studies of Islam commonly focus on its textual
heritage or on visible, official institutions such as mosques. Consequently it is this Islam—the Islam of texts and of mosques—that
becomes visible and that is presented as in some sense legitimate,
whereas most of the Muslims whom I know personally, both in the
Middle East and in Europe and America, would never go near a
mosque or willingly associate themselves with any form of official Islam. Throughout history, official Islam has been our enemy and our
oppressor. We have learned to live with it and to survive it and have
developed dictums such as "There is no priesthood in Islam" to protect ourselves from it; we're not now suddenly and even in these new
lands going to easily befriend it. It is also a particular and bitter irony
to me that the very fashionableness of gender studies is serving to
disseminate and promote medieval men's Islam as the "true" and "authentic" Islam. (It is "true" and "authentic" because it is based on old
texts and represents what the Muslim male powers have considered
to be true for centuries.) Professors, for example, including a number
who have no sympathy whatever for feminism, are now jumping on
the bandwagon of gender studies and directing a plethora of dissertations on this or that medieval text with titles like "Islam and Menstruation." But such dissertations should more aptly have titles along
the lines of "A Study of Medieval Male Beliefs about Menstruation."
For what, after all, do these men's beliefs, and the rules that they laid
down on the basis of their beliefs, have to do with Islam? Just because

they were powerful, privileged men in their societies and knew how to write, does this mean they have the right forever to tell us what Islam is and what the rules should be?

Still, these are merely word wars, wars of ideas that, for the present anyway, are of the most minor significance compared with the devastation unloosed on Muslim societies in our day by fundamentalism. What we are living through now seems to be not merely the erasure of the living oral, ethical, and humane traditions of Islam but the literal destruction and annihilation of the Muslims who are the bearers of those traditions. In Algeria, Iran, Afghanistan, and, alas, in Egypt, this narrow, violent variant of Islam is ravaging its way through the land.

If a day won't come
when the monuments of institutionalized religion are in ruin
. . . then, my beloved,
then we are really in trouble.

Rumi

It has not been only women and simple, unlearned folk who have believed, like the women who raised me, that the ethical heart of Islam is also its core and essential message. Throughout Muslim history, philosophers, visionaries, mystics, and some of the civilization's greatest luminaries have held a similar belief. But throughout history, too, when they have announced their beliefs publicly, they have generally been hounded, persecuted, executed. Or, when they have held fast to their vision but also managed to refrain from overtly challenging the powers that be and thus avoided violent reprisal, they have been at best tolerated and marginalized—accepted as eccentrics outside the tradition of "true" Islam. From almost the earliest days, the Islam that has held sway and that has been supported and enforced by sheikhs, ayatollahs, rulers, states, and armies, has been official, textual Islam. This variant of Islam has wielded absolute power and has not hesitated to eradicate—often with the same brutality as fundamentalism today—all dissent, all differing views, all opposition.

There has never been a time when Muslims, in any significant number, have lived in a land in which freedom of thought and religion were accepted norms. Never, that is, until today. Now, in the wake of the migrations that came with the ending of the European empires, tens of thousands of Muslims are growing up in Europe and America, where they take for granted their right to think and believe whatever they wish and take for granted, most particularly, their right to speak and write openly of their thoughts, beliefs, and unbeliefs.

For Muslims this is, quite simply, a historically unprecedented state of affairs. Whatever Islam will become in this new age, surely it will be something quite other than the religion that has been officially forced on us through all these centuries.

~

All of this is true.

But the fact is that, however genuinely humane and gentle and pacifist my mother's and grandmother's Islam was, it left them and the women among whom they lived wholly accepting of the ways of their society in relation to women, even when those ways were profoundly destructive. They bowed their heads and acquiesced to them even when the people being crushed were their nearest and dearest. Tradition and the conviviality, warmth, companionship, and support of the women of the extended family were rich and fine and nourishing and wonderful so long as things went well and so long as these women were dealing with men whom they loved and who loved them. But when things went wrong, the women were powerless and acquiescent in a silence that seemed to me when I was young awfully like a guilty averting of the eyes, awfully like a kind of connivance.

This, in any case, seems to me to be what my aunt Aida's story points to.

Aida's marriage was absolutely miserable from the very start, but divorce, according to Grandfather, was simply not a permissible thing in his family. And yet his own niece Karima, my mother's cousin twice over (her parents were Grandmother's sister and Grandfather's brother), had divorced twice, and each time by her own volition. The difference was that Karima was an heiress, both her parents having died when she was young. Independent and wealthy, she had married on her own terms, ensuring always that the ʿisma, the right to divorce, was placed by contract in her own hands. (The Islamic legal provision permitting women to make such contracts is one of those details that I mentioned earlier that are written into and buried deep in what is otherwise a body of law overwhelmingly biased in favor of men. Generally only rich women and women with knowledgeable, protective families are able to invoke these laws. Many people don't even know of their existence.) Aunt Aida had not inherited anything as yet and was financially dependent on her husband and her father.

Grandmother, grieving all her life over the cost of Grandfather's intransigence toward their son Fuad, was powerless to alter his decision about Aida. For all I know, Grandmother even acquiesced in the notion that divorce was so great a disgrace that, despite her daughter's misery, she could not bring herself to advocate that course or attempt to persuade Grandfather to relent. Karima, her own niece, always received, of course, with warmth and unconditional affection in their home, was nevertheless regarded by Grandmother and her daughters as somewhat scandalous, or at any rate as someone who was rather unconventional and living dangerously close to the edge of impropriety. Aunt Karima further added to her reputation for unconventionality when she founded an orphanage for illegitimate children. It was scandalous to men like Grandfather for respectable women even to mention such a subject, let alone to be founding a society and openly soliciting funds from him and his cronies to support an organization addressing the matter. She raised substantial funds for it over the course of her life as well as for another society, which she also founded, for the care and training of the blind. Both still flourish today and honor their founder. A bust of her stands in the front garden of the Society for the Blind.

Grandmother would not live to witness Aida's suicide. But she was witness to Aida's sufferings and unhappiness in her marriage, and the electric-shock treatment she underwent.

There is an irony to all this. In the circumstances in which Aida found herself, Islamic law would in fact have granted her the right to a divorce or an annulment. Had she been free to take her case to an Islamic court and had she not been constricted by the conventions of her people, she would have been granted, even by that male-created law, the release that she sought. Not by Grandfather and his customs or by Grandmother and her daughters and their conventions, steeped as they, too, were in the ways of their society, but by Islamic law, in another of those unexpected, startlingly just provisions of this otherwise male-biased construction.

Nor was this the only situation in the various family circumstances I've described when women would have been more justly treated at the hands of Islamic law than they were by the traditions of the society, traditions by which the women of the family, too, were evidently bound. Islamic law, for example, frowned on the practice, entirely accepted by cultural tradition, whereby a man repudiated a woman, as my dying uncle had done, because he doubted her virginity. Asked about such a case, a medieval Islamic judge responded that the man had no right to repudiate a woman by claiming she was not a virgin, since virginity could be lost in many ways—just by jumping about or any such thing. He could divorce her nevertheless, since men had the absolute right of divorce even if in the absence of a good reason, but the woman was entitled to full compensation and could not be regarded or treated as guilty of anything.

And so we cannot simply conclude that what I have called women's Islam is invariably good and to be endorsed. And conversely, everything about what I've called men's Islam is not to be automatically rejected, either.

～

To refuse to veil one's voice and to start "shouting," that was really indecent, real dissidence. For the silence of all the others suddenly lost its charm and revealed itself for what it was: a prison without reprieve. . . .

While I thought I was undertaking a "journey through myself," I find I am simply choosing another veil. While I intended every step forward to make me more clearly iden- tifiable, I find myself progressively sucked down into the an- onymity of those women of old—my ancestors!

Assia Djebar (Algerian novelist), *Fantasia*

If the women of my family were guilty of silence and acquiescence out of their inability to see past their own conditioning, I, too, have fallen in with notions instilled in me by my conditioning—and in ways that I did not even recognize until now, when, thinking about my foremothers, I suddenly saw in what I had myself just written my own unthinking collusion with the attitudes of the society in which I was raised. Writing of Aunt Farida and of how aggrieved and miserable she was when her husband took a second wife, I reproduced here without thinking the stories I'd heard as a youngster about how foolish Aunt Farida was, resorting to magic to bring back her husband. But I see now how those stories in effect rationalized and excused his conduct, implying that even though taking a second wife wasn't a nice way for a man to behave, perhaps he had had some excuse, Aunt Farida being so foolish.

"The mind is so near itself," Emily Dickinson wrote, "it cannot see distinctly." Sometimes even the stories we ourselves tell dissolve before us as if a mist were momentarily lifting, and we glimpse in that instant our own participation in the myths and constructions of our societies.

$\mathcal{S}$CHOOL $\mathcal{D}$AYS

OUR SCHOOL stood on the extreme edge of Heliopolis, a suburb of Cairo about three miles to the west of us. It was a handsome, beige L-shaped building with green shutters occupying a corner on one of the boulevards of Heliopolis, and it was the last building before the desert. About five or six stories high, its walls were embossed at regular intervals with the school's emblem, a laurel wreath enclosing a rose over which were the words *Ducit amor patriae*—Love of our country guide us—an emblem emblazoned also on the upper front pockets of our school blazers, in shades of blue or rose, the different colors signifying athletic achievement or prefecthood or something else, I cannot recall what. Our blazers, worn in winter, were navy blue, like our uniform, a navy tunic over a white shirt and the school tie of gray and navy blue, with a thin line in a different color (purple, green, red, or blue) edging the navy stripe to indicate which house we belonged to—Gloucester, York, Kent, or Windsor for girls, Raleigh, Frobisher, Drake, or Grenville for boys. In summer the uniform was royal blue. And white socks and black shoes, both seasons.

Behind the school were the school grounds and playing fields. The playing fields, of red pressed sand marked with white lines for the running tracks and the football, hockey, and net ball fields, extended a considerable distance. Beyond them, toward the end of the grounds, was a copse of firs and oleanders, the outer boundary marked by a line of taller firs all permanently inclined in one direction because of the prevailing desert wind.

This was the Senior School. Junior School, on the same grounds but at some distance from the main building, had a smaller and less striking building and a series of huts with round tin roofs in which we took some classes.

I moved up to Senior School the year before our trip to Europe. When I returned after that summer, I was promoted two grades instead of one—the effects of my having plunged into reading were beginning to show in my schoolwork. Until then, in Junior School, I was usually among the bottom five students in the class, except at exam times—the only times I took the trouble to read through our books—when I would be in the top three or four. But by and large I was absorbed in play and found schoolwork completely boring. The only class I liked, in fact loved, was English, taught by Mrs. Turner, a frail, dried-up-looking Englishwoman who was in fact friendly and warm. It was a reading and writing class, which I think she taught at all levels of Junior School. On Fridays she would read to us. I remember looking forward to Friday class and the acute pleasure of sitting there listening, and I remember laughing and laughing at *Winnie the Pooh*, and I remember her reading *The Wind in the Willows*, and that we, in turn, would read from it to the rest of the class and that this too was pure pleasure.

And I remember that I was a Brownie in Junior School, an activity for which we wore brown uniforms and gathered in a circle around a wooden Brown Owl, and that the teacher was also the Brown Owl, and that we sang songs—"John Brown's baby had a cold upon his chest, a cold upon his chest, a cold upon his chest." (The cold eventually kills the baby despite all the remedies and rubbings that we sang about.) We also learned to do things whose point was completely mysterious, like tying reef knots, although that was probably among the few things I thought could be handy, at least in the various imagined adventures on which my playmates and I were constantly embarking.

Prior to the English School I had attended the English Mission School for a year. It was there that I learned to sing, and eventually to read and write, the alphabet. I remember learning that A was for apple and seeing a picture of an apple on the board, a fruit I had never seen before. And I remember that we had dolls in a corner of the classroom and that once when I was taken ill I was put on the doll's bed—I think only to comfort and distract me and not because I could fit into it. But I hated this school. I hated having to drink from the taps in the school yard, because of the brown slime on the wall behind them where the water dripped and because of the smell there—the taps were outside the lavatories. And I hated the lunch— wet rice with gristly mincemeat and sometimes artichokes. We had artichokes once a week and every week I would end up having to stand in the corner. We apparently were expected to eat (though this seems incredible to me now) the hard part of the leaves, but I could never chew my way through them and would always get caught trying to sneak them under the table. My sister and I had been sent to the Mission School because it was all girls, but in the year I was there a dispute arose over the school's attempts to Christianize us. The school refused to yield and some parents, including mine, decided to remove their children even if it meant sending them to a mixed school (the only other English choice). I don't know why parents thought it rea- sonable to ask a mission school not to proselytize, but this, as I recall, was what happened.

The English School required that new students already speak English, and there was a small hitch regarding my admission not be- cause I could not speak English but because I refused to speak to the teacher who interviewed me. I was taken to the school for the inter- view and was so overwhelmed with shyness I would not speak. A few days later the school agreed to send a teacher to our house, where it was thought I would feel more comfortable. I hid in the garden but was finally persuaded to approach, though not to enter, the house. I stood by the side balcony, where the milkwoman and her cow would be when they came, and the teacher was up on the balcony, sitting on the parapet and looking down, questioning me. But she asked questions—I do not recall now what—to which the answers were so obvious that I was sure she already knew them. So why was she asking them? I stood contemplating this mystery, looking intently into her eyes, but saying nothing. My father, distressed and frustrated that I had again failed to gain admittance to the school, nevertheless chuckled when I explained to him why I had not answered. Somehow he persuaded them to send the teacher out to us yet again and I suppose he must have impressed on me that I must answer no matter what, because this time I got in.

In Senior School the day started with our standing outside the hall in rows according to our houses; the teachers stood on a raised, covered arcade facing us. The youngest children would be in front, and house prefects would walk up and down the lines checking that we were quiet and properly dressed, our ties and socks straight. Once all the teachers were there, there would be a pause, and then a hush would fall over everyone and the headmaster would sweep out of the school building and onto the arcade, his academic robes flowing behind him. Mr. Brent Price. A new headmaster appointed by the powers in London, he had replaced Mr. Whiting, who had been there many years, much loved by students and parents alike.

On Mondays we would troop up the stairs and into the hall for assembly. The headmaster would make various announcements and generally give a short speech. We would then sing hymns; my favorite was "Teach Me, my God and King." I loved in particular the first stanza and two others:

Teach me, my God and King,
In all things thee to see
And what I do in any thing
To do it as for thee.

A man that looks on glass
On it may stay his eye;

Or if he pleaseth through it pass
And then the heav'n espy.

A servant with this clause
Makes drudgery divine:
Who sweeps a room, as for thy laws,
Makes that and th'action fine.

I wonder now why this last stanza was as arresting to me as it was; I had never myself had to sweep the floor. Perhaps it helped make sense of what I know I sometimes vaguely puzzled over, why it was that some people were servants and how it was that apparently they were not unhappy about it.

We would conclude with the Lord's Prayer. The hymns, referring only to God and specifically chosen from among those that made no reference to Jesus, were, like the Lord's Prayer, considered by the school to be interdenominationally monotheistic and thus as acceptable for Muslim and Jewish children as for Christians. On special occasions we also sang the national anthem—the British one, of course. It included the words "God save our gracious king," and "Send him victorious, happy and glorious, long to reign over us." So far as I recall, we sang them entirely unself-consciously. We must have stopped singing it after the Egyptian Revolution, July 26, 1952, but I seem to remember that we sang "God Save the Queen" for a time, too; Elizabeth ascended the throne a few months before the revolution. The transition from king to queen in England was marked in my own life by a detail that for some reason I still remember. I had been invited to tea at the home of my schoolmate Lucy, who lived close to us, and we learned that afternoon, when Lady Fulton, her mother, came to collect us from where the school bus dropped us off, that the king had died. Lady Fulton looked pale, and stricken, as if a close family member had died. Lucy was perhaps nine and I was about eleven, but for us too, evidently, things could not proceed normally in the face of this tragedy. Lady Fulton did not disinvite me, but our tea proceeded most solemnly. We were not left to play but had to sit quietly at table while the tea was being prepared, and when it was served the amount of food we got was awesomely meager—two small triangular slices each of buttered English white bread and that was all. No cakes as we had had in past teas. And after tea we did not go out into the garden to play as we would normally have. Lady Fulton explained that the family was now in mourning for the king and that Lucy could not go out to play. She looked grave, but she always looked a little grave. Even her daughter, a beautiful child with solemn brown eyes and brown shining hair who looked just like her mother, often had that same air of gravity about her. She was an only child and had come late.

On weekdays other than Mondays we would not go into the hall for assembly. After we had lined up outside and after the headmaster had made his usual entrance, he would make a few brief announcements and then declare, "Jews and Muslims fall out!" At this point, Christian students would troop into the hall to pray and sing Christian hymns, while we Muslims and Jews had the time to ourselves, usually about twenty-five or thirty minutes during which we would walk about with our friends on the school grounds or out onto the playing fields as far as the fir and oleander copse.

This became the time that Joyce and I would spend together. Joyce, who had straight black hair and bright, mischievous brown eyes, had been my best friend from the time I first came to the English School at the age of six, when she also was six. I remember our friendship not, as with Gina, for the games we played but for the way things were between us, the way we would know, for instance, just exchanging glances, what the other thought. And the way we saw things the same, as if we stood together on the edge of things, outside the ordinary stream of life, observing from a space of our own, seeing below the threshold of words that the rules by which adults lived and with which they tried to contain what we thought were not grand and infallible, as the adults would have us believe they were. Joyce was Jewish, and I know that we discussed to our satisfaction what it meant that people were of different religions, and that we watched quizzically (I remember exactly Joyce's expression) the antics of adults, and that we observed, exchanging glances, the convolutions into which they sometimes got on the subject of different religions. At home I was told about Jews what I was told about Christians, that we all believed in the same God but had different religions because people had to be the religions into which they were born. I expect that Joyce was told something similar, probably with the same additional explanations that I got in response to further persistent questioning. It would go something like this: "Are all three religions exactly the same?" "No, not exactly. There are differences, but they are in essence the same." "But are they all exactly equal?" "Well, no, ours is best." "Well then, why doesn't everybody else convert?" "They can't do that. People have to belong to the religion into which they're born." "But if ours is best?" "Well, it's best for Muslims, dear. Why don't you run off and play now?"

The issue of Palestine and Israel was something happening elsewhere, somewhere "out there," and it had no bearing at all, at least insofar as I was aware, on relations among Jews and Muslims and Christians where we lived. In my own perception it would be only after Suez that these would change. But my own perceptions were those of a preteenager and obviously reflected attitudes in my own home and community, and not necessarily those of the country at large. Elsewhere in the country and in Cairo, as I know now (not from memory but from history books), other currents and feelings were afoot, and already for several years before the revolution there had been hostilities and incidents against Jews.

I recall a few details of the kind of play Joyce and I engaged in, for instance, the secret society we formed consisting of just the two of us and modeled, I expect, on the secret societies in Enid Blyton's books. We had a secret symbol, the letter K (because it came between her first initial and mine), which we wore on buttons we made for ourselves by writing the letter on a piece of material and wrapping it around a button and tying it there, attaching it to our clothes with a safety pin; we explained its meaning to no one. We also had secret signs and a secret written language, but it was such a labor composing and deciphering notes in this language we did not resort to it often. I remember, too, that we roller-skated together, and that Joyce broke a front tooth one day when we were skating in the school rink, and that she got up and did not cry, in spite of all the blood—she had also cut her lip—and that we were scared as we ran to the school matron. And I remember her new tooth, whiter than the others, and how she worried that people would know she had a false tooth.

My skipping a grade separated us to some extent, but it did not end our friendship. We kept up our habit of spending that first half hour of the school day together, walking in the school grounds and talking. And we continued seeing each other outside school, Joyce sometimes coming to Ain Shams and I sometimes going to her home, though more rarely, because it was an apartment and we were more confined there. They lived on the main boulevard in Heliopolis, opposite Cinema Roxy, an open-air movie theater to which we would go together. During the intermission we would buy Coca-Colas and the delicious fresh round sesame bread (called *semeet*) sold there with slices of Greek cheese in wax paper, enjoying, as well as the film we had come to see, the always pleasant evenings of Egypt in the seasons in which open-air cinemas were open. Invariably, though, Nanny came with us, as I was not allowed to go anywhere without her, even to the rare parties (usually birthday parties). Later, this would cause me enormous embarrassment since no one else went places with their nannies. Some girls at our school had even stricter families, though, and they were simply not allowed to visit anyone who was not family.

The films we saw were almost always American, and when they were not American they were British: *On Moonlight Bay, Fantasia, The Secret Life of Walter Mitty, Hans Christian Andersen, Annie Get Your Gun, Seven Brides for Seven Brothers, The Greatest Show on Earth, Lassie, The Man with the Golden Arm.* We rarely went to Arabic films, which we did not like, except for those of the famous comedian Naguib el-Rehani, which we loved. Arabic movies, like Arabic music, were looked down on in our circle, although when I say this, I don't know who exactly I mean: my parents rarely went to movies, Arabic or Western. (Now I love old Egyptian movies. Egypt was the Hollywood of the Middle East, and in the thirties and forties, anyway, produced some wonderful films.)

Besides the movies we also went to the Heliopolis Sporting Club, where we swam and sat on the Lido and drank Cokes. Sometimes we took walks in Heliopolis, from Joyce's house to the Baron Empin castle, right next to my aunt Aisha's house, and sometimes I took walks in that area with my aunt Aisha, too, with her great, big, handsome gray dog, Wolf. The baron, a Belgian, was the man who had thought up Heliopolis, buying desert land and designing its layout and persuading the government to build wide European-like boulevards with palms and varieties of trees and grass down the middle, and selling plots for villas. The result was an attractive European-style suburb, called in Arabic Masr el-gedida, New Cairo. Empin amassed a vast fortune and built himself an extraordinary castle that, in all the years that I knew it, was totally deserted. A peculiar, haunting landmark, its grounds were dominated by flights of steps on which stood stone vases and sculptures, and there was little green except for some ornamental palms. Rising above them, the rose-colored castle with its complicated turrets looked exactly like the castles of dribbled sand on the beach.

In my second year in Senior School, the year I was moved up a grade, Mr. Brent Price, the new headmaster, instituted the practice of teaching a class in every grade once every two weeks.

The class he taught was called Civilization. He would talk about world civilizations, and we would read books and write essays for him. One of the first books we read was Samuel Butler's *The Way of All Flesh* (perhaps in a special edition for schools), after which we had to write essays about its subject, parents and children. Butler's book was, I think, the first that revealed to me that one could be critical of the world around one; it freed me to find words for the pained, scathing vision I had formed as a result of the recent events of my own life. I immersed myself in writing and wrote passionately.

When Mr. Price handed back our notebooks he began, as he told us he was doing, with the students with the lowest grades, saving the best essays for last. He called out names and generally made some comment as each student came up. Finally he called the name of my new friend Jean, who, like me, usually got top marks in English. He had given her a very high mark and he said something complimentary as he handed her her book. Then he called my name and smiled the smile he was famous for, a crooked, one-sided smile, and, handing me my book, he said that he had not given me a mark at all because the essay was so good he could not believe it was my own and that, if it was, I must take it as a compliment that he had not graded it. Mr. Price, who was South African, had an accent that was unfamiliar to me and that I had difficulty understanding, and this, coupled with his smile and the fact that mine was the last book he handed back and finally that the essay was indeed my own, meant that I went back to my seat feeling at once very pleased and very confused. I sat through the rest of the class hour with my ears burning, still not quite sure what had happened.

It was Jean who, after class, said, "Don't you understand what he means? He thinks you cheated, that someone wrote it for you."

I was so ashamed even to be thought to be cheating that I never told anyone. This was easy to do, for my parents, though pleased at good end-of-term reports, were not involved in what was going on at school in any daily way.

Mr. Price gave me no grades on my next three essays, always returning them to me with the same smile, the same soft-spoken unctuousness. One of those essays, about an aquarium, I still remember, recalling the pleasure with which I imagined the underwater world and the colors and fronds and sea anemones. After that essay, he apparently accepted that I wrote my own essays and he began giving me grades, always, though, a mark or two below Jean's. Jean had recently joined our school and, despite Mr. Price's attempt to make rivals of us, she and I became best friends and remained so throughout our school days. It was only at the end of my career at the English School that I learned the root of Mr. Price's attitude. The year we took our O levels, Jean was in England for the summer and, calling him to get the results, she asked him for mine as well as hers. In all our subjects we were within a few marks of each other, she ahead in one subject, I in another. Mr. Price told Jean how sorry he was to see me ahead of her in anything; after all, he said, she was a Christian and I only a Muslim. Of course she reported his comments, telling me also of her disgust at them.

It would have been less unsettling if I had understood earlier what had fueled his behavior. But I did not know and I was in awe of him—he was, after all, the headmaster—and though I sensed his unfairness, I must have inwardly discounted that feeling, for I know his views and words did carry weight with me. I recall that I consulted him as to whether I should enter the arts or the sciences and that he was firmly against my entering the sciences, much to my father's annoyance. My science grades were good and my father wanted me to be an engineer, like him, or a physicist, or whatever I wanted, as long as I was a scientist. Mr. Price's opinion swayed me, even though my father for the first time doubted him, questioning the grounds for his advice: he believed that Mr. Price was advising me against the sciences because I was Egyptian, that his attitude was a relic of the old days when the British did not want Egypt to have its own scientists. That, of course, had been his own experience as a young man.

But it was not only Mr. Price who discouraged me. The only kind of scientist I thought I might want to be was an astronomer—we had a telescope at home, which we sometimes mounted in the garden. I went to talk to my math teacher, Miss Minty. She said she could not recommend astronomy, but I was confused as to her reason and that was because she herself conveyed it only very ambiguously. It had something to do with my being a girl—and now I think she was trying to say that even if I did major in math I would never get to be an astronomer because women simply didn't (which I suspect was the case in her day). I think that I felt ambivalent about being a scientist, anyway, because I too thought that science was what boys did and that if I did it it would make me boyish.

No doubt other teachers shared the prejudices that Mr. Price exemplified, but these were not things I was alert to, and even with

Mr. Price, while I had sensed that something was amiss I had not understood what. I remember feeling uneasy, for instance, at his telling us how the art and artifacts of the Egyptians proved that the Egyptians did indeed have a civilization but also showed that they lacked the capacity for abstract thought. This fact became quite obvious, he said (smiling his crooked smile), when Egyptian civilization was compared with that of the Greeks, who had developed philosophies and mathematics and so on, which the Egyptians did not have. Moreover, the Egyptians had a morbid obsession with death—everything they left behind was a tomb, even the pyramids. But though I felt an unease, I could not have said exactly why. The part about morbidity and death seemed true, and why would he say that they lacked the capacity for abstract thought if it were not so? I remember feeling uncomfortable also at a comment made by Miss Hopkins, our biology teacher, who had a human skeleton hanging by the front desk. One day as she was pointing out its various bones, she picked up a mahogany-colored skull from her desk and said that it was an ancient Egyptian skull and that ancient Egyptian skulls were thicker than other human skulls. It may well have been that Miss Hopkins was merely reporting a well-known scientific fact, but I took her to be saying we were thick-skulled in the other sense. If it was mere scientific fact and she was not trying silently to convey something else about Egyptians, some inferiority in them, why didn't she make the distinction clear?

My favorite class in Senior School, as it had been in Junior School, was English, and there were at least two teachers whose classes I positively enjoyed. Mrs. George was both my form teacher and my English teacher when I first moved to Senior School. She had beautiful violet eyes and was married to the athletics master. Mrs. George was young and full of fun and warmth. I remember her praising one of my first essays for her. It was on the subject of heat and included a description of sitting in a car on a stiflingly hot day stuck in a traffic jam, and watching two barefoot children crossing the road, leaping at each step because the road was so hot. She read my essay out to the class, commenting on this passage. I wonder now if she was not trying quietly to foster a social conscience in us. The Georges had only recently come to Egypt, and the contrasts of wealth and open poverty on the streets would perhaps have been new to her.

My other favorite teacher was Mr. Beard, our class teacher in the fifth form, when we were preparing for O levels. Mr. Beard, who was probably in his sixties, had been at the school forever, perhaps from when it started. He walked with a limp, acquired, people said, in the war. He loved Egypt and was a great admirer of T. E. Lawrence. He was single and was known for being a recluse and also very tough. It was he who caned the boys when the headmaster decided that a caning was to be administered. Again, he was also our English teacher, teaching us Shakespeare as well as composition. Gruff in manner, he could make us see subtle and complicated things in our books. I remember writing an essay for him on King Farouk, in which I maintained that the king had been deliberately corrupted by the British as a young man so that they could manipulate him to their own ends; when he handed it back, he looked amused and pleased and said that he thought I was probably quite right.

Mr. Price's prejudices probably did have some negative effect on my sense of myself and my abilities. But the teacher whose behavior toward me would mark me for life was not some British racist but an Arab, our Arabic teacher, Miss Nabih. I never forgot her, because once in class she slapped me. Her action, besides shocking me, caused consternation in the class. Hitting us was not permitted. Caning boys, evidently, was something different. When my parents learned what had happened, they took it up with the school and Miss Nabih was reprimanded.

We had just started learning Arabic in school. It was my first year in Senior School and just a few months after the revolution and passage of the law requiring foreign schools to teach Arabic. Standard written Arabic is completely different grammatically and even in vocabulary from Egyptian Arabic, and studying the language consists essentially in memorizing endless grammatical forms and reading stilted, boring passages in what, we were told, was "real" Arabic, "correct" Arabic—whereas what we spoke was an inferior, corrupt, incorrect Arabic, an Arabic that could hardly be called Arabic at all. For a youngster, endlessly studying grammar and vocabulary and plodding through an alien, unimaginative prose (in what was supposedly "my" language) can be exceedingly tedious work, and I frankly didn't put much effort into it. I was not particularly worse than my classmates in the subject, but for some reason it was I more than anyone who provoked Miss Nabih's anger. My friend Jean was no better at the language than I, but like Miss Nabih a Palestinian, she was always treated cordially by her. In reality Miss Nabih's rage (as I sensed even then) was a rage at her own plight as a refugee and at those she considered responsible for it, among them, presumably, the "corrupt, irresponsible Egyptian upper classes," such as the people just booted out of government by the new men of the Egyptian Revolution. In Miss Nabih's mind, I obscurely sensed, I had come to stand, with my insouciant attitude toward Arabic, for the irresponsibility of those classes and their cavalier attitude toward the Palestinians. For in this era following the revolution, it was widely asserted that it was the corruption of the King and of the military establishment in Egypt that had been responsible for Egypt's ignominious defeat by Israel in 1948.

I have always thought that those moments between me and Miss Nabih were in large part responsible for the feelings of confusion, anger, and guilt that I've felt all my life in connection with the issues of Arabness, identity, the Arabic language, and the like. In reality, though, these incidents were the only tangible things I could fasten onto in the enormous turbulence and upheaval we were then living through. My relations with Miss Nabih were only a symptom of the times: of the battering and reshaping of our identities that the politics of the day were subjecting us to. I would be marked by everything that was happening, not just by Miss Nabih. Only when, in the process of writing this book, I began to examine this memory and others, and the history in which they were entangled, would I come to that realization.

There are two other moments from roughly that same period that I remember, both also touching on these questions of nationalism and identity. One is of my sitting by the radio—aged about thirteen—listening to an address by Abdel Nasser. Nasser was at times an extremely gifted orator, not because he could make flowery speeches but because, dropping into simple, colloquial Egyptian (not the standard Arabic used by radio announcers and people making speeches), he would address his audience with the sense of intimacy of someone addressing close personal friends or his own family. In this instance he was speaking on an Arabic program called *Children's Hour*. Lunch was being served, and I was called to the table, where my parents and sister and brother (it must have been during summer vacation, because they were back) had already sat down.

"I'll come in a minute," I called back from the radio room, which opened onto the dining room. "I have to listen to this. The president is speaking to us."

"Us?" inquired my mother. "Who's us?"

"The children of Egypt," I replied.

Everyone found this amusing—that I had so wholly and so unselfconsciously placed myself in the group that the president was addressing.

I was the only one in the family young enough to be significantly shaped by the notion of Egypt that the revolutionary government was in the process of defining.

A second moment also marked a shift in my consciousness and a growing distance from my background and my family's attitudes; it marked as well a further turn in my induction into this new kind of nationalism and our re-forming identity. This moment, too, occurred in the context of an encounter with Nasser, this time a live encounter. Nanny, my cousin Mona, and I were at the movies. I think the film was *Mutiny on the Bounty*. The auditorium was not very crowded. In the intermission after the news and commercials people suddenly started clapping, looking up to the balcony seats behind us. We turned and looked—and there was Abdel Nasser, sitting with some men and smiling broadly. People lined up to shake his hand and so did we, my cousin and I. He had an extraordinarily attractive, winning presence: compelling yet warm amber-brown eyes, like the golden eyes of a great eagle, and the same quality of ease and sense of intimacy to his presence that his voice and easy colloquial speech sometimes conveyed. I was simply enthralled by him but also completely turned around in my head by the encounter. As we shook hands, he asked us our names and my cousin readily replied "Mona," a perfectly good Egyptian Arab name. I, however, was rooted to the spot, unable to speak. I could not say "Lily," my name at school—not to this man who, I knew, hated the British. How could I, an Egyptian girl, have such a name? How could I confess to such a name? I couldn't say "Nana," either. Nana, I suppose, was too personal, a name for family and intimates only.

I was called Lily at school because my father asked when he was registering me what I wanted to be called, Nana or Lili. My family called me Nana (from Nadine, one of my given names) and Nanny called me Lili, her version of my other given name, Leila. I don't know what was going on in my five-year-old head and why I chose Lili. Perhaps it was a name I had already encountered in stories and movies and that felt to me like a "real" name, whereas I knew no one else called Nana, which felt like a name for intimates only. I don't think I knew my actual given names when I was five.

My daydreams were nearly all, in my early Senior School years, about the rolled red sand of the playing fields and the great oval marked out afresh, in the athletics season, with the brilliant, stark white lines of the running tracks. I remember standing there dreaming, looking out over the playing fields and toward the distant end of the grounds and the line of smoke-gray firs leaning slightly before the wind, feeling the air light on my skin and the heat rising from the earth and the sun on me as I moved out from the shade to begin my training.

The athletics season was in the summer term. In the fall and winter we played hockey and netball and rounders (the last two being British schoolchildren's versions of basketball and baseball), and I was always on the school hockey and netball teams (I do not think there was a rounders team). So I was involved in sports all year. But it was athletics (the British word for track and field sports) I loved, and it was in the summer that I went out daily onto the playing fields with a sense of real excitement.

I had always been fast and at home had outrun everyone, older and younger children, but in Junior School, when I saw myself leading, I would slow down so that others would catch up. This changed—who knows why?—once I got to Senior School. I began to win most running events, the high jump, and sometimes the long jump. And so I would win, too, at the end of the three days of competition, the coveted cup awarded to the *victrix ludorum*, the winner of the most girls' events.

I would go home loaded with medals engraved with the laurel and rose of our school. My father took pleasure in my winning, but I also remember days when I would arrive home after the exhilaration of winning and nobody would ask what had happened. I would show my medals and cup to no one and would put them away, to gather dust in the drawers.

My athletic career came to an end when I was entered by our school in the Cairo competitions and won the hundred-meter dash, setting a new Cairo record. My picture appeared in the paper. My parents, or more exactly my mother, feeling that it was not at all appropriate for a photo of me in shorts to appear in the paper, decreed that I could no longer compete in games—in any public venue, at any rate. It was around that time that the English School closed. It reopened as al-Nasr School, but its sports tradition had declined.

We studied arithmetic in pounds, shillings, and pence and we read about the history and geography of Europe but not about the history and geography of Egypt. I knew all about the flora and fauna of the British Isles and where coal was mined and about the Pennines and the chalk cliffs of Dover but nothing about the Nile and the ancient valley where I lived. Is this really possible, or have I, in the interest of neatness and in some process of internal spring cleaning, simply erased the memory of studying at least the geography of Egypt? I seem to know something about floods and silt and the rains in Ethiopia and the branches of the river and the delta and agriculture and exports and so on—was this not from school? And I knew all about Bismarck and Garibaldi and nationalism in Europe but nothing about Egypt, the Arabs, the Muslims, the Turks. Obviously such schooling had distinct shortcomings for a future citizen of Egypt.

We were intended, the children of the professionals and intellectuals of this society, the children of its middle and upper classes, attending such schools and often going on to universities in Europe and America, to return and put to use in the service of our society and ourselves the know-how we had acquired. We were intended, like the preceding generation of professionals and intellectuals, to be the brokers of the knowledge and expertise of the West, brokers between the two cultures, raised within the ways of our own people yet at ease with the intellectual heritage of Europe. We were intended to be the intermediaries, connecting and mediating between this society and culture and that. This is again the role that intellectuals play to some extent in Egyptian society. Egypt's most prominent economists, its scientists, its social analysts, and many of its writers and other intellectuals are not only fluent in a Western language (many of them are graduates of Western universities) but in command of the work done in their fields in the West and elsewhere.

But for a time in the Nasser era, when Arab nationalism and socialism were the going dogmas, fluency in European languages and Western education became discredited, things that one tried to hide, markers of belonging to the wrong class, the class of the once affluent, privileged, unjust oppressors of "the masses." In those days of unceasing nationalist rhetoric, a rhetoric of denunciatory rage as well as of nationalism, it became quite acceptable to discriminate against, and be openly hostile toward, people who betrayed (by their fluency in a European language, say) that they belonged to these classes. We at home had noticed and knew quite well, as other Egyptians must have noticed and known, that whenever some project of Nasser's failed or ran into problems he would immediately make an impassioned speech denouncing some group or other—feudalists, Zionists, imperialists, forces of regression—inciting people's fury against it and making it a target of rage—and thus, obviously, also deflecting people's rage away from himself. The rhetoric of rage, of justification and delivery (or the promise of delivery) through rage, was the politics of the day.

~

O, for the wings, for the wings of a dove,
Far, far away would I roam,
In the wilderness build me a nest
And remain there forever at rest
O, deep in the wilderness
Build me a nest
And remain there forever at rest.

We had a wonderful collection of records of European classical music. I must have begun listening to them when I was quite young. My cousin Sherif, who dazzled us when we were both eleven by playing the *Moonlight* Sonata, remembers that it was I who introduced him, when we were younger, to *Eine Kleine Nachtmusik.* Sherif's father was an architect and his mother would become a well-known watercolorist. She got the idea of taking up painting the day she watched her youngest son leave for school and found herself alone in an empty house.

I continued to love European classical music and still have (a little grudgingly perhaps) a love for it. But I find myself sometimes yearning for another music, the kind only my mother and her sisters and friends listened to at home when I was a child. I began to appreciate it myself in my late teens. What I hanker for now is hearing it live, Arabic music but also other non-Western music, particularly Indian, and not only classical instrumental Indian music but other varieties too—tabla, dance, *mawali* (ecstatic song), music of presence and community, and of audience and musicians together, and of being here, now, in body, mind, spirit. Not a music to be appreciated silently, intellectually, privately and then discussed in connoisseurs' murmurs as we file out. I go to non-Western concerts whenever I can, and afterward European classical concerts seem peculiar.

At school we sang English songs. My absolute, all-time favorite was "O, for the wings, for the wings of a dove, / Far, far away would I roam."

We lived in fact, throughout our childhoods, easily and unthinkingly crossing thresholds between one place and another—Ain Shams, Zatoun, our school—places that formed their own particular and different worlds with their own particular and different underlying beliefs, ideals, assumptions.

Moving daily among those three different worlds under the blue skies of Egypt, we lived also in our heads and in the books we lost ourselves in, in a world peopled with children called Tom and Jane and Tim and Ann, and where there were moles and hedgehogs and gray skies and caves on the shore and tides that came in and out. And where houses had red roofs. Red roofs that seemed far better and more interesting and intriguing to me than roofs that were like, say, the terraced roof of our house in Alexandria.

We grew up believing that some world over there was better, more interesting, more civilized than this world here.

When I was a schoolgirl in the years immediately following the revolution, Doria Shafik, an Egyptian feminist and Sorbonne graduate, went on a hunger strike, demanding the vote for women. When it was granted, she went on another hunger strike, this time protesting Nasser's dictatorship and demanding the restoration of democracy. Nasser placed her under house arrest. Her actions registered with me in just a vague way. I remember my parents talking about them and Father's supporting her and speaking of her with great admiration.

Shafik was someone who looked always to the West as the measure and source of good things, someone who seemed to be seeking always to escape, to flee this place, this native place, this inferior realm of the native. Understanding this about her, I understood that something similar had been there in my own makeup, at least back then.

That was the unspoken burden maybe, this longing to escape, underlying how much I loved that school song. Longing for wings to fly away.

But after all, many people, and not only "natives" long to flee, to get away, to roam. Look at all the Americans of my generation who went to India in search of gurus and all the people before them, Westerners anyway, who went off hoping to find another culture, another way to live, a different way to be. Perhaps such searching is just another version of our human restlessness. "Through winter-time we call on spring," writes Yeats, "And through the spring on summer call . . . Nor know that what disturbs our blood / Is but its longing for the tomb." Or, as the poet Rumi puts it:

I'm like a bird from another continent, sitting in this aviary.
The day is coming when I fly off.

Besides, the music to that song I so much loved (as I discovered the other day, looking it up nostalgically) was, after all, by Mendelssohn.

I remember walking along the beach in Alexandria one sunset with two of my cousins and our sitting down in the sand and having our fortunes told by a wandering fortune-teller. Each of us in turn took the shells he gave us and shook them, saying something over them that he told us to say, then casting them on the sand. When my turn came he said, "You will die in foreign parts."

"You mean I will die soon?" I asked, alarmed.

"No," he said. "You will live in foreign parts, and you will die there."

I remember that as we had walked on along the edge of the sea and I turned to watch the waves erasing our footsteps, I yearned for those other shores and other worlds, pleased with his words, praying that he was right.

I remembered this recently walking along the shore on Cape Cod, and I stopped still in my tracks and stood looking back now, as it were, to that other shore. Two images came to me. The first was of my mother, the way she was in a photo I have of her taken on the beach in Alexandria. The golden light of sunset falls on her, and her dress, caught by the wind, streams before her; half running, half stumbling on the scuffed sand, she is reaching out with a racket. I do not remember my mother playing badminton on the beach—Aunt Aisha, yes, but not my mother—but here she is, slim still and young, at least to my eyes now. And then, just as I was about to turn and walk on, came this second image—myself, the young girl that I was, aged fourteen, fifteen, looking out from that shore and looking now directly at me, eyes clear and stern as ever, judging me now with that same sternness that she had once directed at my mother.

"But you didn't have to live it," I remonstrate, for she is judging me. "You didn't have to stumble on, find a way somehow, keep going. Figure things out on the spot, in the instant. Get through whatever had to be got through. It's all very well from there on the sidelines."

Why did you settle, compromise, accept? she seems to be saying. She herself, she seems to think, would have stood her ground. Would never have settled, never have compromised.

Another memory from that era. We'd gone on a trip to Agami, Aunt Aisha and her children and I. We drove along the Corniche and out of Alexandria and onto the desert road that headed toward Libya, a road that ran along the sea most of the way. Bedouins along the route held up eggs and *simman*—quail—for sale, small birds caught in nets as they arrived exhausted from their migration across the Mediterranean from Italy. We stopped to buy a basket of figs freshly picked from the trees that grew in small, low plantations along the white sands. At Agami we swam and ate a picnic lunch (in those days there were no hotels or houses there, just empty beaches) and then Aunt Aisha decided that we should drive on to Sidi Abdel Rahman, a famous beach we had never been to. It was about another hour's drive along the coast, the sea there shades of azure and turquoise because of the whiteness of the sands. Just before Sidi Abdel Rahman we passed through Alamein. A vast expanse of crosses, marshaled row upon row, white symmetrical crosses receding as if without end toward sea on this side and desert on that. An archway over the entrance and beside it a small white building surmounted by a cross and a low wall along which grew clambering red roses. In front of it, oleanders.

Getting out of the car into the stillness, we saw that the different cemeteries were alongside one another—British, German, Italian. We walked a little ways into the British one, reading the names and dates of the buried—many of them only a few years older than I—the sound of gently breaking waves in the distance. To come to this foreign shore to die, so young, here where the Mediterranean was so blue. And this, I thought to myself, is what civilization was? Civilization?

I knew something by then about the Second World War, enough to have some vague sense of why it had been fought, even if no clear idea of why these young men had come all the way to these perfect shores of Africa to die. I believe now that I was unconsciously echoing, with my portentous thoughts about "civilization," words I had heard as a young child years earlier when my parents, speaking of Hitler and Auschwitz and Hiroshima, had wondered what, after all, this project of European civilization was.

ſUEZ

THE SUMMER of 1956, leading up to the Suez invasion, was a smoldering one. I remember it as the hottest summer ever in Alexandria, though perhaps I remember it that way only because we did not stay at Siouf, Grandfather's house, but in a rented villa near the beach of Sidi Bishr, which had a direct view of the sea but thin walls and terrible insulation, so that when we came home from the beach for lunch the house would be like an oven no matter how wide open the balcony doors and the windows. In the evening the sea wind, so strong it would snatch doors and windows out of one's hand, would sweep through the house and it would be cool again. The thin walls were a problem, too, because it seemed sometimes that in almost every room of that house there was anger, voices kept down but still coming through so that one caught words, or their edginess, anyway. Those first weeks of summer were our worst ever as a family. My brothers and sister were home for the summer, my eldest brother, Omar, having brought his wife, who was visiting Egypt for the first time. We took the villa because there were too many of us to stay at Siouf.

Doris, my brother's wife, who was English, seemed to be when she first came in a constant state of irritation, and often became, to my teenage eyes, unintelligibly angry at all sorts of things—just the way things were in Egypt, the way we did things, the way we were, and the way, in particular, that my mother was and did things. Poor Doris turned red at the slightest exposure to the sun and couldn't enjoy swimming and being outdoors all the time as the rest of us did, and that in itself is enough to drive anyone crazy.

She seemed first of all not only distressed but also angry at the poverty around us and by our apparent insensitivity to it. In Alexandria one did not see—either along the Corniche, with its elegant and occasionally quite palatial villas, or in the center of the city, with its handsome colonial-style buildings—people living in deprivation, as one did in Cairo. Even in the narrow cobbled streets of Old Alexandria one did not see what was evident in Cairo—dusty, derelict houses, shacks made of tin cans and cardboard, sometimes perched on vast rubbish heaps combed, as one saw even from a passing car, by the ragged inhabitants for anything salvageable. But what was evident in Alexandria, vividly and glaringly, was the contrast between the well-to-do and the poor, not because one saw where the poor lived but because the entrances to the beaches, beaches open only to those who had cabins, were always thronged with beggars. Consequently, on the Corniche and at the gateways to the city's exclusive beaches, one saw the rich of Egypt arriving in their long American cars, some of them very flashily dressed in high heels and hats and the latest (Western) fashions, and, at the same moment, a good many beggars, some blind or crippled or both. There were beggars without legs who sat on boards on wheels by the doorways and who propelled themselves by pushing on the ground with two wood pads held in their hands, skittering and darting between people's legs and even between cars with great speed, pursuing a person scrambling in a purse here, a badly aimed coin there. There were also those without boards, with legs twisted and useless, who could also move agilely, darting and scampering crablike across the pavement. And there were women, old women, blind women, women with infants, and women so wrapped in black *milayyas* that one couldn't tell what was wrong with them. Of course the stories in Alexandria, sometimes reported in the papers, were that the beggars were organized and run by gangs that made millions, and that some of the beggars were themselves very rich, and that the spots by the beach entrances were extremely lucrative, and that some people were deliberately mutilated, particularly children.

Whatever the stories claimed, one could not go to the beach without seeing people, dressed in rags, who were crippled or blind and destitute. And it *was* hard, even for those of us who had never known things to be otherwise. Arriving at the entrance trying not to see, trying to drop our coins without seeing too precisely what was wrong, turning our heads away, forced at the start of every carefree day at the beach to be aware, even as we tried to shut out such thoughts, of what we did not want to be aware of: the injustice of life and the terribleness of some people's lives, the awful things that can befall people and that could at any moment befall any of us. The injustice of life—not, as we saw it, *our* injustice. It was not we who had made the world the way it was, not we who made the poor poor, any more than it was we who were responsible for people's having accidents or falling sick or being born blind or anything else. That was the way life was. The idea that we were responsible for society or that there was anything, besides giving generously, that we could do about the inequality was unfamiliar to me then. And so, though I found Doris's horror intelligible, I could not understand why she was so angry with us about the poverty and why she thought we were insensitive to it. I too thought it was terrible that the poor had the lives they had, and I too hated seeing them, and I always gave them coins when I passed them. What else could I, could any of us, do?

And yet I was aware, or I was beginning to be aware, that society as a whole could and should try to change and improve conditions for everyone. Ideas about social justice and about a society of equality and opportunity and prosperity for all Egyptians were being proclaimed by the new revolutionary government, and they were ideas that appealed to me, whatever the family adults were saying. The members of my mother's family, who lost considerable property and land to the government, were, understandably, not great enthusiasts of socialism—in fact, they were constantly muttering against Abdel

Nasser and his "socialism." But I, at fifteen and sixteen, thought them selfish.

Doris would get irritated at things that were even less intelligible to me—when the chauffeur opened the car door for her, for instance. The chauffeur was then specifically instructed not to open the door for her, but he often forgot or else thought the instruction too bizarre to be abided by. And so she would get angry again, directing her words at her husband but intending them, I thought, for all of us. At home the thing that had her fleeing from the lunch table was the way my mother would press her to have a bit of this or a bit more of that, a gesture, to us, of common courtesy. We kept explaining to Doris that Mother did not mean any harm by it, that she thought she was just being hospitable and polite, and that Doris should just ignore it. And we kept telling my mother to stop, not to urge her to eat anything, and my mother would restrain herself for a time and then forget and lapse once more into offering her some dish. I did not understand then why it was so irritating to be pressed to eat, but I understand it somewhat more now. I returned to Egypt on a visit after a long absence and found myself snapping at my hosts for continually urging me to eat, particularly as I was watching my weight and, faced with the feasts with which tables are habitually laid among both the barely comfortable and the well-to-do, I was having a hard enough time of it as it was.

But Doris also apparently put various constructions on my mother's behavior, taking her, at one moment, to be implying that she was too thin and therefore unattractive and wondering, at another, whether my mother was not, by pressing her to eat, underhandedly criticizing her for not having got pregnant after three years of marriage. Doris would even protest the fact that there was so much to eat, so much waste. And we would explain that the food was not wasted, that the servants would eat it. It was still waste to her: people did not need so much variety, they did not need to eat so much.

Of course I can now appreciate what I had little awareness of then, the enormous stress in Doris's situation of having to cope at once with a new country, a new culture, and a new family in the midst of whom she found herself now having to live and the meanings of whose ways and words were still unknown to her. And within weeks in fact she was transformed, at ease and relaxed and positively appreciating Alexandria and the pleasures of Alexandria. By the end of the summer she had forged bonds of real affection with all of us, and in particular with my mother, bonds that would prove lifelong.

But at first, my brother's and her room was one of the ones from which one would hear suppressed, edgy exchanges. And, to begin with, it was a summer filled with general fractiousness. My second brother, Karim, just graduated as an engineer, was out to prove himself, and he argued constantly with Father about every point of engineering. He argued whenever Father was back from Cairo, settling finally on taking issue with him over his analysis of why the High Dam—not yet built or even begun—would be a disaster. Father's attachment to things like Nile silt was old-fashioned, artificial fertilizer was just as good and better, science had changed and Father's ideas were now irrelevant. Exasperated, Father responded by giving Karim his calculations to go over for himself. And so these arguments, too, soon enough would stop, for as Karim worked his way through the evidence, he would do a complete turnaround on the matter. Although we did not know it then, Father was engaged in trying to persuade the government and Nasser not to go forward with the dam's construction and didn't know yet whether he was succeeding.

Arguments were constantly erupting, too, between my mother and my sister. Magda, also just back from Cambridge, continually took up the issue of whether she had the right, if she wanted to, to marry a Christian. It was against the law, Mother said, and in any case she would never permit it. Unless, of course, the man converted to Islam, which would make the marriage legal. Magda would not leave the matter alone. Why was she harping on the subject, Mother would sharply ask, did she have any particular person in mind? No, Magda would say, she was just arguing the principle of the thing. On and on they went, their words often fierce and intense.

I hated being home and hated the constant sound of muffled

bickering. I would sit, hands over my ears, by the window of my tiny room, outside of which grew a large, stiff cactus pointing at the sky, or I would lie on my bed and put a pillow over my head, or I'd go out into the villa's small garden—but that was not far enough away. We were not on the Corniche, but there was nothing between us and the sea except for a tract of vacant land, its chalky, stony, dusty earth overgrown here and there with a succulent, cactuslike grass with little purple flowers. The drive along the road from the house to the beach was a couple of miles. By footpath it was only ten minutes, and so sometimes I would walk down on my own to the beach. Sometimes, too, I'd go to my aunt Aisha's cabin rather than ours, and occasionally I'd go back to Siouf with her family for lunch and sometimes overnight to get away, chiefly, from things at home.

On one of those occasions I went with Aunt Aisha and her daughter Mona to the open-air cinema at San Stefano to see a haunting film whose images remain with me today. It was the movie version of a novel, *Dua al-Karawan*, "The Call of the Curlew," by Egypt's foremost writer in those days, Taha Husain. It is about a village girl who goes to work as a servant for a young man and is seduced by him. When she returns home pregnant, the men of her family murder her for having sullied their honor. Set in a village on the edge of the desert, the film is full of stark images of women in black, of the desert, and of a well surrounded by palm trees where all the talk and decisions occur, including the decision by the men of the family to kill the young woman. A sense of doom hangs over everything, and the film is threaded through with the *karawan*'s haunting, mournful call: that call, heard only in the twilight in Egypt, that I so loved.

I am sure now that I found the film compelling because it put into story form the underlying reality of the world in which I was living, the sense of violence, of deadly violence that was there beneath the surface of ordinary pleasant living when matters of sexuality and sexual transgression were concerned. The violence, after all, had already, in a small but devastating way, been part of my own life. I remember talking of all this with Fatma, a spinster and distant relative who supported herself by making all the casual wear for the family—

pajamas, nightdresses, housedresses. She would come to stay at our house, or at the aunts' houses, or at Zatoun or Alexandria, bringing her Singer sewing machine, and would remain until she'd finished all the sewing we needed. Fatma was the only adult with whom I felt I could speak fairly freely. She seemed more able to see through conventions, possibly because of her own marginality and her own dependent and yet free-floating social status. I loved her visits above all because of the moments of deep laughter that we invariably shared. She was at Siouf that summer for a few weeks and I remember sitting with her the day after seeing the movie. It was the siesta hour—Fatma was one of the few adults who did not retire for the siesta—and we sat in the shade of the downstairs balcony overlooking the front garden, its white paving stones, with vivid ornamental grass demarcating them, dazzling in the afternoon sun.

꙳

Such was the summer we were having when Nasser made his speech nationalizing the Suez Canal on the twenty-sixth of July, the fourth anniversary of the revolution. He was speaking in the main square in Alexandria and one could hear on the radio the surges of euphoric applause breaking in as he spoke—and he spoke for several hours. There was no euphoria in our home. Even back in the days of the revolution, the news of it, of the coup that had sent the king into exile, had been received somberly at home, much to my incomprehension. I'd often heard my parents lament the corruption of the king, and so logically they should be pleased now, I thought. But to them it was a military coup—a group of officers had cut through the democratic process and forcibly seized power. Democracy in Egypt, they feared, was at the very least in jeopardy, and perhaps at an end. And of course they were right. By 1956 the country was a dictatorship, though it was not called that: Nasser was the country's "democratically" elected president and he would continue for the rest of his life to be "democratically" elected and re-elected, always receiving 99 percent of the vote.

The speech he now delivered—speaking in colloquial Egyptian—was a rousing one, describing British oppression of Egyptians since the building of the canal, the construction of which had cost, he said, hundreds of thousands of Egyptian lives. And ever since then imperialists had taken for themselves, as they continued to this day to take, the revenue of millions generated by the canal, continuing meanwhile in every way to frustrate Egypt's hopes, selling arms to Israel, refusing to sell them to Egypt, and deciding now—as America had just announced—to withdraw the funds they had promised for the building of the High Dam. And so the answer—and there could be only one answer now, he said—was to throw off the imperialist yoke and take possession of what was rightfully ours, the canal. Its revenue, he said, would be used to finance the dam.

This fiery speech, exhilarating in its defiance of tyranny and imperialism, was received in our home with deep gloom, principally because of Nasser's linking of the nationalization and the dam. Only in the course of hearing it did my father realize that, contrary to his hopes, Nasser meant to go ahead with the dam despite the enormous damage that my father had warned him would ensue. Years later I would learn that Nasser had not informed the Egyptian cabinet—the body supposedly governing Egypt—of his intention to nationalize the canal until hours before his speech and that many cabinet members had been opposed to the action because they opposed pursuing a course of seizure rather than of negotiation and law. And so we were not the only Egyptians in the country who were less than euphoric over the nationalization. But at the time it felt as if we were. How I wished that we could just for once be like everybody else, that we could be nationalistic and anti-imperialist and just support Abdel Nasser. But I knew too by then, because my parents had drummed it into me, that I must reveal to no one what they said at home: already the society was beginning to be riddled with "secret police" and informers who would report critics to the government; already we had heard the rumors of people being tortured in jails and knew of people who had disappeared.

The nationalization speech was to be the first shot in an unfolding drama that would become a landmark in world history, bringing about an end to old-style imperialism and, above all, to the old-style assumptions and attitudes of imperialism that had been the norm. The nationalization of the canal and, even more directly, the British and French reactions to it would also transform Nasser from a dictator in Egypt who had begun to resort to repressive measures to control discontent at home and with, as yet, only a relatively small following abroad, to a Third World hero and the uncontested leader of the Arab world.

At home, over the rest of the summer, things grew subdued. Father's trips to Cairo continued, and he continued, as I learned only years later, to try to dissuade Nasser from proceeding with the dam, despite Nasser's announcement that the canal revenues would be used now to finance its construction.

I remember the very moment that we saw the planes. It was a golden October day. We were sitting, Joyce and I, on the bench outside the gym, looking out toward the playing fields and the line of firs on the edge of the desert. A light wind rose and fell, making a great whirl of dust on the fields and tugging at our skirts so that we had to hold them down. A group of girls passed behind us, one of them singing, "Merrily, merrily, merrily, merrily, life is a but a dream," a drone from above threading her last words. We looked up, shading our eyes, and saw two silver planes gleaming in the depths of the sky. They must have been recognizably different from ordinary planes even to us, because watching them pass we said to each other, "Maybe we're going to have a war!" We laughed because we were joking, but there was enough going on to bring the possibility to our minds.

The nationalization of the canal was still a live issue and various political exchanges had been reported in the news—exchanges that we schoolgirls paid no attention to but would undoubtedly have been vaguely aware of. More important and immediate was the fact that since we'd returned to school at the beginning of October our school days had been filled with all sorts of emergency arrangements and unexpected free periods because many of our British teachers—specifically all the women—had failed to come back. The headmaster had announced at the beginning of the term that they had not returned on the instructions of the British government, which was always extremely cautious, he said—overly so in this case, he added with that smile of his. He fully expected that they would be joining us shortly. It was now late October.

The bombing began the following morning, October 29, 1956. The planes we had seen had been British RAF reconnaissance planes. French planes, Cairo Radio told us, had been seen in action over the Suez Canal region. The planes bombing Cairo were British. The attack on Egypt was not, the radio said, as had been thought at first, an Israeli attack. The Israeli incursions in Sinai were simply a pretext and a distraction, an excuse for the British and French attack.

Air-raid sirens and all clears sounded throughout the day, and throughout the day there was the sound of bombs and anti-aircraft fire. At home we stocked up on candles and papered our windows and car lights as instructed on the radio, to which we were glued, my father taking control of it, twirling the knob so we could piece together from the BBC, Cairo Radio, and other stations what was actually happening. A British station came on, not the BBC, broadcasting from Cyprus, explaining that only airports and military installations were being targeted and that the station would announce the times and targets of the attacks so that the people could stay away. Once we'd established that the times they gave for the raids were accurate, we packed some essentials and set off, during one of the brief scheduled intervals in the bombings, for Zatoun, with its thick stone walls a sturdier house than ours and less likely, my father thought, to collapse if a bomb fell too close. My aunts Aisha and Nazli were already there with their children. We all slept in the basement, considered safest, making our beds on the sofas that lined those downstairs rooms.

Cairo Radio said that all our planes had been flown to safety in Sudan and Saudi Arabia, and it issued bulletins of the number of British and French planes shot down; but other stations we picked up, including the BBC, said that the entire Egyptian air force had been wiped out and that there had been no British losses. Nasser made speeches saying that we were under attack by two of the world's mightiest military powers but that if they thought we were going to bow to their tyranny and injustice they were wrong. We would fight, we would fight (*Hanharib! Hanharib!*) for our freedom and dignity, every single Egyptian would fight, we would all be issued arms, and we would all, every single one of us, fight. We were a small country and had no military power compared with theirs, but we would not be defeated. They would see, we would not be defeated. *Hanharib! Hanharib!* From village to village and house to house, we would fight and never surrender. All the world, he said, was on our side against the tyrants, the imperialists. His friend Nehru had sent him a cable saying that all the people of Asia and Africa were with us, that the aggression of the imperialists against the small, newly liberated country of Egypt was a shock to the whole world. The Soviet Union was on our side, and even America, usually the ally of the British, even America was on our side.

And it was true—we got the same thing from the BBC. All the world, apart from the aggressors, seemed to be supporting us and all were outraged at the British and French attack. Sir Anthony Eden, the British prime minister, had been declaring that they were coming in to separate the warring sides, Israel and Egypt, and that they were going to land in the main cities on the Suez Canal to safeguard it. But nobody believed Eden. The British parliament was in an uproar, as we heard on the BBC. People were shouting at Eden, calling him a liar, demanding to be told the truth and demanding that he resign. Eisenhower issued a statement condemning the aggression, and America sponsored a UN resolution supported by all the nations— except for the aggressors—demanding an immediate cease-fire.

But the bombing continued night and day. At night, to the sound of bombs, now muffled and distant and now close, and the sound, sporadically, of anti-aircraft fire, I would listen to the radio and watch the searchlights' pencil-thin beams raking the sky over a city and suburbs unfamiliarly black. My brother went off to serve in the Suez area as an ambulance driver. My mother, kissing him solemnly on the head, did not, to my amazement, make a scene or try to get him out altogether of serving in a dangerous area. It was his duty to serve his country, she said, and she would be praying every moment for his safe return.

I continued to spend my time by the radio in the basement of Zatoun, reporting to the adults, who now spent their days upstairs and no longer followed every version of what was happening on the ground, the targets that had been hit, the number of planes downed according to Cairo Radio and according to the BBC, the ships sunk in the canal. After a first ship was unintentionally sunk in the canal by the British, the Egyptian side deliberately scuttled several more in order to totally block this canal that they were bombing us to "safeguard."

I slept at night with the radio beside me and would listen to it whenever I was awakened in the night by sirens and bombs, keeping the volume low so that it was just a murmur that only I could hear, waking to listen to it in the gray light of dawn and in the pitch dark of night when the faint light of the radio dial was the only light there was. Until the British bombing and subsequent invasion of Port Said, when thousands died, there were few civilian casualties. And so the bombings and searchlights with which we lived in those first days, and the constant and varied reports from the radio, imparted to life not a sense of the horror and tragedy of war but chiefly a sense of general excitement and of the heightened danger with which life was now edged. Above all, there was the exhilaration of feeling that here we were, a small nation unjustly and immorally beleaguered by two of the world's mightiest powers and greatest bullies, heroically fighting on to the support and applause, as we learned from the radio, of the entire world.

And so I followed through those days, riveted not only by news of the developments on the ground but also by every detail of what was happening internationally: America again denouncing the French and British, the African National Congress issuing a declaration of solidarity with the people of Egypt, huge demonstrations in Trafalgar Square against Anthony Eden and the British attack, speeches made against the British government by British members of parliament, all reported in full on the BBC—the BBC, often in the past jammed by the government in Cairo, now coming through loud and clear. We heard all about the battles in parliament, how Hugh Gaitskell, leader of the opposition, denounced the aggression as an act of folly and immorality and how Anthony Nutting, another minister, had resigned, saying that the British government was acting against all its traditions. For the first time I learned the names of British ministers. Nutting and Gaitskell became heroes in my mind.

For in addition to the drama I was living through with everyone else in Cairo, there was for me, as I think for many English Schoolers, an inner drama, a personal drama about loyalty abused and trust betrayed. We would say to one another afterward, we English Schoolers, how shocked we had been to see the British behaving in this way, with such brazen injustice and to see them being so immoral and so openly, cynically acting on the principle that might is right. The British, who had taught us that what they stood for was morality and uprightness and fairness! I remember feeling grown up saying this, how I had believed in them and trusted them, and yet they had done this to us, a small country like us, bombed us, invaded us. I felt, I said, that I could not believe anyone or anything anymore.

My sense of having been betrayed was deeply personal. I was hurt the way one is when one has trusted and been betrayed by a friend, when one had believed in the goodness and uprightness of someone and then discovered that they have after all been deceiving one.

I wonder now, looking back, at the anatomy of that sense of belief in the British despite the fact that I was living, as I was by then, in an environment pervaded with anti-imperialist and anti-British sentiment. First of all, obviously, I was a schoolgirl and knew nothing about history other than what we learned in school, about battles and the Magna Carta and William the Conqueror and Bismarck and Cavour. Second, the political speeches all around us were made in that declamatory tone that made one automatically discount whatever was being said as untrue—as a lie or at the very least a wild exaggeration. And the attitude at home would have confirmed my sense of the falseness and manipulativeness of the political rhetoric. It was well known at home that, if something or other went wrong in the country or there was some political fiasco or failure, Nasser would immediately deliver one of his long diatribes blaming everything on "the imperialists," "the feudalists," "the Zionists," "the forces of regression." My parents always listened carefully to his speeches to glean, from the various codes of political discourse and from the subjects he harped on, what the country was in for next. His routine was so familiar at home that my mother, when he started in on the imperialists, would say, "Ah yes, now we're next," and would brace herself for his attack on the feudalists, which she always took personally, as if they were direct attacks on her and her family. She would sit there fuming, countering his every charge. She did not believe they had been oppressors at all; on the contrary, they had been, she was convinced, enormously responsible, conscientious landlords, generous to a fault toward the people living and working on their land. By the end of his tirades she would be furiously invoking curses on his head. *Allah yell'anak ya Abdel Nasser!* God's curses upon you, Abdel Nasser!

In addition to all this was the fact that I knew "the enemy"—the imperialists—all too intimately. I was at home in English books, English ideas, Jane Austen, Dickens, Winnie the Pooh, George Eliot, Adam Bede. There was no way that I could reduce what I knew to some cardboard caricature called imperialism and come to hate and reject everything English, as the rhetoric around us enjoined us to do.

Besides, even with what we had just lived through, what had been reinforced for me—in a way that of course I would not have known how to say then—was how multilayered and complicated everything was and how even the evil imperialist British were not all just one thing or another. There had been Anthony Eden and the attack on us and the perfidy and injustice of that, but there had also been demonstrations in Trafalgar Square, and resignations from the British parliament, and people passionately denouncing their leader, and the BBC reporting things as they were, often things that were totally in our favor.

I emerged, then, from those packed few days lived in the semi-underground rooms of Zatoun probably somewhat more nationalistic than before but probably, too, with an enhanced rather than a diminished sense of how complicated things were—politics, justice, truth.

～

On a Saturday, five days after the British planes had begun their bombing, British ships began the bombardment of Port Said. News of civilian deaths and casualties and of overflowing hospitals began to pour in, reported, though in slightly lesser numbers, by the BBC as well as by Cairo Radio. On Monday, British and French troops began landing in Port Said. The governor of Port Said refused to surrender and the numbers of civilian deaths and casualties rose into the thousands. The Soviet Union threatened attacks on Paris and London and the United States, refusing Britain the oil and funds it now desperately needed, demanded an immediate cease-fire. The cease-fire went into effect at midnight on Tuesday, November 6, 1956. At American insistence, the British and French began a total withdrawal from Egypt and Israel gave up the territory it had captured in Sinai and returned to its prior borders. Sir Anthony Eden left for Jamaica "on doctor's orders" and shortly afterward resigned as prime minister. Nasser, the man who had stood up to imperialism and tyranny, was hero to the entire Third World and its friends, and undisputed leader, too, of the entire Arab world. In Egypt henceforth there would be no bar to Nasser's doing whatever he wanted—anyone even mildly critical of him was purged or somehow or other silenced or got rid of.

～

When we were back at Ain Shams I called my friends; the phone line had been down at Zatoun almost from the day we got there. All our teachers had left, I learned, when the British were ordered out of the country a few days after the attack began. I talked to Jean and heard her news but got no reply when I called Joyce. Soon, though, she called me. They were just back, having gone to stay with relatives in Alexandria; there were too many airports near Heliopolis, her parents felt, and Alexandria, they thought, would be safer. I said that we, too, had left our house and gone to my grandfather's place. I paused.

There was something I had sensed in her voice that prevented me from launching into ordinary conversation, talking in our normal way about what we were feeling and thinking. There was a silence. When the phone had rung I had been upstairs and I was speaking now from the upstairs phone, which was in my father's room. Both my parents were there, my father in front of the mirror buttoning his crisp white shirt and stiff collar and putting on his tie and braces and talking to my mother, who was sitting in an armchair on that side of the room glancing through the paper. They were not paying attention to me but I still felt inhibited. I said to Joyce, "Hold on, I'm going to go down to the downstairs phone."

"No, don't," she said, "my father's waiting to use the phone, so I can't stay on long."

"Oh," I said, mystified, wondering why she hadn't let him make his call and then called me, so that we could talk at length, as we usually did.

Then she told me that they were leaving Egypt—immediately, the very next day.

Her words threw me into a turbulence of feelings. My own best friend Joyce and her family were, apparently, on the wrong side. Instead of supporting us and standing with us, they were on the wrong side.

I recall the general feel of what happened between us but not our exact words. I must have responded stiffly, my hurt and withdrawal obvious to her. Joyce explained that she had nothing to do with the decision, it was her parents who were deciding. If she could choose, she'd stay, she said, but her parents thought it would be dangerous for them. She didn't succeed in persuading me of anything and I remained stiff and distant and hung up, saying a cool goodbye.

My mother, however, made me call her back. Putting the phone down I'd announced that Joyce was leaving and my mother at once remarked how surprised she was to hear that it had been Joyce that I'd been speaking to in that tone of voice. She thought Joyce's parents' decision to leave was an entirely sensible one.

"But the president said the Jews were welcome to stay," I said.

I'd heard him myself on the radio. Many Jews thought of Egypt as their homeland, he'd said, and they were welcome to stay, but if they did they must be with us all the way and give up their foreign passports and accept Egyptian nationality. That had sounded fair to me. If you lived in Egypt and considered it your home, then you should accept Egyptian nationality. Why not?

But my mother didn't see it this way at all. "What if they give up their passports and he changes his mind and turns against them?" she said. "Why should they trust him? Why should they take such a risk?"

"But why should he change his mind?" I asked. "He said that they're welcome in Egypt. He *said* that."

She continued to argue with me, saying that of course he wasn't to be trusted and that the decision that Joyce's parents were making was a very hard one to make, and probably they were right. And in any case it was not Joyce's decision, and she was my friend and she was leaving. I'd be very sorry later if I didn't call her up now and say goodbye properly.

I didn't want to. I looked at my father.

"Your mother is absolutely right," he said. "Do as she says."

I did call her. And this time, by the end of our conversation, we were both in tears, promising each other that we would write.

Months after they left, Joyce wrote to me from England saying that they still did not know where they were going to be. They had been temporarily placed in a house with people they did not know, and her brother had gone to France, where a family friend had secured a job for him. Her parents had been trying to arrange for her to go to school but she was not sure, she said, that she wanted to go to school anymore and they were arguing about it. She wrote again some months later to say they were in their own apartment in London and she was going to secretarial school but was not sure she would finish there because they might be moving again, to France this time because that was where her father had a job. I meant to write back but I procrastinated. Months later I heard from her again, just a card this time with her address, in Paris, and the words "Why don't you write?"

I procrastinated again. I was beginning to plan my own move to England, where I was going to college, and I put off writing until I knew when exactly I was going to be traveling, as I thought that maybe we could plan to meet. I could perhaps, I thought, stop in Paris on the way and we could meet. And so finally I wrote to her with my plans.

My letter came back stamped "Unknown at this address."

I never heard from her again or from anyone who knew her.

School, when we went back in January, was no longer the English School. Taken over by the Egyptian government, it was renamed al-Nasr—Victory—School. Documents had been discovered in the basement, it was said, that indicated that the school had served as a British spy center. Probably, people said, the school had branched into spying with the advent of Mr. Price and probably he had been appointed by the British government specifically for the purpose of beginning this operation. This explained both the abrupt recall of his predecessor and the British government's break with precedent in appointing someone unfamiliar with Egypt—a white South African, at that. Who knows, though, if any of this was true or if it was just propaganda.

The new teaching staff at the school, all Egyptians, had been hastily recruited by the government, and the academic level was now far below what it had been. Having just passed my O levels, I was nominally in my first year of preparing for my A levels, exams that one usually sat for two years after O levels, but the work I was doing was easier than preparing for O levels. In the past, both exams had come from England; now they were going to be set by the Egyptian Ministry of Education.

Many students had left—all the British children and nearly all the Jews. And once the school reopened and it was clear how poor the academic standards were, others also left, including my remaining friend, Jean Said. After a few weeks at al-Nasr she left to complete her schooling in America so that she'd be able to go on to Vassar, which was where her parents had always intended her to go.

I do not know why my parents did not think, as Jean's did, of

sending me abroad to finish school. It would have been logical to send
me to England, since the plan had always been that I would go to
college there. Instead, my father entered into discussion with Girton
College, my sister's college, as to what should be done about me, given
that my education had been interrupted by politics, matters outside
anyone's control. The college decided to permit me to sit for the next
entrance exam the following November, even though A levels were
normally required and there was no expectation that I would have
passed them.

In June of that year I sat for the Egyptian A levels and passed
with flying colors. For the next year I just stayed home, hanging out
occasionally with the new friends I had made. Two in particular were
important to me, Amr and Nawal. Both were a couple of years older
than I. Amr had been in his final year of preparing for A levels, and
Nawal had entered our school just before the Suez invasion, having
passed her baccalaureate at a French school and having come to ours
to spend a year improving her English. Books played a major part in
both friendships. I would take long walks on the school grounds with
Amr. We would talk—or rather he would talk and I would listen—
about Dostoyevsky, symbolism, and the meaning of good and evil. I
think now, hearing the name Dostoyevsky, not of those brooding novels but of oleanders and firs and desert and red playing fields. We
would walk along the edge of the fields to the copse at the end of the
grounds, where the firs leaned against the desert, and once there we
would continue to stroll, now daringly holding hands. There would be
other couples strolling there also, though not many, for there were
weighty taboos among us, the students as a whole, against having
boyfriends and girlfriends. Occasionally, late in the school day, after
games, when the dusk was beginning to close in, one might sometimes
see a really daring couple sitting interlaced behind an oleander bush.
Since I was of course not permitted to have a boyfriend, my friendship
with Amr remained confined to school.

Like Amr, Nawal took the lead intellectually, dazzling me with
her French-style literary analysis and her ease with philosophy. Because of her I now read Proust and Gide and Camus and Colette,

names I had heard my cousin Samia and my mother mention but had not until then thought to exert myself to read. My friendship with Nawal (whose father was a well-known doctor) would eventually lead to connections I would have for the rest of my life. Her family, particularly her mother, Soheir, who treated me almost like a daughter, regularly included me in their projects. I began in this way to discover aspects of Cairo life that I had not hitherto encountered. My first visit to Khan Khalili, the famous Cairo bazaar with its winding alleys in the medieval section of the city, was with Nawal, her four sisters, and her mother, who were visiting it to browse through the craft shops and to purchase jewelry. And through Soheir I met Um Kulsum, who was a close friend of hers. She took us to one of Um Kulsum's concerts, and hearing the famous Egyptian singer live, I finally understood how truly marvelous her singing was.

Soheir took us too to the annual charity bazaars held in the Semiramis Hotel. These events were run by society women, who embroidered various things or baked cakes or donated jewelry and other items for sale. Besides raising funds for charities, these affairs had an unofficial objective. Frequented only by women, they were a kind of marriage bazaar, for the stalls where the goods were laid out were manned by the society matrons' daughters, *"jeunes filles de bonne famille."* In this way they would be shown off to the women of other society families, who were there, among other reasons, to scout out brides for their sons. Um Kulsum, too, was a regular at these affairs, not because she had sons but because she herself (it was said) enjoyed seeing the new crop of pretty girls. Among my own relatives, only Aunt Karima took part in these charity activities and the lively socialite life they involved. This life was, I think, too much part of the public domain, too nontraditional and too Westernized for the more conservative women of my own direct family, my mother and aunts and of course Grandmother.

My friendship with Nawal's mother and sisters would endure over the years, so that when I finally returned to Egypt it would be with them that I would stay. My friendship with Nawal would continue too, but not in the way that it had begun—as a passionate intellectual companionship. Her life was soon overtaken by tragedy. Already in those first years of our friendship she began to suffer from a mysterious illness. It proved to be multiple sclerosis and it eventually affected her mind, clouding its once dazzling clarity.

While I stayed home waiting to take the Girton entrance exam, Amr and Nawal began attending Cairo University. When November finally came I sat for the exam in the bizarre setting of the Swiss embassy. In those post-Suez days there was no British embassy and no British institution in Egypt to which Girton felt they could entrust their exam and its supervision.

I didn't want to go to Cairo University or to the American University in Cairo. I knew from friends at Cairo University that there was a kind of rote approach there, that one was expected to put down what the lecturer said verbatim and not what one thought for oneself, and to me that sounded deadly. The American University had a somewhat better reputation, but for some reason I didn't want to go there, either. I wanted to go to England and to Cambridge.

"Place offered Stop Peace," the telegram from Girton read. Peace, I learned from my sister, was not part of the message: it just happened to be the name of the college admissions secretary.

$\mathscr{T}$HE $\mathscr{H}$AREM $\mathscr{P}$ERFECTED?

I LOVED GIRTON from the moment of my arrival on a day in early October as dusk was falling, the taxi turning into the college driveway and pulling up under the red brick tower with its college crest. I remember pushing open for the first time the heavy wooden door to the porter's lodge and how busy it was with people—students arriving, parents saying goodbye—and then coming out again with my room assignment into the failing October light, glimmering now in a dramatic streak of brilliance over the buildings. I followed the assistant porter as he trundled my luggage diagonally across the main courtyard with its shadowy trees and bicycle racks. We entered the buildings by another heavy wooden door, leading into what I would come to know as the East Wing Gyp, the gyp being what they called the area containing the laundry rooms and bathrooms. "Gyp" was also what they called the college cleaning women. ("Gyp: at Cambridge and Durham, a college servant"—Oxford Dictionary. Possibly, the dictionary notes, from gippo, varlet, or from gypsy. Gypsy: "a wandering race . . . believed to have come from Egypt.")

I loved it all: huge, heavy doors, corridors that went on forever, overlooking courtyards and lawns and woods and hazy, distant meadows, Victorian Gothic turrets and towers and spiral stairs, secret words—words like "gyp"—known only to initiates. It was like arriving in a Brontë novel—some combination of *Jane Eyre* and *Wuthering Heights*—and being immediately taken in, accepted at once as one who belonged.

Of course this was "England," a place, with its red roofs and woods and fogs and rain, that I'd already lived in, in my mind, through all those years of losing myself in English books. This was one reason, no doubt, that I took so easily to Girton and instantly felt at home. Another, of course, was that my brothers and sister had also been students at Cambridge and I'd grown up hearing them talk about it. Even the people who were to be the key presences in my own life at Girton, Miss Bradbrook and Miss Duke, director of studies and tutor respectively, were people I'd heard about before I ever got there because my sister had been at Girton and they'd had the same role in her life. Indeed they too, I found, knew about me. Miss Bradbrook, for instance, knew that I had been a champion runner and that I had, that summer, read and loved *A Room of One's Own*—my sister had written to her telling her about me. Magda had surely thought that this latter fact would impress her, but for some reason I found Miss Bradbrook's knowing it deeply embarrassing, feeling that my sister had given away something about me that was very private. What was it about loving that book of Woolf's that I felt it was so important for me to be secretive about? Its feminism, when feminism had not yet become a living idea again? Certainly I wasn't consciously a feminist in those days. I think it must have been something to do with that that made me both love the book—whereas I thought then that what I liked about it was the way she wrote—and feel that I had to be secretive about it.

There were other, less obvious, less tangible reasons why Girton felt so familiar to me. For, in fact, life at Girton was in fundamental ways deeply continuous with the assumptions, beliefs, and ways of living that had hitherto framed the world as I knew it. The meditative, inward mood of Girton, for instance—this place of books, gardens, quiet, trees—was very like that of Ain Shams. Although infinitely less grand and lovely, Ain Shams was a place essentially given over to reading and to a sense of the overriding reality of inner worlds of imagination. Even visitors felt this about Ain Shams. People who

came would say that they felt they had entered the world of Proust
—or whoever their favorite writer happened to be. As if the place
were somehow located exactly on the edge and borderland between
imagination and the ordinary world.

Girton then, spectacularly more lovely, was this too, and so naturally I felt at home. (To this day, probably because of Girton, I love
the English landscape around Cambridge as much as I love any
landscape—even Egypt's. Different as they are, for me they share an
underlying similarity. Flat, dark earth, rich, fertile, furrowed fields
cracked and parched—even in Cambridge—in a dry summer. One of
the pleasures of finding myself in Cambridge again recently was that
of living once more in a place where the look of the earth and trees
and the shapes of leaves and the shadows they cast on the ground
were deeply familiar—and of hearing again familiar birds, some of
which I recognized from childhood in Cairo, birds going back and
forth in their migrations between Europe and Africa.)

Then also the order that framed and regulated our ordinary lives
was one that I was perfectly at home in. I found myself living, just as
I had in Alexandria, in a place where women, presiding over the young
in their charge, were the authorities. This is how it had been from
when I first came into the world, and here it was, the same underlying reality, at Girton. Girton, that is to say, was a version of the
community of women—the harem—as I had lived it every summer
in Alexandria.

Moreover, the order undergirding this reality was familiar in other
and equally fundamental ways, though I would not have known how
to speak of it then. Here, too, we were marked off from others as
special, privileged people. Wearing gowns, for example, in the town
after dusk—gowns that distinguished us from mere townspeople,
marking us as insiders, initiates, members of this ancient, exclusive
university. Wearing them to dinner in hall. Standing, waiting for grace
to be said in Latin from High Table and sitting down, in a great
scraping of chairs and amid the rising hubbub of chatter, to English
food—food that I now, initiated into it at eighteen, have quite a fond-
ness for: roast beef and Yorkshire pudding, shepherd's pie, prunes and

custard, bread pudding. Eating under the eye of the women whose por-
traits lined the paneled hall, women in plain white bonnets, stern
women in dark gowns with frills at the neck, founders, mistresses, our
foremothers. Mine as well, now that I was member and initiate. Sitting
eating, being served not by Saleh and his assistants but by the Girton
kitchen staff, women in black dresses with white collars and aprons.

For here, too, our lives were sustained, as we pursued our quest
of meaning, ideas, truth, by a troupe of others, called not servants but
gyps and staff and workers and groundsmen and gardeners and assistants. These were words that professionalized and also sanitized and
rendered psychologically and emotionally acceptable the realities of
power and class. They were words that, while they allowed the comfortable classes of Western societies to be sustained by the labor and
service of others, simultaneously allowed them (somewhat mysteriously to someone not raised in this system and so not wearing those
particular spectacles) to feel self-righteous and to believe that they,
unlike the backward, oppressive middle and upper classes of Third
World societies, lived in classless, democratic societies and did not
oppress people. (Other common words for this pool of laborers include "helpers," "agricultural workers," and "illegal immigrants"—
never, of course, "servants" or "peasants," though such people sometimes live, even in this founding land of democracy, in conditions as
bleak as those endured by people that other societies designate that
way. For Westerners, apparently, it's okay and democratic to have
servants—people whose labor, both directly and indirectly, sustains
your lifestyle—provided you use the right words and never call them
that. Betty Friedan, for example, unabashedly recommends in *The
Feminine Mystique* that the government subsidize university-educated
women so that they can hire "household help"—of what color, I wonder, and what class in this classless society?—and thus be free to
fulfill their artistic and intellectual potential.)

In Girton, then, this life devoted to the pursuit of "higher things"
sustained by the labor of others could be lived guilt-free and—so long
as you stuck to the right words—without any sense that you were
oppressing or exploiting anybody. And it was free of the bonds of

intimacy and personal involvement with which the servant-master relationship was liable to be fraught in those Third World, "backward" societies. I never saw Brad or Miss Duke or any other faculty member sitting talking intimately, quietly with a member of the staff, let alone with someone as lowly as a gyp—as I had many times seen Grandmother sitting with Umm Said, and Mother with Fat-hia. There were no relationships here of servant and mistress going back to girlhoods, no mutual knowledge and sharing and companionship between them, no reaching out to comfort with the touch of long affection. And no gyp or member of the staff, so far as I know, asked when Brad or any other faculty member died, as Fat-hia would ask when Mother died, for a photo of her to hang in her home and have always before her. (I don't, on the other hand, want to romanticize servant-master relations in the Third World: they were without question relations of power and were surely mired in all the imbalances and injustices in which such relations are typically mired.)

But in any case, it was a deeply familiar world to me. In some ways, indeed, Girton represented the harem perfected. Not the harem of Western male sexual fantasy or even the harem of Muslim men, fantasy or reality, but the harem as I had lived it, the harem of older women presiding over the young. Even the servers here—gyps, cooks, staff—were women, and from these grounds, these precincts, the absence of male authority was permanent. For unlike Smith and other women's colleges in America, the Girton fellowship—the professors —was from the start exclusively female. Girton would remain exclusively female until the late sixties, when I was a graduate student. Consequently I have been privileged to live in two harem communities, a Turco-Egyptian one and a British one. And it has been my destiny, too, alas, to live through the ending of both the Turco-Egyptian harem world and the hundred-year-long British experiment in women's communities as practiced at Girton.

⁓

Going to supervisions: putting on my gown, taking along the essay I had just scrambled to finish, arriving at the door, opening the outer door, knocking on the inner one.

"Come in!"

Miss Bradbrook's high, birdlike voice.

My fellow supervisees already there or arriving a moment later. Usually there were two or three of us, no more.

Reading our essays aloud, listening to Brad's comments, watching her expressions and reactions as she listened.

"Ye-e-es," she would say, suddenly alert, leaning forward to poke the fire.

She might say nothing for a good few moments or begin a sentence and trail off, looking intently into the fire or just into the air before her. Then she would follow out her thought, and almost always the experience of watching her do this was riveting. The sense one had was of being in the presence of someone who nearly always homed in on the essence of the issue before us and never handled it facilely, simplistically. Whatever we were contemplating, we became aware—listening to her probing reflections and her spare, exact words, interrupted by her own long silences—of the multiple universes of meaning in which this object before us existed, as if it were a gem that she was slowly turning before us to catch now this light, now that.

Sometimes she offered us coffee or sherry. For some reason her sitting room, to which we went for supervisions, was always quite dark, although there were windows all along one wall and French doors opening onto the courtyard, which she left open on fine days. There would be some light on where we sat and a fire in the winter. Books lined all the walls right to the ceiling and there was a somewhat cluttered feel to the place, with its occasional tables, lamps, and stools as well as chairs, one of these, her favorite, a rocking chair. There were photos on one of the tables in oval silver-gilt frames of Victorian-looking people in Victorian and Edwardian clothes.

Mrs. Madge's room was quite different, spare, like a Japanese painting. Mrs. Madge was (is) the distinguished British poet Kathleen Raine, and her room had something of the distilled, uncluttered loveliness of her poems. She was a botanist by training (she and Brad had been undergraduates together at Girton). The first thing one noticed

on entering her room were the perfect plants that she always had—
a hyacinth or a white cyclamen in exquisite bloom. In her fifties then,
she was quite beautiful in a painterly, poetic way, sitting awaiting us,
the diamond-shaped windows behind her, vivid blue eyes the color of
the sky. A research fellow rather than a permanent fellow at Girton,
a poet in this academic world, Kathleen Raine self-consciously occupied an alternative space. She was scornful of academics and above
all of critics, although she did value, she said, the work done by true
scholars, people like Brad. Such scholarship was useful, even though
it was not knowledge in the deepest sense of the word. Raine defined
herself as belonging to a different tradition of knowledge, distinctly
in opposition to the "knowledge" pursued in universities, which she
regarded as a barren, dead, destructive, desiccated, rationalistic, su-
premely arrogant, and ultimately deadly enterprise. Real knowledge
was the knowledge of prophets, poets, visionaries; it was there in
Blake and Yeats and in the world's ancient traditions (I think India came into this, and possibly ancient Egypt) and in Plato and
Plotinus—but not in Aristotle, definitely not in rationalist Aristotle.
But what exactly this alternative knowledge and tradition was I was
never quite able to grasp, not in a way that I would have been able
to explain to anyone or even to articulate for myself. But intuitively I
was enormously drawn to what I sensed, rather than clearly understood, she was saying.

Brad, too, deferred to Mrs. Madge's superior ways of knowing and
in terms that affirmed the innate mysteriousness of this other process
of knowing, the poet's vision. She would say, suggesting that we
take some question up with Mrs. Madge rather than with her, "Mrs.
Madge is a poet, you know." The statement was at once explanatory
and conclusive. In Brad's vocabulary, poets seemed to be people with
special vision, so that her words were at once recognition and affirmation.

Thus I had already back then a model of someone who openly
despised academic knowledge, indeed despised this entire enterprise
of what we call knowledge.

I know now more clearly than I knew at the time why, during a particularly difficult time soon after I'd arrived in America, I went out and bought myself a copy of Kathleen Raine's latest collection of poems and had found such solace in them. And why then I bought, in the local supermarket, a white cyclamen, its unfolding flowers in the ensuing days becoming for me like living presences, candles on an altar, invoking the memory of people I'd known, keeping alive the remembrance of a clarity and steadfastness, a holding on, against another tide, to the truth of their own vision.

Miss Bradbrook and Mrs. Madge were the teachers I saw the most of. Both were generous teachers, the best kind one can have: they were passionate about pursuing what was true to them and understanding and defining it as exactly as they knew how. In supervisions they did this in our presence and without concessions to us. (And yet if I were to grade them according to the teaching evaluations that students are asked to fill out these days—Did the professor make the course objectives clear? What significant learning took place for you? How did the course help you better understand the intersection of race, gender, class?—both would fail abysmally.)

Brad would leave me little Christmas gifts in my pigeonhole, once a handkerchief in an envelope. The college would be almost empty in the last days before Christmas, everyone except a handful of people from abroad like myself having gone home. Both Brad and Mrs. Madge, along with my other supervisors, gave me excellent grades on my essays, although I never did well on the university exams at the end of the year. I was exceedingly shy and terrified of speaking in supervisions, and having missed out on two years of study that everyone else at Cambridge had been through for their A levels, I was exceedingly ignorant and unsophisticated, compared with my fellow students. Particularly with Mrs. Madge, though, this seemed to be a point distinctly in my favor: she could be scathingly dismissive of my fellow supervisees, particularly those who were most sophisticated and knowing, and conversely was often very affirming of things I said— those few things I managed to say. Sometimes now, when I have a student who comes from a less "good" school than others in the class,

I understand what it was that she appreciated, and I appreciate it myself in those students. Addressing things out of their deep need to understand, they bring a freshness and directness to their readings; they seem less cluttered in their thought and less entangled than others by what they are expected to think and say—everything the others have been taught in the "good," fast-track schools is the right thing to think, to say.

While Brad and Mrs. Madge interested themselves only in the higher realms of things, my other supervisors, Mrs. Bennett and Dr. Radzinowicz, took enough interest in the practicalities of life to teach me a few elementary but essential skills, like how to structure an essay and even how to take notes, Dr. Radzinowicz showing me the index cards on which she'd mapped out the entire *Faerie Queene* in all its essential themes. The kind of intellectual attention that Joan Bennett brought to bear on whatever we were reading, steady, clear, like a lighthouse, was quite different from the effect of complexity and of sheer contradiction—of light and dark being there inseparably and at once—that Brad's attention brought out in texts. With Bennett one could believe that, provided one thought clearly enough, steadfastly enough, everything could be brought within the compass of our understanding, within the compass of rational thought and human understanding. Not so Brad. Or Kathleen Raine. Radzinowicz was somewhere in between.

Besides the women who taught me, I also saw my tutor (responsible for one's "moral" welfare) fairly regularly. A classicist who had been in Egypt briefly during World War II, Miss Duke conveyed a sense that she was familiar with Mediterranean ways. I don't recall going to her with any difficulties, and yet I remember her as at least indirectly addressing issues that I was worrying about, and saw her as a benign presence in my life. She had a wonderful painting in her room by Winifred Nicholson, Ben Nicholson's less well-known wife, to whose work she'd been introduced by Kathleen Raine. Raine, as we knew from the names she mentioned in supervisions, was at home in the artistic and literary world of England.

After my first term or two at Girton I hardly attended university lectures. This was ordinary at Girton, among students of English, anyway. Lecturers often just talked about their specialties and usually quite unintelligibly to most undergraduates. We read the books, which were generally much clearer, by the various famous people lecturing there in those days but rarely went to more than one or two of their lectures. All the significant learning happened at Girton.

We were in my room late one evening, the two other Muslims in the college, Selma and Hamida, and myself, and I think a couple of English friends. I was sitting on the floor, my typewriter on the coffee table before me, talking with them and then typing what we decided I should type. We were concocting a story about how we were Muslim women whom Girton was holding prisoner, at the behest of our parents, forbidding us to go out on our own, and we had been protesting this and had in consequence been locked up together by the college, which had also deprived us even of paper. Hence I was typing this message appealing for help on the back of a Players cigarette box. We were planning on sending this absurd, transparently concocted story to a newspaper, calling it "S.O.S. from Girton's Muslim Women." Of course it was absurd—who would believe that Girton was colluding in holding Muslim young women prisoner? But there was evidently no limit to the nonsense that the Western—or, anyway, the British —press was capable of believing—or at least to what it was willing to print and sell, in connection with Muslim women—provided such words as "prisoners" and "oppression" were liberally sprinkled about. We mailed the piece off to one of the tabloid newspapers, and to our incredulity and embarrassment the newspaper proposed to send a reporter down to talk to us. I explained on the phone that the story was a hoax and we were really awfully sorry, but he said he wanted to come down and talk to us anyway, could he take us out to dinner? He did. We were all extremely sheepish. No newspaper story ensued.

Obviously we were aware of and making fun of how people in the culture in which we found ourselves seemed to see Muslim women. But none of us, and certainly not I, had a developed or critical understanding of racism, which, in the England of my day and in the milieu of Cambridge, did not exist as a word or as something that people were analytically conscious of. It is true that we did cluster together at times, not specifically the Muslim women but the group of us from abroad and especially from the former British Empire, from the places once shaded pink and deeper pink on the map—British colonies and protectorates. There was Olu from Nigeria, Selma from Iraq, Achla and Primula from India, Hamida and Farida from Pakistan (although Farida's relation to the group was more ambiguous, possibly because she had converted to Christianity; the issue was not her religion, for Olu too was Christian, but presumably something entailed in the process of conversion). Sometimes we clustered together at breakfast or lunch, not exactly as friends, at least not as close friends, but as people with some recognizable connection, particularly if someone had a story about something odd and uncomfortable—racist, as we would call it now—that had happened. Olu, for instance, shortly after she arrived, came down to breakfast aghast—another student, a white woman from South Africa, had knocked on her door and asked her to bring her morning tea! And Selma and I at different times had experiences with fellow students trying to "save," or convert, us. And the hope of seeing us converted was there even among some of the dons (the college fellows), including one I was particularly attached to. There would be some implied —and sometimes not only implied—suggestion that becoming Christian would be the proof and mark of our having found our way to true morality and civilization.

Talking recently to an American friend who had been at Cambridge at the time that I was, I heard of the racism he had witnessed. People at his college, Pembroke, would often in his presence make derogatory remarks about Jews, not realizing that he was Jewish. I never overheard such remarks about Arabs, but obviously both my appearance and my name made my Arabness visible.

This is not to say that I never encountered overt racism in Cambridge. A man spat at me on a bus once when, thinking I was Israeli, he discovered I was an Arab. And once at a College Feast at King's College, where I had gone as someone's guest, one of the young fellows of the college sitting at the head of our table told me that he was a staunch supporter of Anthony Eden and that the Suez Canal should be in British hands—the Egyptians didn't have the engineering capacities to keep the canal open. It would no doubt shortly clog up and the British would have to take over running it again.

~

Of course there were other things going on in my life in those years. I was eighteen and free to do what I liked without supervision for the first time. And of course, too, I had brought myself with me —and all the baggage of attitudes, beliefs, notions of morality, and wariness that had been instilled into me in Cairo. Still there were, undeniably, interesting moments also.

Convention says that it is one's romantic involvements that make up the story of one's life. Unthinkingly assuming that I must inevitably fall in with this convention, I dutifully set forth on what is for me now just an exercise in archaeology—and then asked myself why I was even attempting it. For the truth is that the most unforgettable, lyrical experience in those years was not a moment of either romantic or erotic involvement. Rather it was a moment of intense presence and connection with the living world around us and also of companionship. There were three of us. We'd been sitting up talking past midnight, the window open onto a balmy, scented night of sudden spring. On the spur of the moment we decided to climb out (the college locked its doors at ten and we were not officially allowed out of the building after that) for no other reason than to be out on such a night, running across the moonlit lawn to the safety of the woods. Here we just wandered about, whispering and laughing, picking for ourselves in the clearings bright with moonlight handfuls of dew-heavy violets. If someone had told me then that thirty years later I would easily remember this night—and not so easily remember who it was, in a given year, I'd been involved with—I would never have believed it.

And then, too, no matter what convention says, the people that I have remembered over the years and that I continued to have some relation with were the people who taught me and who were in authority in the college community. It is they whose words and presence and attitudes and ways of seeing I have returned to many times in my mind—in the way that I have returned (without necessarily registering what I was doing) to what Grandmother or Aunt Aisha or my parents once said or how they looked at this moment or that.

Those moments spent in Kathleen Raine's room and Brad's, and a few others, have something of that same charge and richness and sheer pleasure of those starlit dusks and nights spent on the balcony in Alexandria—that rounded balcony shaped like the prow of a ship, a ship cleaving the dark around us—listening to my aunts and grandmother and their company of women. In Alexandria, as at Girton, the women devoted a good part of their time to analyzing, discussing, and taking apart words, meanings, motives, characters, consequences, responsibilities (though in Alexandria their seriousness was leavened with much laughter) and to reflecting on where the moral heart of an issue lay and what it might all mean. In Alexandria, though, it was real people's actual words and real people's characters, motives, and intentions that were taken apart and put together again. And in Alexandria it was real people whose lives might well be profoundly affected as a result of the burden of their talk, the conclusions they came to, the advice they gave, the actions they then took. Sometimes, no doubt, through the resolutions they arrived at, children were saved the devastation of divorce, husbands kept monogamous, and women appeased (for good or ill) so as to endure some unendurable situation. At Alexandria and at Zatoun this activity that engrossed them daily, with both gravity and laughter, was part of the job of sustaining life and sustaining the community in its ongoing life across the generations.

At Girton, on the other hand, it was fictional people, people in books and novels and plays, whose words and actions and motives and moral characters we analyzed endlessly. Obviously this was not an activity that, in any direct sense anyway, sustained anybody's life or actual circumstances. Also, of course, at Girton we got degrees at the end of it. That same activity essentially, practiced at Alexandria and Zatoun orally and on living texts to sustain the life of the community, was called by outsiders to the process—by men of the official Arabic culture and by Westerners, men and women—idle gossip, the empty and even sometimes evil, malicious talk of women, harem women. That same activity, however, practiced by the women of Girton on written, not oral, texts and on fictional, not living, people was regarded as honorable, serious, important work. For the women of Girton no longer practiced it in the age-old, traditional manner that women in their culture, too, once did—orally and to sustain life. They practiced it in the manner and tradition of men, as their own colleagues (and men down the centuries) had—in relation to written texts rather than living people, as a profession, and to earn money rather than to sustain life. Performed by men for these purposes and in this manner, that same activity becomes suddenly a great and important and worthy and honorable occupation. (There is similar difference between cooking for the family and cooking as a chef: the same activity masculinized becomes a profession and worthy of esteem, honor, remuneration.)

Why are we doing this? Virginia Woolf asked, contemplating women in her day entering the ancient, venerable universities and coming to form the tail end of what she called the "procession of the sons of educated men," with their ribbons and gowns and tufts of fur on their shoulders and their arrogance and self-importance. Why are we doing this? she asked. Is this really what we want? What kind of knowledge is it that these men have developed and passed on in those institutions, why are we following in the wake of men's professions— what *are* these professions and why should we, following in these men's footsteps, pursue them? "What are these ceremonies and why should we take part in them?" Woolf herself, offered several honorary degrees over the course of her life, including from the University of Cambridge, consistently turned them down.

A place to pursue the professions of men in a community of women, Girton had offered for a moment perhaps a kind of transitional space.

Foremothers I called those founders of Girton; my own foremothers, too, I said of them. But these foremothers had looked down on my other foremothers and had held them in contempt. They had adopted the same attitudes toward these subjects—as to what was idle gossip and what was worthy, important thought—as their own men had, and they now combined these attitudes with the feelings of superiority that Europeans and white people, men and women, felt toward the cultures of the "inferior" non-European peoples generally. Harriet Martineau, a prominent nineteenth-century intellectual, visited Egypt and was hospitably received in their harem quarters by a group of women who were probably just like the women among whom I grew up. Returning home, she wrote of how ignorant these Muslim women were and how worthless and mindless their harem talk. Of course, Martineau spoke no Arabic. And the harem women, naturally, spoke no English. So how exactly was this woman of (supposedly, by the measures of her society) austere, superior intellect judging them, and how exactly was she setting about assessing, with that fine, discerning, superior intellect of hers, the value of their talk? And she is just one of a steady stream of Europeans who looked down on and thought of Muslim harem women as mindless.

But I too internalized the low regard in which Westerners and also traditional men of the local culture at large held women and the activities of women. In childhood, I'd picked up this sense of contempt for women, and in particular the women around me—just from the air, from the books we read, the films we saw, the intangible attitudes at school and those in the world around me. It is quite clear to me that my mother distinctly enters the fabric of my own memories in the negative. "She was not a professional anything," I wrote earlier in these pages, remembering my own inarticulate, internalized contempt as a youngster. I too saw those women, and above all my mother, as people who "did" nothing, and I too took their "endless" talk as idleness, gossip, as "doing" nothing. In a world where doing—doing, not being—was everything. Men *did* things, *were* something or somebody, and Western women too, at least Western women in books and films, could be something or someone, compared with the women around me in childhood, who just *were*. In the fabric of my own consciousness the women among whom I lived and most of all my mother were everything that I didn't want to be. The only escape from this, the only way out, I must have concluded at some level, would be for me to grow up to become either a man or a Westerner.

· II ·

"RUNNING FROM THE
FLAMES THAT LIT THE SKY"

. . . A damn plot you might think.
Yes indeed, it was called
colonial-ization,
spelt with a z.
The prince of the plot was called Brit Ain
But actually he had many brothers.

. . .

After much time
and many millions of £s later
they leased us back our land
through a deed called In-Dee-pendence
This meant the land was ours,
But everything we produced,
was theirs.
We even got our own leaders.

. . .

Meanwhile,
another plot called Imperial-Ization
had worked its way through the world
and the earth was carved up
and re-aligned.

Back on the Plantation
We all fought each other
(with a little help from outside).

We squabbled over what would remain
when the In-Dee-pendence deed was passed
and the prince departed for home.

And so,
in the midst of the troubles
my parents packed their bags.
They followed the general recruitment drive
to the imperial palace itself.

We arrived in the Northern Hemisphere
when Summer was set in its way
running from the flames that lit the sky
over the plantation.
We were a straggly bunch of immigrants
in a lily white landscape.
We made our home among strangers,
knowing no one but ourselves.

. . .

One day I learnt
A secret art,
Invisible-Ness it was called.
I think it worked . . .

Meiling Jin (black British poet),
"Strangers in a Hostile Landscape"

9

PENALTIES OF DISSENT

THE CAIRO life I returned to after those rich, sheltered under-graduate years was far different from the life we had when I left for England. I knew from my parents' letters—always brief rather than effusive, and arriving always with the censorship tape along one side —that things were hard. Still, the bleakness of their lives came as a shock to me. All the downstairs rooms except for the dining room and hall were closed off and shuttered, my parents occupying just the upstairs rooms at one end of the house. The garden was derelict, overgrown in places and desiccated in others, fruit lying rotting in the grass. Amm Suleiman, the aging gardener, still lived in his room at the bottom of the garden and tended to the garden, but now, with no young assistant, only sporadically.

Most of the time now my father was ill, lying in the corner room upstairs. And Mother was permanently gray-faced, permanently anx-ious. Nanny, of course, was gone. I slept in the room we had shared when I was a child, in the bed we had shared—and in which she had died. I would lie listening to the familiar night sounds—the frogs, the waterwheel—seeing, when I woke in the night, the same dance of leaves on the walls, eucalyptus, mimosa, shadows cast by the street lamp, the shutters standing open.

Nanny's ghost was there, I think, one summer night. Not in the room with me but in the hallway. I woke up about two and heard the heavy, solid footsteps of someone pacing up and down the hall from one end, where my room was, to the other. Back and forth, back and forth. I assumed it was Mother, who had a habit of pacing thus whenever Father's health took a particularly bad turn. I got up to see what had happened. There was nobody in the hall. I went through the middle room to my mother's room. "Maman?" I said, at the door, "Maman?" No response. I pushed the door open. I suppose there must have been moonlight or something, because I could see quite clearly—she was in her bed and sound asleep. Puzzled, I went back to the hall and looked into Father's room in case it had been he; it must have been a time when he was not ill so that it was conceivable that it had been he who had been pacing about. But he was asleep. The pacing, meanwhile, had stopped.

I went back to bed, and the pacing began again. Loud footsteps, back and forth, now just outside my door, now retreating to the other end of the hall and then returning again. Again I got up and went to Mother's room. Sound asleep. I stood there listening. The sound began again. I woke Mother, and she too listened. She said she couldn't hear anything but she looked as if she could. I was sure she heard them but had decided not to distress me by agreeing, since footsteps could only be explained by the presence of a ghost, what else? That was the kind of thing Mother might well do. But it is true that she was slightly deaf, so maybe she really didn't hear anything. A light had now come on in Father's room and we went in and found him, unaware that we were up, settling down to read on the sofa, as he often did when he woke at night. I explained what was happening and, as we fell quiet, he listened for the footsteps. Yes, he agreed, exchanging glances with Mother, he did hear them. Houses creak at night, he said, wood creaks, that was probably all it was. Okay, I said, wood creaks, but randomly, not in this way, like footsteps receding and returning, receding and returning.

"Well, you know it could," he said. "It could be the points of stress where footsteps have habitually fallen, you know, releasing that stress."

I couldn't believe it. "No, it wouldn't do that, sound exactly like somebody walking. Listen, it's footsteps, not just wood creaking. There—now they're at this end, listen, and now . . . Do you think it's a ghost?"

He listened. "I don't know," he said finally.

We all went back to bed. I never heard the footsteps again after that night. And I do not know now why I was so certain the next morning that it had been Nanny and that it had something to do with purgatory and having to retrace things done in one's life. I suppose I dreamed it—or, more exactly, felt that Nanny had communicated something to me in my dreams.

This was a period in my life when all the expectations, assumptions, certainties I had grown up with were dissolving. True, some of the changes I lived through in those years were changes such as we all undergo—the death of the older people one is close to, the illness and decline, quite perceptibly now toward death, of parents. And even at the best of times and even for people much older than I—twenty-one—such events, natural though they are, expected, some day, some time though they are, still are hard to take in and adjust to. But in my case, these natural events were taking place within the context of a completely unexpected reversal of circumstances.

I wrote earlier of how I would listen skeptically, disbelievingly to my mother's anxieties about money, supposing these inordinate terrors to be the result of her having been born to wealth and not knowing now how to cope with less. But in fact I did not know exactly what the family revenues were, and it may be that her fears were justified. Inquiring into one's parents' financial affairs was "not done." It was not done anyway, I must have felt, in relation to Mother, for by the time finances were a problem in our lives it was Mother exclusively who dealt with money matters. My father left all these affairs to her, and even when he was not ill there was a distinct sense at home that money worries were to be kept from him.

In fact there was something surreal about the situation and about Mother's anxieties about money, whether or not my skepticism was justified. For example, I remember a day when Mother arranged for

Gaafar, the chauffeur, to purchase half a kilo of apples because Father, feeling better, had awakened craving an apple. As soon as Gaafar was off, she fretted about how we really couldn't afford apples, which were indeed expensive in those days in Egypt. How, I thought, could someone who lived in a house like this, even if most of it was shut up and neglected, someone who had a chauffeur to send to market, be unable to afford half a kilo of apples?

But the surrealism was really only on the surface. In fact, it is quite possible to live in the fine house in which you have always lived—and have no money. And it is not so easy, when one of you is ill, to up and move, find a smaller, less expensive place. Even the chauffeur, in their circumstances, was hardly a luxury. They lived a considerable distance from shops and markets and pharmacies and the place where they got Father's heavy oxygen tank. Father could drive, but most of the time now was unable to, and Mother could not drive. Besides, there was a whole other layer: Gaafar had been with them for many years and was married to a woman whose family had worked on Grandfather's estate, and these were bonds and responsibilities that could not just casually and simply be dissolved. (When I returned to Egypt more than twenty years later, Gaafar, who had retired to farm a small plot of land after my mother died, made a six-hour journey to see me and to honor the memory of my parents.)

Also underlying my skeptical attitude toward Mother's anxieties, I realize now, were my own fears of having no money. I think the prospect terrified me. I had a job, as good a job as I could get; I was a lecturer at one of Cairo's main universities, the Islamic Women's College, which was part of al-Azhar University. But the pay was low, barely enough to cover the rent for my tiny rent-controlled apartment. I was dependent for everything else—food, clothes, transportation, medical treatment, pocket money—on my parents. It was more bearable, less terrifying to believe that my mother's fears were fantastic, exaggerated than to believe that they really didn't have money and that I was a burden, too great a burden, on them. The terror of not having money is inversely proportional to the remedies and options one has. And if my options and my capacities to go out and earn money in that moment and that society were limited, how much more so were my mother's? What job could she have got?

My having an apartment on my own, a young, unmarried woman, in that society and in those days, I should explain, was itself very unusual and even slightly improper. The situation came about because the Islamic Women's College was in Maadi, a Cairo suburb on the other side of the city from Ain Shams, and so the commute, from Ain Shams by train to Cairo and then by tram to Maadi, was a long one, about two hours. And as it happened—I think none of us would have even considered the possibility otherwise—a flat became available in Zamalek (a central residential district of Cairo) in the same apartment block and right next door to where a close family friend, Madame Sherifa, lived with her two grown children. Her being there helped lend an air of propriety to this enterprise: a responsible older person was close by to keep an eye on me. Yet such was the unusualness and air of slight impropriety that my parents probably would not have agreed to the arrangement had things not been so gloomy at Ain Shams and had they not also been worried about how miserable I was about being unable to leave Egypt. For those were the years that I was trapped in the country, referred from office to office in the Mugammaa, the vast government building dominating the center of Cairo.

And all this, all these obstacles and miseries, were not things that just happened to be occurring—they were being deliberately dealt us, courtesy of the government. "He himself is old and ill? Then get his wife, get his daughter." All this because of some vindictive, malicious person or persons, people who, to curry favor with the *rayyis*, the leader, wanted to punish my father. And for what, what was he guilty of? Speaking out when he was ordered not to be a tyrant? Refusing to be silenced because he feared the costs of his silence would be too great for his country?

All this was happening because we had an unscrupulous government, a government that, in its totally controlled media, spouted an endless rhetoric of liberation, socialism, Arab nationalism, and the Glorious Revolution; a government that ill-treated and abused the rights of its powerless citizens simply because it could.

But these were grim years for others too in Egypt. For one thing, a fair proportion of the people whom my parents knew or who had been part of their broad network of social and professional connections were also in difficult circumstances, also struggling with unfamiliar poverty. Mostly they were people whose properties had been nationalized or placed under sequestration (under government control) and mostly they, too, were elderly people, their children abroad. Socializing now was rare, but it might occasionally happen that I would see at Ain Shams an elderly woman or couple, sitting talking quietly over tea with my mother, and that when they were gone I would hear from her about how this or that person had just stopped taking some heart or other medication because the family could no longer afford it or about how the such-and-such family, living still in its palatial old home because families under sequestration did not have the right to sell property, was now being supported by its chauffeur. The chauffeur lived still in his old room over the garage and shared with his former masters the salary from his job with a newly rich family.

Cairo was full of such stories. These were the years (the late fifties and early sixties) of the Nasser regime's worst repression, when Egypt's prisons bulged with political prisoners—Muslim Brothers and (ironically for a regime that proclaimed itself socialist and was an ally of the Soviet Union) Marxists and Communists. It was a time when Cairo was riddled with *mukhabarat*, the secret police, and their army of informers, ordinary people recruited to report (and eventually rewarded for reporting) any criticism of the government, and it was the era when people suspected of being disloyal to the revolution were being jailed or were disappearing; rumor had it that people could be jailed or disappeared for even the most trivial or oblique comment. Basil, our childhood friend and neighbor, was one such case. He disappeared while doing military service; his mother, desperate to find out what had happened, appealed to the army and the government for information. After two years in prison, he reappeared, the scars of torture on him. He had been in a military hospital after breaking his leg in a parachute jump. One day a radio was blaring in the background when he was trying to sleep, and he called out, "Turn that damn radio down!" It was Nasser making a speech. For those unpatriotic words Basil was thrown in jail for two years, tortured, and beaten.

Stories of government persecution of political enemies, abuse of power, greed, corruption, violence, and general thuggery were rife in Cairo. A man who had disappeared was found by his wife in a garbage bag on their doorstep months later. An officer (and broadly speaking it was the military that was the new class in power) had driven to a grocery store, ordered the owner to fill numerous bags, and driven off without paying. Protesting or disobeying could be costly. People suddenly got rich for no discernible reason, while acquaintances of theirs and sometimes even family members were taken off to prison. Hidayat, a Syrian woman I had met in England, an ardent Arab nationalist and Nasserite, appeared in Cairo and, though a woman of modest means who had never been to Egypt, took up residence in a plush Zamalek apartment. Meanwhile a mutual acquaintance who, in our presence, had been openly critical of Nasser, was in prison. Egyptians abroad knew that they had to watch what they said to other Egyptians—it was well known that Egyptian student bodies in the West were riddled with *mukhabarat*. But it obviously had not occurred to this person—as, until this incident it had not occurred to me— that one needed to watch what one said before other Arabs, too, in this era when Nasser had become the idol of Arab nationalists.

Of course much of this was rumor and speculation; there could be no proof, or no proof that ordinary people could have access to. I myself have no idea which of the rumors were true. But this is a work of memory, not of history, and of the memory of what it was like to live through the aftermath of the Glorious Revolution, rumors and all. An atmosphere of government terrorism was the reality of our world.

Something else happened to the feel of Cairo in those days—as if once you make hatred and derision (that particular derision toward enemies that Nasser was so good at injecting into his speeches) normal and acceptable in one area, they become generalized to everything else. One saw things unimaginable before, small things, details that nevertheless seemed to mark a vast gulf between the old Cairo and this Cairo of the aftermath of the revolution. An old man who just happened to be passing, shuffling slowly by on the pavement, sneered at by two young men simply because he was old: unimaginable before in this society where respect for the elderly was so ingrained and where for the young to address the elderly disrespectfully was something so extraordinary that I had never actually witnessed it. I remember the shock of seeing this now and the feeling I had that I was witnessing the breakdown of a major human taboo. (I know, though, that I cannot succeed in conveying the shock of this scene in a society where the idea that respect for the elderly is a fundamental human value seems weird and not particularly meaningful.) In the old days, too, other people in the street would never have tolerated this behavior; someone would have told those young men off. I remember observing with the same kind of shock as a group of boys threw stones at two women, a mother and daughter, stepping out of an old-fashioned and clearly once-grand car. "Your days are over," they called out, "or don't you know it yet?"

I am not an apologist for feudalism or class privilege or even in some vague way for the old order. I am sure that the revolution brought about many good things and that for other people and in other parts of society doors were opening and new, golden opportunities offering themselves. But not in my neck of the woods.

I know too, familiar as I now am with the history of many revolutions in our own and in earlier times, that as revolutions go this revolution was very mild in its consequences for political enemies and the old displaced classes. There were no guillotines, no mass executions. And I know that all revolutions bring about justice and liberty and equality first of all and above all for the revolutionaries themselves. The French Revolution executed not only the aristocrats but also those who presumed to ask for a little liberty and equality for their own groups—Olympe de Gouges, for example, executed for the crime of daring to ask for a little liberty and equality for women. And I know that ideals become tarnished and that hordes of small-minded, greedy people ride in on the coattails of revolutionaries, abusing power and further tarnishing the ideals of the revolution. And that in the end leaders come to depend on these sycophants and hangers-on, even if they are not themselves corrupt. There were never, for instance, any rumors in Cairo that Nasser himself was greedy or venal. On the contrary he lived, everyone always said, a simple, even an austerely simple, life. There were rumors that he was vindictive and ruthless toward those that he deemed political enemies, yes, but venal, no.

But this was the only revolution I lived through. Whether I liked it or not, words like *ishtirakiyya, al-wataniyya al-Arabiyya*—socialism, Arab nationalism—and the Glorious Revolution, became for me redolent of fraud. This was not an analytical reaction and I don't believe I even consciously registered it intellectually. It was merely an emotional, lived perception. And the fact is, too, that over these years those people in my experience who took principled stands and who were honest and upright and did not abuse others were not the revolutionaries, not the Nasserites or the Arab nationalists, not the new rich, busily lining their pockets.

10

*I*N THE *G*ROVES OF *W*HITE *A*CADEME

I WAS SITTING on a plane at Cairo airport within days of getting my passport. I'd gone out to Ain Shams to say goodbye to my parents: saying farewell to my father for what we both knew would be the last time.

Finally. I just wanted the engines to start up, the plane to take off. I wanted to be out of Egypt.

But it was a precarious, uncertain moment, too. My scholarship was for just one year, which was simply how British Council scholarships were. What then? Would I get the funds to continue? Cambridge (and most other British universities) did not allow students to work part-time while getting their degrees. My student visa, in any case, didn't allow me to work in England, and it was unimaginable, with all the problems in the news about immigration, that the British would give me a work permit. Cambridge had accepted me only for the M.Litt. degree, not the Ph.D., on the understanding that they would review my status after a probationary period. Everything, I felt, depended on my work's being good enough in the next few months for them to upgrade me. It was desperately important that I succeed: there was no safety net, only a black hole under my feet. No Egypt to go back to now and no one to turn to if I failed. My sister was in England, at Oxford. A student herself, with family responsibilities, she was in no position to help me. And my brothers were in Switzerland, struggling to establish their own lives, and we were not much in touch, anyway. I couldn't imagine turning to any of my siblings if things didn't work out.

It was January. Gray and raining in England. At the station, waiting for the train to Cambridge, I sat watching a black woman, from Africa or the Caribbean, I assumed, sweeping the platform and wondered if coming to England had turned out to be the right move for her. Was it better to be sweeping a platform in London than to be trapped in some other life in another, sunnier world?

Now there are many British-born black people in England but that was not the case then, in the latter part of the sixties. In the sixties, these years of the aftermath of the British Empire, black immigration—and in British English "black" meant all of us, all non-Europeans—had become the major political issue of the day. Politicians talked endlessly about how to stop it, curb it, this flood of blacks coming to their shores. Right-wing extremists, among them Enoch Powell, who had a mass following, advocated deportation, forced mass repatriation, for the presence of these "niggers," these savages—us— threatened not only British jobs but the very fabric of civilization. These issues, continually in the news, and this kind of language formed the ambiance and backdrop against which I now began my life as a graduate student.

I had been assigned the ground-floor room in the Girton graduate hostel on Trumpington Street, the only room that happened to be vacant. It smelled of traffic fumes even with the window closed, and the roar and rumble of traffic was as constant as the sea—Trumpington Street is one of the major arteries into Cambridge. A far cry, then, from the woods and lawns of Girton. And in fact, although I was attached to Girton, I would have little connection with the college apart from occasionally going out there for dinner. As I discovered, college affiliations were essentially nominal at the graduate level.

There were two entirely fortuitous circumstances that, looking back, I see were essential to my survival. Without them I doubt I would have made it through those years or managed to get my degree.

Oddly enough, those years were as hard, emotionally and psychologically, as the preceding difficult years in Egypt. I say "oddly" because
outwardly and in concrete terms they were not particularly hard in
the way that being in Egypt in that last period had been. Nobody here
was denying me a passport, nobody was forcibly preventing me from
pursuing the life I wanted to pursue.

The first piece of good fortune that now fell into my life was that
I was assigned Professor Arberry as my supervisor. He would be my
supervisor until a few months into my second year, when he became
too ill to see students. He died a few months later. Arberry, the Sir
Thomas Adams Professor of Arabic at Cambridge, was a scholar in
the tradition and possibly of the stature of the great British Oriental-
ists. Among other things, his translation of the Quran was, and probably still is, one of the finest English versions, and his translations of
Sufi poets, and of Rumi in particular, are still highly regarded.

Arberry had Parkinson's disease and was by this stage in his life
in a wheelchair. He never came to the faculty building so I would
cycle out to his home on Gilbert Road for supervisions, where I would
sometimes glimpse his wife, who herself was disabled, her hands quite
crippled by arthritis. Working on mysticism, he himself had a gentle,
mystical air about him and I felt at the time—as I do today—that it
was a rare, special gift to have known him. He was never harsh or
brusque in his responses to my work and almost always encouraging,
although I was very tentative in what I did and only just beginning to
learn what research was. He managed always to seem positively interested in what I had to say in the papers—the outline of my research
project and then the draft chapters—that I wrote for him. No doubt
this was partly because the subject I was focusing on—the life and
work of Edward William Lane, probably the finest British Orientalist
of the nineteenth century—was a subject that he himself had written
about.

The second piece of good fortune to fall into my life just then
was that, within the first few weeks, I met Alan, the man I would
later marry. The marriage would not last, probably most of all because
of the stresses that overtook our lives and that neither of us knew

how to handle. Still, Alan's affection and friendship through that year of my arrival and then through the first year or two of our marriage were crucial to me. His warmth and support, his ability to laugh, and the fact that with him I was able to be completely myself and also to laugh, not least at my own anxieties, gave me a fundamental base of connection and stability.

Alan and I met at a party at the house of another student, like Alan an American. It was rather a fine house on Panton Street— Americans on the whole had more money than the rest of us. I had been standing before a large, murky painting, trying to make out what it was, when he came up beside me, stood studying it a moment, then offered a mock-Freudian, pseudo-artsy analysis that was at once intelligent and funny. We spent the rest of the evening together. The following weekend he arrived, looking spruce and scrubbed and shy and keen-eyed, bearing an African violet, to take me out to dinner.

The connection we made was immediate. We began to see each other regularly. He, too, was a graduate student—in American history—and had already done a postgraduate degree in America. He was four years older than I and had brown eyes and black, deep black hair. I thought he might be part Native American, but he said the black hair came from a Welsh ancestor.

The African violet flourished. I took that as a sign. I'd never before managed to keep a plant alive for long.

It was the Vietnam era. Americans seemed to make up a significant proportion of the graduate students (several that I knew were there as a way, somehow or other, of avoiding the draft). Vietnam and happenings in America—protests, sit-ins, confrontations with the establishment, Kent State, Woodstock, flower people—were followed in their every detail by everyone in the circles I moved in, British as well as American. Knowing about these things and knowing the language and issues and debates that went with them was part of the graduate student culture of the day.

Radicalism was in the air, anyway. Though less in England than elsewhere, in Europe too this was the era of student protests and sit-ins that often made the headlines. Marxist student leaders (Daniel Cohn-Bendit in France, for example, "Danny the Red," as he was dubbed in newspapers) become household names, and in the strike of 1968, which brought Paris to a standstill, students joined with the workers.

But it was America, and events there, that set the tone. For me, of course, the day-to-day happenings in America and the import and significance of the issues they raised were all quite new. To make connections and friends in this community and understand the political and intellectual issues, I had to scramble to learn about the American scene, from understanding what "institutional violence" meant and why it was important to oppose it to learning about Che Guevara and reading Marx's critique of imperialism, which friends told me had changed their lives and their understanding of American involvement in Vietnam.

These events and perspectives set the tone academically as well. At the seminars I now began attending, where Americans were among the smartest and most articulate people, the language of Marxist theory was often the language used by the senior graduate students and those who were intellectually in the lead. To me, this too was new, a language and theory that I hastened to master. While Marxist analysis was new to me, many of the ideas and terms that were part of the political and intellectual radicalism of the moment and of the language of the day were in fact familiar to me and had for me a quite different ring and meaning than they did for my American and English cohorts in Cambridge, all of whom were, broadly speaking, from the middle and upper classes and had lived their lives in stable, democratic societies where they were free to say what they liked and to go where they liked. (All the Americans I met in Cambridge in that era —as well, of course, as all the English people who were there—were white.) Words like "revolution," "socialism," "liberation struggles," "class oppression," "the struggle against imperialism" represented, for my classmates, great shining ideals. But for me they had quite another undertow. According to the theories that my classmates were advocating as superior intellectual truth, on the face of it anyhow, my parents and family and all those who had suffered in the revolution were on the wrong side, distinctly on the side of the bad, whereas the unjust people in power, spouting their rhetoric of revolution, socialism, *al-ishtirakiyya*, the struggle against *al-imperialiyya*, and so on, apparently were on the side of the good. I knew naturally that it was more complicated than that and that Marxist analysis did not mean endorsement of injustice and tyranny. But the resonances that this theoretical perspective and language had for me in relation to my own experience doubtless made me more reluctant to embrace it than I might otherwise have been.

At any rate, then, for my classmates the popular theories were those that exposed and explained their governments' "wrongful" imperialist policies and conduct and that deeply and directly spoke to and addressed their own situations and their own moral, political, and intellectual dilemmas. These same ideas and theories, however, did not in a parallel way or in any simple sense directly explain or illuminate my own life and the history I had lived. Connecting to them entailed for me, personally and analytically, a much more complex and complicated negotiation than it did for my fellow students.

I realize now that the process that I underwent as a graduate student—of having, first, to learn the facts and realities of other people's lives, the lives of those in whose history and experience the current academic theories were grounded, and of having, second, to master theories that explained their experience but that needed considerable refining and transforming to have meaning for my own life —must have been the typical, indeed the *defining* experience for students from the Third World coming to the West. Many of us from the Third World arrived having lived through political upheavals that traumatically affected our lives—for this quite simply has been the legacy of imperialism for most of our countries. But it was not those histories that we had lived that were at the center of our studies, nor was it the perspectives arising from those histories that defined the intellectual agenda and preoccupations of our academic environment. Of course, the histories and perspectives that defined not only the curriculum but also the theoretical perspectives and issues of the day were those of the countries to which we had come, societies that were at the very center of the Western world. Moreover, it was not only the old academic establishment that reflected the perspectives of these powerful, dominant societies; even the oppositional, anti-establishment, countercultural, "radical" intellectual trends and critiques of the day also in fact represented the views of the powerful classes in those societies—the white middle classes—but, now, of the new generation of those classes. For, obviously, it was not the concerns of black or working-class Americans or Britons that defined our agenda in the academic world or that we needed to learn about in order to get on with our studies, it was not those groups who were generating the theories and critiques that we needed now to acquire. Blacks and working-class people and others on the margins of Western societies who joined the academic world had, just like us, to scramble to learn the experiences and histories and perspectives of others—of the Western white middle class, which set the academic agenda—and to learn to put those first, intellectually. We *had* to do this, *needed* to do it to make our way in the academic world.

All these kinds of issues, inhering in my situation and in what I was living through as I pursued my work and life as a graduate student, we would eventually identify, address, explore, and analyze, as my own generation and the generation just ahead of my own began to mature as academics and intellectuals. For what I was living and passively learning was exactly the kind of experience that would fuel the intellectual revolution that would come, particularly in the American academic world, as those from the margins—blacks, women, people from other cultures and from minority cultures in the West— understood their exclusion from the academic curriculum and set to work to make their own perspectives and histories academically visible. And thus they began to rework old theories and devise new ones grounded in the lives and histories of their own people, and to make sense of the processes and currents of history and society from the perspective of their own—our own—lives.

But this revolution had not yet happened. I know that there was for me a sense of fundamental disconnection between what I was grappling with academically and my own life and entirely private and isolated struggle to make sense of what I'd lived. I remember concluding vaguely sometime in those years that Theory must have nothing to do with Life, or that my life, anyway, was obviously completely irrelevant to theory and vice versa. I think I also had some intuitive understanding of the connection between geography, power, and the making of academic knowledge, for I would occasionally wonder—waking, say, in the middle of the night—why American lives and knowing what was happening to Americans were so important to theory and to everything else, whereas the lives of people in Ghana or Egypt or India, for example, were apparently completely irrelevant. But in the day I dismissed these as midnight thoughts that had nothing to do with anything.

Preoccupied in my daylight life with learning, mastering, understanding, writing all the things that I needed to learn, master, understand, and write in order to survive as a graduate student, I relegated such things to the margins, the edges of consciousness. What, for example, did I make of finding myself defined as black? And what did I make of the enormous negative significance with which my identity and race—whether Arab or black—were quite unambiguously charged in this culture? These, too, no doubt were subjects that I pondered only in those wakeful moments in the night, waiting for sleep or for the dawn.

It is extraordinary to think that it was exactly these kinds of concerns, relegated to the margins, dismissed as of no consequence to anything, that today make up the very questions that we often directly wrestle with, particularly those of us working on feminist issues and in black and cultural studies. What, for instance, from *our* perspectives today, is the meaning of race and racial identity? Who is it that defines what constitutes "true" knowledge? Does the white male academic canon, and the white male perspective on other cultures and other races or on women, represent a "truer," more valid, more universal understanding of human experience than any other perspective? Whose experience and whose perspective should be at the center of our studies in the academy? Whose lives? Men's? Women's? Which men and which women? Native Americans? Blacks? White middle-class women? And whose perspective and theories should weigh with us? Does an intellectual in Cambridge or New York have a truer, more valid, more authoritative understanding of our world and the processes shaping our lives than someone who lives, say, in Delhi or Cairo or Lagos and who works out of those different cultural perspectives, experiences, theories? Can it really be the case that it is only us here in the Western world (including those of us who migrated to this world from the "periphery") who have some special, privileged relation to true knowledge, true understanding, true theory? (Or only us and those abroad who ground themselves in the same assumptions and knowledge systems as we do?) How do we define what "knowledge" is and what it is that we should be learning and believing and studying and passing on as the essential, cherished heritage to the next generations? Whose lives, whose values, whose histories?

So this was how I occupied myself in those first months: I spent my days reading in the library, writing papers for Arberry, seeing Alan, going to seminars. As time went on and I began, as graduate students normally do, to acquire new analytical and theoretical vocabularies, the experience of attending seminars nevertheless continued, occasionally at least, to be an experience of straining to grasp what was being said in what seemed to be an increasingly abstract language. And indeed the late sixties was the era when the language of French theory and French theorists—structuralism, poststructuralism, Lévi-Strauss, Barthes, Foucault, Derrida—was just beginning to be used by the rising young stars among the Cambridge faculty and even by one or two of the smartest graduate students. At any rate, this was the language occasionally spoken in English department seminars. In my other department, Oriental Studies (I was affiliated with both), they spoke only the old-style, perfectly comprehensible academic language.

By the end of the summer I moved to the room at the top of the hostel, larger than the one on the ground floor and with a view of the tops of trees as well as of buildings. I had come to know the other

hostel residents and had become particularly friendly with Veena, who was from India and occupied the room below mine, and with Barbara, an American. When I came home in the evening I would often come down from my room and stand chatting with Veena while she cooked her supper—nearly always lentils and rice—on the stove on the landing outside her room. Veena was a theoretical biochemist. She was from a poor family in the south of India and had arrived where she was through scholarships and sheer native brilliance. She was a vegetarian and a practicing Hindu and had on her desk a picture of Ganesh, the deity whose form is that of a benignly smiling, humanlike elephant. The small space around it was arranged like an altar, with a few flowers always and a stick of incense. Barbara, who was also a scientist, a physiologist who did experiments on rats, tried valiantly to engage with Veena, who was eager to talk about her work with a fellow scientist. But Barbara, who was utterly committed to rational scientific methods and for whom religious belief was simply superstition, could not overcome her prejudice about Veena's devotion to Ganesh. It tainted for her the value of Veena's work and she could not bring herself to take her seriously as a scientist.

I too, actually, was prejudiced about Ganesh. I knew almost nothing about Hinduism and I had still essentially the prejudices of my own upbringing, which regarded monotheistic religions as infinitely superior to other religions. I had no conception at all that for theists like Hindus, God was One, too. But I liked Veena and I did try to understand how she prayed to what, in my ignorance, was simply an image of an elephant. "Everything is symbolic," Veena explained, all religious images, Christ on the cross was a symbol, Ganesh was symbolic as well. This was to me an unfamiliar but perfectly plausible idea.

❧

Over the ensuing months, the following events take place.

One evening when I get home there is a message from my sister to call her. I call from the coin-operated phone on the ground floor of the hostel and hear of the various difficulties besetting her life.

❧

On my way up to my room I find Veena on the landing, cooking as usual, but this time there are tears pouring down her face. She has been thinking about Ivan, the Czech man who worked in the same lab with her and with whom she was in love—and with whom she is obviously still in love. He was in love with her, but when he finished his thesis and went back to Czechoslovakia and told his parents he wanted to marry an Indian, they would not hear of it. He was sorry, his letter said, but he could not bring himself to defy them.

I end up sharing her supper and by the end of the evening we are laughing and laughing, doubling up with laughter. She's been trying to explain to me what it is exactly she's working on and why this is an exciting time for her. She thinks she is on the point of making a real breakthrough. If her calculations prove correct and she is able to substantiate her theory, it could be very exciting. She tries to explain the equation that is her basic premise. "Y equals such and such," she says, trying to convey to me why it matters.

"Why?" I ask her. And somehow the noncommunication that ensues as she tries to explain some mathematical formula and I flounder in this sea of incomprehensibility, trying to grasp what she is saying, seems suddenly hilarious to us both. We laugh and laugh until the tears run down our faces.

～

I am at the Arberrys' house on Gilbert Road. There are rattling and banging noises coming from the kitchen. The woman who cleans for them puts her head round the door and asks me if I would like a cup of coffee. A few moments later she returns with two cups.

Arberry, handing me back my chapter, says, "This is really good. I'll have no difficulty recommending to the board that they register you for the Ph.D."

～

Early in the morning I am urgently called down to the phone. It's Cairo. My mother. After asking how I am, she says my father wants to talk to me. After a moment I hear his voice.

"Hello, Nana darling!"

"Hello, Dad! How are you?"

Silence. Then my mother's voice again. "He's too tired to talk anymore now, *ya habibti* [darling]. We'll call you again soon."

The next day when I get home I find a telegram waiting for me, informing me that Father passed away the previous afternoon.

It seems odd over the following days that nothing is different. There is nothing in the world around me to indicate that anything of any significance whatever has happened. Everything is just as it was, people's eyes today look just as they did yesterday. Nothing is different for anyone here. Life, everything, seems just the same.

I find myself reading intensively, searchingly through Yeats's works. Yeats, whom I studied years ago with Mrs. Madge, believed in reincarnation—as, I think, did Mrs. Madge. He believed, too, that spirits manifest themselves in all sorts of ways, as scents, for instance—the scent, suddenly, inexplicably, of roses maybe. Yeats himself experienced spirit presences. I read *A Vision*, Yeats's book based on spirit revelations made through his wife's automatic writing.

I decide to try automatic writing myself, holding my pen and invoking the spirits in the way that Yeats described. And almost at once, shocking me but not at that point frightening me, my hand begins to move. I watch the letters taking shape under my pen, not knowing what word I am about to make and gradually (for the writing is slow) I see, forming across the page in writing not my own, the words, "I've just died!" And again and again the same words, "I've just died!" And I feel, as my hand moves, the shock and disbelief of the spirit, David, who—as I feel—is using my hand to write. He has just died in a car crash in Cornwall and cannot believe that he is dead; he just cannot believe it. He is young, in his twenties. Then another spirit takes over. A French woman. She writes the *F* of "France" with a great flourish. She is some kind of aristocrat. She died in the seventeenth century and is here now to look for an ivory cross that belonged to her and that somehow—it has something to do with William and Mary—had been unjustly taken from her. Why has it taken her so long to come for it, I ask, what has she been doing all this time? Resting, she replies. I ask her if she has met Yeats, or Freud or Jung, or if she knows where they are. Freud is in purgatory, she says. Where is she? Purgatory. Why is she talking to me? She is lonely, she says, spirits get lonely for the living. Is it permissible, is it all right for the dead and the living to communicate like this? Does God permit it? By which I mean not can it happen but is it all right, acceptable to do it. A long pause. By now I can sense her replies even before they appear on the page. I sense her reluctance to answer. No, she writes at last. Then I will have to end this, I say, I don't want to do it if God doesn't want us to. I must stop now. I can feel her departing loneliness. She is gone. I put my pen down.

It is dawn by now. I go to bed and fall asleep immediately. Waking in broad daylight, I find myself terrified. Am I going mad? What does it mean that this has happened, that I have stayed up all night doing automatic writing, communicating, apparently, with spirits, sensing their feelings, their thoughts?

I tell Alan. "No, I don't think you're going crazy, it's just stress," he says. "You know, your father's death and everything." But it doesn't reassure me. I call a psychiatrist I know, saying on the phone now that I am very worried that I am losing my mind and need to see him immediately. He sees me that afternoon. Benson, the psychiatrist, is actually quite wonderful. He seems to find the entire matter fascinating and much of it enormously amusing, as I recount the details of our exchanges: that the woman had been "resting" for a couple of hundred years or so and was, for some reason—something to do with an ivory cross—thoroughly irritated with William and Mary. Freud's being in purgatory is a detail he seems particularly to relish. No, he says, he doesn't think I am going crazy. Now, if I had come in wearing a crown or claiming to be myself a French aristocrat . . . but this, no. He doesn't know what it is—subconscious, spirits, he doesn't know —but he is not concerned as to my sanity and doesn't see any reason for me to continue seeing him. But should I feel I want to I can always give him a call.

How *does* one deal with death? How does one think about it? How does one think about those who are gone?

꿴

I am back once more into the rhythm of regular work. Focusing essentially now on my own research, I have given up going to most seminars.

I spend several weeks in Oxford reading manuscripts in the Bodleian. Staying in lodgings a long bus ride from the center of town, I see my sister a couple of times. On weekends I return to Cambridge.

꿴

I've decided to attend a lecture by the head of Barbara's department, a brilliant, internationally known scientist whom Barbara thinks I should hear. It is an open lecture, intended for nonspecialists. It's about suicide—genes and suicide. The gist of the talk is that suicide can quite legitimately be thought of as "nature's" way—the way of the genes—to cleanse and purify the species of the psychologically weak. I am shocked, feeling there is something terribly wrong with this, and also, in some scarcely acknowledged recess of myself, startled as well as appalled—as someone might be who on occasion has secretly been drawn to thoughts of suicide. But I can't think how to respond intelligently to Barbara's enthusiasm for the talk or to say why exactly I found the talk lacking in compassion, inhumane, wrongheaded.

꿴

A letter arrives from my mother saying she is planning a trip to Europe to visit us all and expects to spend a few days in Cambridge. Alan and I decide to get married while she is here, even though it is only recently that Father died. It would be good, we feel, to have Mother here for the event and who knows when she will next be out of Egypt? We had already talked of marrying before this. Mindful of the bitter arguments between my mother and sister on the subject, I long ago told Alan that as long as my parents were alive I couldn't consider marrying him unless, just as a formality, he converted to Islam. Alan is completely secular and he has no problem with the idea and apparently even quite likes it. I don't know exactly why, other than that it is for him perhaps just a bit of an adventure. Anyway, he enjoys telling his friends and, now that my mother is coming and we have to do something about it, he embarks on the project with gusto, choosing a Muslim name for himself, Ishmael, of course—in Arabic, Ismael. He is delighted that he will be able to say to his friends, "Call me Ishmael!" We seek out a sheikh in London and Alan learns to recite the *fat-ha* (the equivalent of the Lord's Prayer), although this is not a requirement, and he learns the formula that a convert is required to utter as a mark of conversion: *La illahi illa Allah, wa Muhammad rasul Allah*—There is no God but God, and Muhammad is his Prophet.

Mother arrives. She stays with me, literally with me, in my room. I borrow a sleeping bag from Barbara and sleep on the floor. In the old days when my parents came to Cambridge they stayed at the University Arms or the Garden House Hotel. Miss Duke, who knew my parents from then, now invites us to lunch. At some point when we're in her garden and out of earshot of the others, Miss Duke tells me about friends of hers in Greece who lost everything in a political upheaval and about how she loaned them money, which eventually, when things were all right again, they returned. Knowing how difficult things must be for my mother, Miss Duke goes on, she would be quite happy to lend us some money, "until, you know, things sort themselves out."

I am touched by Miss Duke's thoughtfulness and generosity, as is my mother when I tell her of our conversation. My mother of course declines the kind offer. Who knows, she says, when things will "sort themselves out"?

Most of the time my mother is like someone in a daze, as if she is not quite taking in where she is and what is happening. At one point I cross the street ahead of her, absorbed, talking to Alan about something, and when I look back I notice that she seems to be staggering, lurching as she walks. She is, as we will later learn, already ill.

As I look back to those days I am sure that she was suffering, too, from what must have been depression. That was why she often seemed disconnected and unable to take a positive interest in anything, although she was, I think for our sakes, making heroic efforts to be, or at least to seem, involved. It seems so obvious now that this must have been her condition. She had lost, after all, the one person who had been her companion, friend, intimate all of her adult life, and this following those last harrowing years in Cairo.

Nothing, at any rate, seemed to truly rouse her interest, not Alan's conversion or even our marriage.

There was only one moment in all that time when she seemed fully present and engaged in our exchange. We'd been talking about Father and she began to tell me how she had been out of the room when he actually died. She had left his bedside for a moment, to go to the bathroom, and had come back to find him gone. The same thing had happened with her mother. "It was as if," she ruminated, "they couldn't bear to go while I was there, couldn't bear to leave me, so they waited till I was out of the room."

Alan and I got married, at the Guildhall, with my mother and Miss Duke and a few friends in attendance. Mother then left for Oxford, to see my sister.

When Alan and I registered our marriage at the Egyptian embassy, formalizing it in an Islamic contract, remembering my Aunt Aida's difficulties around divorce, I did not fail to invoke the clause that it is the right of every Muslim woman to invoke—transferring the power of divorce from husband to wife.

Alan and I then went for a week to St. Ives in Cornwall.

On the evening we got back Barbara came up to my room. "I thought I heard you," she said. "I have some news. They've taken Veena to Fulbourne." Fulbourne was the Cambridge mental hospital.

"Good God!" I said. Why, what had happened?

Barbara didn't know exactly. Veena had had some kind of psychotic breakdown. Among other things, Veena apparently had been telling colleagues that she had discovered the secret of the universe.

Barbara herself was shaken and we stayed up late in my room, talking. Despite her reservations about Veena as a scientist, she had grown fond of her.

~

I plunged into my work now, working on my dissertation, thinking about almost nothing else. I was going down to London almost daily, to the British Museum, to read manuscripts, unpublished works, letters by Lane and his circle of friends.

In the early fall Dr. Radzinowicz, tutor to graduate students, gave a party at Girton to celebrate our marriage. I invited Husain, an Egyptian psychiatrist who had been at Cambridge with my brothers and whom I liked a lot. He and my sister fell in love immediately and soon married.

~

A few months later my mother returned to England, this time going straight into a hospital in London. She had cancer, although apparently, though we knew it, she did not. She thought she was being treated for damage caused by an overdose of radiation that had been wrongly given to her in the first place. Once the confusion was in place in my mind, I could never again feel entirely certain as to what she died of. Still to this day I wonder—was it an overdose of radiation or cancer? But to begin with I thought it was cancer and I was unaware that she did not know, so when she said to me, when I went up to see her, "Imagine! They thought I had cancer!" I simulated surprise and disbelief but not, I think, well enough, not quickly enough. I gave away, I believe, what I then thought was the truth, for I saw a kind of shadow come into her eyes, a dark understanding suddenly clouding them as she lowered them away from mine. For the rest of my life I would remember that look, for the rest of my life I would ask myself whether it was I who had unwittingly given my mother a knowledge that she did not want.

In the next few weeks in London, Mother regained her looks, becoming now, as she must have been as a young girl, extraordinarily beautiful. Her cheekbones grew prominent as she lost weight, and her eyes, blue-gray like the sea, seemed to grow more luminous.

I said my last goodbye to her in London airport, where she was taken onto the plane in a wheelchair. She died a couple of months later in a hospital in Cairo. Fat-hia, her maid, had moved in with her, sleeping on a cot in her room. Fat-hia, my aunts told me, had said to them, as they sat through the days outside Mother's room, that she loved my mother more than she did her own mother and that, when she was going through her divorce, Mother had saved her from suicide.

In her last days, I was told, Mother seemed not to recognize anyone. She seemed to be seeing only those who had already died— Grandmother, her brother Fuad, her sister Aida. That was just in the last day or two. It was no doubt delirium, my sister interjected as my aunts talked of Mother's death. Probably, darling, my aunt Nazli said, and then Aisha, too, chimed in, Yes, *ah daruri, ya habibti*, no doubt, darling.

"But still, you know," Nazli resumed after an interval, the wonder back in her voice, "the way she was talking to them, it was exactly as if she could see them." As if they had come, those who had already died, as if they had come now to receive her as she came over to them, to greet and receive her and gather her to them and love her as they had always loved her.

Anyway, she was gone.

It was spring when she died.

As I write these words, aware of the sound of my hand across the page, the scratch of a pen, a great wind outside bends everything before it, baring the underside of leaves, tossing them down in great bunches, flinging down small branches, tugging at the house. I imagine the house tossing, coming free, as it did once in a dream. In fact it is sturdy, fixed, like a well-planted tent. But I feel a sense of darkness. I know now, I find myself saying to myself, that the road leads to death, and more precipitously, it seems, than I had yet realized.

Veena and her breakdown. Veena and her picture of Ganesh.

When I think back to Veena and to that period in my own life, I think of the silent costs of the lives that we were living.

I think of the events and words that made up the news in those days and that were the ordinary backdrop to our lives. Enoch Powell holding forth about black immigration and the menace and danger that blacks (all of us non-Europeans) represented and how they must be turned back and those already in Britain deported. And headlines about white youths going on "paki-bashing" rampages. "Paki-bashing" was the term for attacks on Pakistanis and Indians, who in those days formed the largest group of recent immigrants to Britain. Such were the words and events that we routinely took in with our morning coffee. We took in this open racism, lived with it, and yet never once spoke of it. I do not remember a single conversation I had with Veena or anyone else either about racism or about ourselves as actually touched by, and implicated in, these racist words.

Why? How was it that we apparently were not able, did not know how, to speak about racism? Racism was not, in the Cambridge in which I lived, a subject that was openly talked about, at least not as an issue that might touch *us*. For one thing, there was the myth that racism existed only "out there," not in civilized Cambridge. Cambridge was indeed too well-bred for the crass and overt racism of an Enoch Powell or of paki-bashing, and most people I knew and had dealings with openly deplored these ghastly, appalling happenings. But there was undoubtedly, too, the sense that we were not quite what they were and that our cultures and religions and race (but that word most particularly would never have surfaced) were not quite up to theirs and would be best left outside the door.

I think that there were other reasons why both Veena and I, reading and hearing about the overt racism that was out there, did not fully identify ourselves as among its targets. To begin with, we were not direct targets. There were no physical attacks on nonwhite people in Cambridge. There was never a moment, going out into the streets, that I was fearful of being attacked. Paki-bashing violence happened not in Cambridge but in places like Leicester and London's Notting Hill Gate, working-class cities and neighborhoods. And there was the silent implication in Cambridge and probably in the liberal British press generally that it was working-class blacks who were not only the targets of racism but who were probably in fact somewhat inferior: "them," the working class, and not people like us here in Cambridge. And it was an implication that, unconsciously, we were probably only too eager to seize on and ourselves believe and accept.

Nevertheless we would have known at some level that we were indeed implicated by these prejudices, even if less fully and directly than working-class blacks. I am perfectly sure that, though I never spoke of it, I knew full well that even civilized Cambridge did not regard us as equals.

But we didn't talk of it.

And so, privileged though we were and living in the world of the superprivileged, we lacked the psychological sustenance that the presence, perspectives, and words of other people like ourselves would have afforded us, not only people of our own particular group but all those subjected to these insidious or overt assaults of racism. Veena was the only other black person I knew well in Cambridge. There was a Pakistani graduate student at Girton whom I knew slightly, and there must have been other blacks in other colleges, but we were few and far between. This too, I expect, must be a distinguishing aspect of the experience of middle-class academic immigrants, who nearly always come from their countries without family and live, then, isolated in predominantly white communities. No one living on our street, no one we might meet at a bus stop was living through what we were living just as an ordinary part of our lives. We had no community with whom to exchange words about common experiences, no one to joke with, to make some connection with that would break the sense of isolation. And there was no one with whom, shutting the door on this assaultive world and its demeaning tide, we could share and affirm our own feelings and beliefs and ways of being.

There was another dimension that defined the perspectives, beliefs, and values that were the norms in the societies from which we came as implicitly but distinctly inferior. This was the pronounced and almost aggressive secularism of the Cambridge of my graduate student days. There was no doubt that people who were religious were not regarded as quite on a par intellectually with those who were unambiguously and forthrightly secular. Even Christians were marked in some sense as intellectually lesser in this ethos. And anyone who belonged to and actually believed in any of those "other" religions like Islam or Hinduism was completely outside the realm of those who were to be taken seriously.

And so Veena, engaging in what in her home society was the simple, ordinary act of putting an altar before Ganesh, here found herself the target of the scarcely veiled contempt of her peers. And no doubt she sensed it as clearly and surely as I knew that I would not be considered an equal by my peers and would not be taken seriously as an academic had I defined myself as a believing Muslim.

Veena and I (and thousands of other nonwhite women immigrants into the academic societies of the Western world) were living through our own version of the experience of Betty Friedan's generation of women in America, what Friedan called "the problem that had no name." We too were living in a society that insidiously and pervasively undermined our own experience, our own perspective, and our own sense of reality, and in ways that we too did not know how to speak of, and that undermined and denied too, in our case, our own histories and cultures and the foundational beliefs of our societies. The Friedan generation of middle-class women flocked to psychiatrists, took Valium, felt suicidal, and eventually, as they began to find words for what they had lived, would transform not only their own consciousness but also that of their class and society.

A similar quiet revolution is, I believe, now under way as academic women and writers and other women of color, who as yet live scattered and isolated through white academia, continue steadfastly to map and name and make visible the territory of our own different experiences.

It is no wonder, then, that Veena had a nervous breakdown.

And perhaps these kinds of unspoken stresses played some part in bringing about the physical illness from which I now began to suffer. Sometime between my mother's first visit and her death, I began to suffer a vague, mysterious illness that trailed me and that I would not be able to shake off for the remainder of my days in Cambridge.

It didn't feel like anything particularly serious. Slightly swollen glands, a bit of a temperature, exhaustion, so that doing any little thing was a chore. When the symptoms didn't go away, I went to the doctor. Probably glandular fever, he said. It didn't show up in the tests he'd done, but I could still have had it—it generally took a while to clear.

I don't know how long I waited, a month or two, before going back, but I did eventually go back. It had not cleared. The GP referred me to a specialist at Addenbrooks, the Cambridge hospital. They took me in for a few days for observation. Blood samples, chest X ray, and so on. Dr. James, the specialist, came by with a bevy of young men. They picked up my chart and flicked through it as they stood exchanging comments. James put my X ray up on one of those light boxes, gesturing and talking. They were just out of earshot. Then they were gone. No one had addressed a single word to me, James only briefly nodding when they first came in.

Then I was sent home. They hadn't come up with anything but were going to continue to observe me, the nurse told me. I was to keep a diary of my symptoms and a daily chart of my temperature and return in two weeks.

Weeks passed. No change and no diagnosis. Now I reported to Addenbrooks every month instead of every fortnight. When I had first gone in, Addenbrooks had been on Trumpington Street, just down the road from where I lived. Then the hospital moved to its new site, a long bus ride down Hill's Road; it was something of a walk, too, from where I lived to the bus stop. In the rain and cold the trip was no fun, nor was having to sit for an hour or two waiting for James in the gloom of the out-patient department. Nor, for that matter, was always feeling tired and unwell.

Somewhere along the line I complained to Husain, my new brother-in-law and a doctor, that nothing was happening and I was fed up at not getting better. He offered to make me an appointment with Sir Ronald Firth, physician to the queen, whom he happened to know. I eagerly agreed.

Reviewing my record and running some tests himself, Firth told me that, although the results were not absolutely conclusive, he believed that what I had was rheumatoid arthritis. It was a benign chronic disease, he said (I knew nothing about it in those days), which could usually be controlled by medication. He suggested putting me on steroids, and I was entirely happy to fall in with this plan. At last someone was doing something.

I thought, over the next couple of weeks, that I was getting better, and I returned for my regular Addenbrooks appointment. I mentioned either to James or his nurse that I'd seen Firth and was taking steroids and feeling better. As I was leaving, James's nurse told me that James wanted to see me the next week and that he wanted to see my husband and my brother-in-law. He also ordered an eyelid biopsy.

This request to see my relatives of course made me extremely anxious. Why would he want to see them unless there was something very seriously wrong? Tuesday rolled round again, and the four of us—my sister, Alan, Husain, and I—met for lunch before setting off for Addenbrooks. But I was feeling far too anxious to eat.

And then at the hospital, after we had sat waiting for a while, James's nurse came up to us and asked Alan and Husain to go into James's office—only them, not me.

For me that instant confirmed the absolute worst. Obviously this was the end. I had some awful disease and he was going to tell them about it and they would have to tell me—why else would he want to see them and not me? Finally the door opened and I was asked to join them. James's face was red and Husain and Alan, Husain particularly, were quite pale. James said, "I don't agree with Firth, I don't think it's rheumatoid arthritis. I believe it's sarcoidosis. The evidence is not completely conclusive but I believe that that's what it is."

"What?" I said. I couldn't catch the word he was saying, which, of course, I'd never heard before.

He said it again, barking it out, as if furious.

"Could you please write it down?" I was still stunned and could not grasp what he was saying.

He scribbled the word on a piece of paper and handed it to me, still apparently furious.

"What is it?" I asked.

It was, as I now learned, like rheumatoid arthritis, an autoimmune disease, which meant a disease in which the body for some reason attacks itself. And it also meant that, unlike, say, an infection, it wasn't something whose progress could be stopped or altered; treatment essentially was just to alleviate symptoms as they arose. In most cases, James said, it ran a benign course, and he fully expected it to in my case. They were going to continue to see me regularly and to treat me as need arose. Meanwhile he wanted me off the steroids.

That was the end of our meeting.

Outside I naturally immediately wanted to know what awful things he had told them about this illness and what was about to happen to me. No, no, they said, he hadn't said anything at all about any awful thing that he expected to happen. Well, what had he said then? I couldn't get anything out of them, just rambling meaningless nothings. Why were they, and Husain particularly, looking so upset? Well, he hadn't been pleased about Husain's taking me to Firth— Husain should have consulted with him first. For this he had called them in and left me out there and subjected me to this terror? I couldn't believe it, simply couldn't believe it. But I never got any other answer from either of them, so I suppose that that really is what happened. Alan later told me that James had actually bawled Husain out quite sharply, and that Husain had privately told Alan that he had in fact notified James, leaving a message with James's secretary, but had felt that it would be ungentlemanly to point this out.

Still, to this day I find James's insensitivity as a doctor quite extraordinary. This was British patriarchy, medical establishment—style, at work, as I know now. Perfectly standard and ordinary behavior in that setting. But for me it was new. I'd never been treated before, certainly never by any doctor in Egypt, as someone not to be considered or directly addressed in the deliberations that passed between men. Different patriarchies evidently had their different styles and their different forms of casual, ordinary, acceptable erasures.

Dr. James's treatment blighted my life for the next couple of years, for it was emotionally devastating. It was as if he had put a curse on me. For the next few years I could not free myself of the terror that I had felt in those moments outside his room or of the conviction that at any moment this disease whose name he'd barked out at me would take a fatal or a devastatingly crippling turn. For it could indeed be, as I learned from my reading—for of course Alan and I both read up on it—a very serious, sometimes crippling, and sometimes swiftly fatal disease. Its course, however, was unpredictable. You just had to wait and see.

Had I had a decent doctor, I like to think, I would not have become the anxious, terrified person I now became, afraid that any little change in my health was augury of impending disaster. And had it not been for my anxiety about this illness and the stress it placed on me and Alan, we might never have divorced.

But there it is.

Alan was having problems with his thesis. He was told he had either to revise and resubmit it or accept an M.Litt. instead of a Ph.D. He had no precise idea how they wanted him to revise it and he was getting little help from his supervisor. And he had just accepted a job in Hull, his first teaching job, and he was in terror of lecturing—a terror I had no understanding of until the day that I had to deliver my first lectures.

A hundred problems came up. Where would we live, who would commute? He felt I was not there when he needed me, and I felt the same about him. And once he was no longer a student he changed—and began to pressure me to fit into the conventional role of wife, the person who would be there for him when he got home from his job.

It was a miserable time.

What got me through it was my work. Reading deeply in the history of the period, I began piecing together from the boxes of notes I had all around me, the material I'd gathered in my trips to Oxford and the British Museum, the life of the man whose work I was studying. And this, I suppose, was my third and hitherto uncounted piece of good fortune. Lane, after all, could have been someone who, though living in and writing about Egypt and Islam and becoming an authority on them, disliked the country, its culture, people, religion. He could have been someone who, at least privately, wrote condescendingly or even contemptuously of it. And it could, therefore, have been a distasteful exercise for me to spend so much time thinking about him, so much time in his company—as one does writing someone's biography. But fortunately Lane loved Egypt, unreservedly loved almost everything about it. From his arrival, his entire life and the work he undertook would be an act of devotion and service to this country and culture that he so much loved and in which he felt, almost from the start, more at home than he did in his own land. He had first fallen in love with the idea of Egypt as a young boy, simply through reading about it (which I understood perfectly, longing as I had as a youngster for the red roofs of England rather than our own flat, boring roofs). Scraping and saving for years to make the voyage to Egypt, he finally arrived at the age of twenty-four, and it would prove to be all and more than he had hoped.

By the time I was done working on Lane I would feel about him rather the way I did about Arberry, that I'd been in the company of an extraordinary human being and that it had been a privilege and gift to come to know him. Of course I knew Lane, in important ways, far more intimately than I knew Arberry: I'd read his private journals and letters. It's a peculiar and quite poignant relation, that of biographer and subject, at least it is if you come to feel, as I did, a great liking for the person. Reading someone's private words you share his hopes, fears, longings, knowing all the while what he does not—which book will be published, which will succeed, which illness will prove fatal.

Working on Lane at this time in my life was also a gift to me in some quite specific ways. Lane's love for Egypt, after my own recent alienating experiences there, brought it back into my life in a positive, restorative way. His letters, whenever he was away from Egypt, were full of sighs and aches and longings for that country—as well as of endless complaints about England. Egypt, Egypt, Egypt! *Ah ya Masr!* Oh, Egypt! Oh, to be back there. Oh, to be sitting once more taking supper on the bank with the boatmen. Oh, to be there in those summer nights, listening to the croaking of frogs, breathing in the scent of its orange groves! In Cairo his pleasures were talking to people, learning things, studying things, drawing them (he was a fine draftsman, a trained engraver), hearing stories from his friend the bookseller, looking over his manuscripts, joining in prayers at the mosque, sitting on there afterward in meditation.

I learned from Lane too—at a moment when it was valuable for me to learn it—how totally a person could be devoted to and absorbed in work, just work. I got to know his daily routine exactly. Going to his desk every morning after an early breakfast, he would begin his workday with the words *"Bismillah al-rahman al-rahim"*—In the name of God, the Compassionate, the Merciful—the words that devout Muslims utter on beginning a task, dedicating their labor to God and in the service of His purposes. Lane would break only for his daily half-hour stroll and for meals with his family—his sister, Sophia Poole, who, when she was abandoned by her husband, came with him to Egypt, and his wife, Nefeeseh, a Greek or Greek-Egyptian—meals that would begin always with the utterance of the Christian grace.

Lane's deeply religious temperament and his unconventional but also deeply religious habits, interweaving Islam and Christianity, were also valuable to me in that I was going through a tremendous inner crisis, a crisis about loss of meaning and about the kinds of things that we tend to define as "spiritual." It was a time of depression and near despair—not surprisingly, given the losses I'd suffered in just two or three years and the anxiety over my health. I remember standing one day at the bus stop outside Addenbrooks, holding down my coat against a sudden cold blast, watching the wind pick up and whirl on the edge of the road a circlet of leaves, feeling myself whirled, too, and as if spiraling into vast interstellar spaces empty with meaninglessness.

I was desperate for, craving, some religious faith, something that would say to me that all this, what I was living, was meaningful. I went to church a lot and read deeply in Christianity—Bultmann, Tillich, Teilhard de Chardin. And I came close, really quite close to converting. I did not, in the end, go through with it—and I was right not to do so. It would have solved nothing and would have only muddied things further. For my crisis was not in fact about which religion to belong to. In reality I have never had any difficulty feeling that one could perfectly well believe both Islam and Christianity at the same time, although I recognize, of course, that for many Christians and Muslims such a view is completely unacceptable. And as I have gotten older and learned more about other religions, I feel the same way about those too, including, of course, Veena's Ganesh and Hinduism more generally.

No, my crisis was grounded in two things. First, it was a crisis about faith, just religious faith in itself. For I was no Veena. Unlike her, I was thoroughly pervious to and permeated by the secular assumptions of my time. And this in the end—because I could not sustain religious belief and could not shake myself free of the conviction that no reasonable thinking person could possibly believe in religion—was the reason I did not go through with conversion—and not because I had understood that the real issue was not *which* faith but any faith at all—simply faith itself.

Second, my crisis and my attempt to resolve it by turning to Christianity had been my response to, and my attempt to remedy, a loss I had suffered—without knowing that I had suffered it, without knowing that I had lost anything. Until now I had lived in communities for whom religious belief was just a given, an ordinary part of life. This had been true, of course, in Egypt, but it had also been true of my years at Girton. There too, people, and in particular the people who had been most important in my life, had been deeply religious. Miss Duke and Brad were devout, practicing Christians, and Mrs. Madge, although she was not Christian (on the contrary, for her, Christianity, the beast slouching toward Bethlehem, marked the beginning of the dark ages) was definitely Something. For the first time now in my graduate student years I was living bereft of a community of belief and bereft of the sense of sustenance and reassurance that such communities can provide whether we are active believers or not. Such communities buoy and sustain us, without our necessarily even being aware of it, by their sense of the meaningfulness of all our lives.

~

I finished my thesis, got divorced, and began to apply for jobs. I continued to have physical problems but they did not get worse. In addition I was freed now from James's curse as a result of a visit to an Egyptian doctor in London to whom I was taken by a friend from Cairo who was briefly in England. This doctor, who was a chiropractor as well as a conventional doctor, spoke utterly persuasively of the limits of regular medicine and of how little doctors knew particularly about such vague sub-clinical ailments where the medical evidence remained inconclusive, and he began for me the process of dismantling the authority of James's pronouncements about my own life and body and future.

~

Veena recovered. She completed her thesis and defended it successfully. Ivan, her Czech boyfriend, came to see her and, drawing strength from what she had been through, found the courage to tell his parents that he loved this woman and would not abandon her. Veena left for Prague to marry Ivan.

~

I began working part-time, teaching at the Cambridge College of Arts and Technology (now Anglia University) as well as doing some college supervising. I got no offers of full-time jobs but I did receive a letter from a publisher to say that they would be interested in considering my thesis for publication. Like most of my cohorts, and just as a routine part of the business of finishing one's doctorate and applying for jobs, I'd sent an outline and sample chapters of my thesis to various publishers—and now I had had this astonishing reply. I sent the manuscript off, feeling certain, though, that they would reject it. But I was wrong. They liked it and in due course published it.

Still, the end point of this process of education that in Cairo I had pursued with such yearning did not after all give me what I had so craved. It was interesting enough, the work that I had learned to do in Cambridge, but it was essentially academic. Neither the questions that we asked nor the theories that we studied seemed to connect much with anything that was real for me or to take up or truly address the concerns that were at the heart of my own life and thought—thought that remained private, unarticulated, relegated to the midnight hours and the margins of consciousness.

One day I learnt
A secret art,
Invisible-Ness, it was called.
I think it worked . . .

—Meiling Jin

But I forgot what those years in Cambridge had been for me. I forgot the disconnection that had gradually come about for me between my academic work and the ideas and questions that had meaning in my life, and I forgot the feeling of unease and silence and limbo in which I had existed in those years—until I returned just this last year for a fellowship year in Cambridge.

It all began to come back to me within days. It was triggered by who knows what—just being in that familiar space. Walking down the corridors of the university library, going to the tearoom, looking out on familiar vistas, all places and vistas redolent for me of the people and feelings that had made up my life in those years. And walking and cycling into town through the familiar Backs (the meadows along the river and the backs of colleges) and the familiar colleges.

As it turned out, of course, my own experience of disconnection and of unease and discontent in relation to academic work was a common experience among many of my generation, particularly people of color and white women. A sense of unease and discontent with what was being purveyed to us as knowledge in our universities, and the feeling that the real issues were being bypassed, were not even visible in the curriculum, would shortly fuel, particularly in America, a major intellectual and academic revolution. Through the seventies, black studies and then women's studies programs sprang up on campuses throughout the States. The founding of such programs reflected the growing understanding that what was being purveyed to us as "knowledge" and "objectivity" and grand transcendent truths represented in fact neither "truth" nor "objectivity" but rather merely the intellectual traditions, beliefs, and perspectives of white middle-class men.

For ours had been the era when we were taught, more or less as gospel truth (academic gospel truth), that writers like D. H. Lawrence represented great moral visionaries—the very writers whom Kate Millett would expose for their misogyny in what in 1970 was a radically iconoclastic book, *Sexual Politics*. Not only, Millett showed, did such writers openly endorse the "natural" inferiority of women but their works were thoroughly riddled with contemptuous views of women and even glorified rape and other abuses of women as ordinary, acceptable norms. Until then we had been routinely taught (and for some time after would continue to be taught—it took a while for the feminist challenge to be taken seriously) that such men were not only great writers but writers who modeled for us, out of their deep human vision, the true nature and ideals of relations between men and women. This was the era, too, of the Kohlberg study on human moral development (published in the early seventies), in which Harvard psychologists maintained that the "rigorous," "objective" research they had conducted showed that women were deficient in their sense of justice and thus morally defective. These were the conclusions that Carol Gilligan in another groundbreaking book (*In a Different Voice*, 1982) would take on and expose for their outright prejudice. She showed how the male bias of the researchers in this so-called objective study was there in the very conception of the experiment, and in its questions and terms and conclusions, and finally also in the researchers' inability to grasp, even when their own evidence pointed that way, that women's moral reasoning proceeded from a different ethic, an ethic of "care" rather than of "principle"—but an ethic that was in no sense less "moral" than that of the men in the study.

It was these kinds of things, presented as "neutral" and "objective" truth, that were our ordinary academic fare. These were the texts and the views that we read and studied and versed ourselves in for exams. This insidious, built-in denigration of women was what we lived with and imbibed. In exactly the same way in those days the steadfast, insidious, built-in denigration of blacks, Muslims, Arabs, and people of other cultures and the colonized generally, was just the ordinary academic fare. (Not that studies written from this perspective are not produced today, but today there is a thriving culture of challenge and dissent that did not exist then.) In that scholarship, blacks, women, Muslims, and so on could be the *objects* of study, as in the Kohlberg study, for instance. But they could not be its subjects. The perspective through which they were understood, measured, analyzed, judged, had to be that of white men. Otherwise, the conclusions arrived at could not be considered "objective."

In America, social ferment and activism formed the backdrop to the new intellectual perspectives that were emerging. In England, or at any rate in Cambridge, there was no parallel ferment either on issues of race or of gender that I might have connected with. By the end of my graduate student days I had essentially acquiesced in and accepted my own proper invisibility from scholarship and the proper invisibility and object status of my kind. The passion and joy of thought and understanding would come back into my life only after I had gone to Abu Dhabi to work and begun to feel driven by my need to understand, as the Iranian revolution crested, our history as Muslim women, and what possibilities lay ahead; simultaneously I began to read the exhilarating feminist books coming out of America. Placing Muslim women at the heart of my own work was in a way, and among other things, (as I see it now) a refusal of our invisibility.

"One is not born but rather becomes a woman," goes Simone de Beauvoir's famous dictum. I obviously was not born but became black when I went to England. Similarly, of course, I was not born but became a woman of color when I went to America. Whereas these are political identities that carry, for me, a positive charge, revealing and affirming connection and commonality, my identity as an Arab, no less a political construction, is an identity that, in contrast, I experience as deeply and perhaps irretrievably fraught with angst and confusion.

It was in Cambridge and in these graduate student years that I first began to suffer the mute, complicated confusions of my exilic Arab identity, my identity as an Arab in the West.

Why now rather than when I first came to England? Many things now were different. I was no longer merely a visitor with a home in another land to go back to. As a visitor, I could let racism, insofar as I encountered it, slip by as of no great moment to my life, which would be lived out elsewhere. This, obviously, was no longer the case. And England was in a different time in its history. Undergoing its first significant black immigration, England was for the first time dealing (somewhat hysterically) with the issue of color and race on home soil rather than in the far-flung colonies. Racism, consequently, was far more insistently and inescapably in the air now than it had been just a few years back. And I was myself older and read the papers more regularly. And then, too, there was the 1967 Arab-Israeli war, which unleashed in the press a deluge of frenetic, ignorant, biased, and outright racist views of Arabs.

All of these in themselves would have been hard enough to deal with for a young woman with little experience of racism and no family or community to turn to and talk with about these strange, unsavory happenings. I don't think there were many Arabs in Cambridge in those days. I knew one Egyptian, a Nasser enthusiast who had a government scholarship and was friendly with the Egyptian consul. I was exceedingly polite to him when I ran into him but I also avoided him: it was routine in those days, as we all knew, for Egyptians abroad to act as government informers on one another.

My own recent history and experience then in relation to the rhetoric of Arab nationalism and to that great hero and leader of the

Arab world, Nasser, was part of the difficult, immensely complicating underlay to my experience at this point of what it was to be an Arab in the West. For where exactly was it now that I could take my stand? I certainly felt no loyalty toward or solidarity with Nasser, with his endless, empty, fraudulent rantings about *al-Uraba*—Arabness—and all that awful, badgering nonsense that I read about in the papers but was fortunately no longer being directly battered by. On the other hand, the racism and ignorance and bigoted imperialist perspective with which both Nasser and the Arabs were often presented in the British press were, on an emotional level certainly, perfectly plain to me. I hated Nasser, but at the same time I knew that what they were saying about him was imperialist, racist rubbish. And the flagrant heartlessness and injustice with which the British press often wrote of the Palestinians was also perfectly plain to me. I knew all these things well. But I did not know how to explain nor even understand myself the complicatedness of my position and feelings. Emotionally I couldn't fully side with the Arabs insofar as Nasser was their spokesman and universally adulated hero. But it was even less possible for me to side with the bigoted British racists and their stupid diatribes against Nasser and the Arabs.

Not only did I have no community of people from my own background with whom to discuss these sorts of things, but in those days we did not as yet have a language with which to speak subtly and complexly and in ways that would enable us to make fine but crucial distinctions in reflecting on the highly fraught and complicated subject of being Arab. Touching as it does on matters of identity, race, nationalism, loyalty, betrayal, it had all the emotional and psychological ingredients that make a subject almost impossibly difficult to think about clearly. And over and above this, being Arab was profoundly implicated, of course, in what has proven to be one of the most painful and intractable political problems of our day, the Palestinian–Israeli conflict.

It is not at all surprising to me now that I did not know back then how to address this subject, given my own complicated awareness of it. As if all this were not enough, there was for me a further layer of complexity and conflictedness to the matter that had been inscribed into my own life and history in ways that I would only come to understand fully in the process of writing this memoir.

Edward Said's *Orientalism* appeared after I left Cambridge and when I was in the Arab Gulf. This work, analyzing colonial discourse and its part in the consolidation of colonial hegemony, which today has justly taken its place as a major text of our times, gave us (among many other things) a language with which to begin to talk of some aspects of the experience of being Arab. Most particularly it gave us a way to speak of being Arab in the West and of what it was to live embattled in a sea of prejudices, prejudices that came at us as "knowledge" and as "objective," "neutral," "transcendent," "unbiased," "truths."

And yet the burden of my own history layered my experience of this text with a degree of unease. Most difficult of all probably was *Orientalism*'s profound resonance to my ears with the perspectives and rhetoric of Arab nationalism. Nasser, for instance, figures in its pages only fleetingly, but he is there as hero and only as hero. Even Said's general thesis echoed for me Arab nationalist rhetoric, for of course the notion that European attitudes and policies toward Arabs were rooted in a European hatred that went back to the Crusades was a commonplace of that rhetoric. The book even echoed, too closely to me, the overly simple binary view of Arab nationalism, which represented imperialism as uniformly and comprehensively negative. I knew from my own life that, for all the real injustices of imperialism, its legacy had also meant that I had had choices when my mother, and my aunt Aida most vividly and unforgettably, had had none. No doubt it is part of the nature of grand, overarching theories, theories that redefine, as *Orientalism* did, ways of seeing of an entire era, that they will overlook or erase particular terrains of experience. Still, for me then, a theoretical analysis of imperialism that did not seem to allow for the complexities that had been part of my own experience could not ring entirely true.

Then there was also the way that the book intersected with my own scholarship. Lane, whom I had studied with such closeness, appears in Said's pages as one of the villains of Orientalism. Knowing Lane's work as well as I did, I had no doubt at all that Said's interpretation was not accurate. Said, after all, deals in this book with scores of writers and centuries of history, and naturally he could not have studied all these writers and all that history in specific and meticulous detail. Nor indeed does the inaccuracy of this or that particular reading alter the validity of Said's broad thesis. It would be very easy today to demonstrate how my own different reading of Lane does not in fact contradict Said's thesis: all that is required is that one complicate that thesis a little to show how writers working within the Western tradition both reproduced and affirmed the views and assumptions of their times and also, sometimes, endeavored to work against them. But back then this detail further contributed to my sense of unease with the book.

And finally, too, although *Orientalism* did give us a language with which to speak of what it was to be Arab in the West, for myself it seemed simultaneously to flatten and erase other aspects of being Arab. Powerfully and forcefully written from this base in the West— this place of exile and embattlement—the book did not at all address (nor, of course, had it set out to address) or simplify for me the problem of how to think about, speak about, or make my way through the broader, more complicated territory of what it was to be Arab.

I write these words, obviously, in the context of a memoir and to set down some of the ways that this major text of our age intersected at that time with my own consciousness and experience, and not at all, of course, with the intention of offering here a comprehensive analysis of this complex work. In addition, like the vast majority of academics working today in the Western world, I am naturally enormously indebted intellectually to Said's work more generally and to *Orientalism* specifically. I write them now not to register a belated criticism but out of the need to voice and to recognize the complexity of the field—and the world and experiences—with which we all struggle in our ongoing endeavor to speak and write of the realities that make up our lives and our world. Said's *Orientalism* itself, in a sense, might be said to be, among other things, the monumental product of Said's own heroic and transformative struggle—transforming the intellectual landscape for all of us—with the fraught and specific complexity of what it was for him to be Arab.

11

ON BECOMING AN ARAB

I remember the very day that I became colored.

Zora Neale Hurston

THE TEACHER called on me to read. I started haltingly. She began interrupting me, correcting me, quietly at first but gradually, as I stumbled on, with more and more irritation, leaving her desk now to stand over me and pounce on every mistake I made. She was an irascible woman, and I had not prepared my homework.

"You're an Arab!" she finally screamed at me. "An Arab! And you don't know your own language!"

"I am not an Arab!" I said, suddenly furious myself. "I am Egyptian! And anyway we don't speak like this!" And I banged my book shut.

"Read!"

I sat on stonily, arms folded.

"Read!"

I didn't move.

She struck me across the face. The moment afterward seemed to go on forever, like something in slow motion.

I was twelve and I'd never been hit before by a teacher and never slapped across the face by anyone. Miss Nabih, the teacher, was a Palestinian. A refugee.

The year was 1952, the year of the revolution. What Miss Nabih was doing to me in class the government was doing to us through the media. I remember how I hated that incessant rhetoric. *Al-qawmiyya al-Arabiyya! Al-Uraba! Nahnu al-Arab!* Arab nationalism! Arabness! We the Arabs! Even now, just remembering those words, I feel again a surge of mingled irritation and resentment. Propaganda *is* unpleasant. And one could not escape it. The moment one turned on the radio, there it was: military songs, nationalistic songs, and endless, endless speeches in that frenetic, crazed voice of exhortation. In public places, in the street, it filled the air, blaring at one from the grocery, the newsstand, the café, the garage, for it became patriotic to have it on at full volume.

Imagine what it would be like if, say, the British or French were incessantly told, with nobody allowed to contest, question, or protest, that they were now European, and only European. European! European! European! And endless songs about it. But for us it was actually worse and certainly more complicated. Its equivalent would be if the British or French were being told that they were white. White! White! White! Because the new definition of who we were unsettled and undercut the old understanding of who we were and silently excluded people who had been included in the old definition of Egyptian. Copts, for example, were not Arab. In fact, they were Copts precisely because they had refused to convert to the religion of the Arabs and had refused, unlike us Muslims, to intermarry with Arabs. As a result, Copts (members of the ancient Christian church of Egypt) were the only truly indigenous inhabitants of Egypt and as such, in our home anyway and in the notion of Egypt with which I grew up, Copts had a very special place in the country. In the new definition of us, however, they were included as speakers of Arabic but they were not at the heart of the definition in the way that we were.

But of course the people who were most directly, although as yet only implicitly, being excluded by the redefinition were the Jews of Egypt, for the whole point of the revolutionary government's harping insistence that we were Arab, in those first years following the founding of Israel, and following the takeover of Egypt's government by New Men with a new vision and new commitments, was to proclaim our unequivocal alignments: on the side of the Palestinians and Arabs and against Israel, against Zionism. Ever since, this issue has been the key issue determining the different emphases Egypt's leaders have placed on its identity. If they have proclaimed insistently and emphatically (as Nasser did) that we were Arab, it has meant that we would take a confrontational, unyielding line on Israel and that we would "never deal with the Zionists." If we were Egyptians above all (Sadat), then we could talk, negotiate.

Our new identity proclaimed openly our opposition to Israel and Zionism—and proclaimed implicitly our opposition to the "Zionists" in our midst, Egyptian Jews. For although explicitly Zionism was distinguished from Jewishness, an undercurrent meaning "Jewish" was also contained in the word. The word "Arab," emerging at this moment to define our identity, silently carried within it its polar opposite—Zionist/Jew—without which hidden, silent connotation it actually had no meaning. For the whole purpose of its emergence now was precisely to tell us of our new alignments and realignments in relation to both terms, Arab and Jew.

Jews and Copts were not, to me, abstractions. They were people my parents knew and saw and talked about, and they were my brothers' friends and my sister's and my own, including my best friend, Joyce. I am sure I sensed these insidious, subterranean shifts and rearrangements of our feelings that this new bludgeoning propaganda was effecting, or trying to effect, in us. And I am sure that this, as well as the sheer hatefulness of being endlessly subjected to propaganda, was part of the reason I so much disliked and resisted the idea that I was an Arab.

Nor was it only through the media that the government was pressuring us into acceptance of its broad political agenda and coercing us into being Arab. For this was the era, too, of growing political repression and of the proliferation of the *mukhabarat*, the secret police—the era when political opponents and people suspected of being disloyal to the revolution were being jailed or disappearing. In this atmosphere, being disloyal to the revolution and to the Arab cause (being, as it were, un-Arab) became as charged and dangerous for Egyptians as being un-American was for Americans in the McCarthy era.

The propaganda worked on me and on others. To question our Arabness and all that our Arabness implied became unthinkable. Only despicable, unprincipled traitors would do such a thing. And it is with this complicated legacy that my own sense of identity as Egyptian and as Arab is entangled.

The following pages recount a personal odyssey through the politics, emotions, and history of our becoming Arab. For no matter how carefully I examined my memories and feelings, they remained opaque until I took this journey into history and into the history of the world of my childhood. These pages both describe the information that I discovered and pieced together—some of it quite surprising and even shocking to me—and trace the process and voyage of discovery itself and my new understandings of my past.

Thinking back to the incident with which I began this chapter, I asked myself what this scene between me and Miss Nabih told me about my parents and family, from whom, certainly, I got my understanding of what it meant to be Egyptian. Why was it that I was so stubborn, so convinced that I was Egyptian and not Arab, definitely not Arab? Presumably this was what my parents thought, but why? Was this a class issue? Were they part of some elite milieu which imagined they were Egyptian while "the masses" knew all along that they were Arabs? When, in fact, did Egyptians become Arab—or have we always been Arab?

The answer to this question, which I assumed I would find simply by looking up a book or two on the history of Egypt, actually took quite a lot of detective work, for it was not clearly or fully addressed in any of the books where I had expected to find it. It felt as if I had embarked in search of some esoteric secret. In the last few years there has begun to be a scholarship piecing together the history of the rise of Arab nationalism, but as regards Egypt, it is a history as yet only barely sketched in.

The story, anyway, begins in Syria, in the late nineteenth century, where the idea of an Arab identity and Arab nationalism first arose. Prior to this, "Arab" had referred throughout the Middle East only to the inhabitants of Arabia and to bedouins of the region's deserts. It was among the Christians of Syria, and in particular among a group of Syrian men who had attended French missionary schools, that the idea of Arab nationalism first appeared, in part as a movement of literary and cultural revival and in part as a way of mobilizing both Christian and Muslim Syrians to throw off the domination of the Islamic Ottoman Empire.

Egyptians, who in that era were preoccupied with getting rid of the British, not the Ottomans, were either uninterested in or positively hostile to this strange Syrian idea of an Arab identity. Mustapha Kamil, the leading nationalist of the day in Egypt, strongly pro-Ottoman and pro-Islamic, denounced Arab nationalism as an idea invented and fomented by the Europeans to hasten the destruction of the Ottoman Empire. And paranoid though Kamil's notion sounds, there may have been some truth to it. Historical records suggest that British officials were indeed already encouraging and supporting the idea of Arabism even before World War I (that they did so during the war is well known).

Well into the first decades of this century, neither the self-defined new Arabs nor the Egyptians themselves thought that this new identity had anything to do with Egyptians. For example, in 1913 an Arab conference was organized in Paris. When an Egyptian who was attending as an observer asked permission to speak, he was refused on the grounds that the floor was open only to Arabs.

During World War I, the idea of Arab nationalism emerged again as an important idea—and again as an idea mobilizing people against the Turks and their Islamic Empire. This time it took the form of the British-instigated "Arab revolt," led by T. E. Lawrence. (The fact that this famous revolt was led by an Englishman makes obvious, of course, Britain's political interest in promoting Arabism as a way of fighting the Ottoman Empire and bringing about its final dissolution.) Once more, as with the Syrian form of Arab nationalism, not only were Egyptians not part of this movement, they were, if anything, inclined to be sympathetic to the other side. For one thing, this Arab movement now involved mainly the Arabs of Arabia and nomadic tribal Arabs, people whom Egyptians regarded as even more different from themselves than the Syrians. The distinction between settled and nomad is, in the Middle East, one of the fundamental divides. For Egyptians it is a distinction that has marked off their society from that of "the Arabs" (Arabians, nomads) since the beginning of their civilization.

In addition, these Arabs were fighting *with* the hated British, the oppressors of Egypt, and *against* the Islamic Empire and the caliph of Islam. Egypt's Khedive Abbas had been sent into exile by the British for his open sympathies with the Turks and the Islamic Empire, and so also had the leader of the Nationalist Party, Mohamad Farid. The Egyptian writer Naguib Mahfouz, in his novel *Bain al-Qasrain* (*Palace Walk*), set in World War I, portrays his characters, the "common folk" of Egypt, as praying for the return of Abbas and for the Turks to "emerge victorious" and as declaring that "the most important thing of all is that we get rid of the "English nightmare" and that the caliphate return to its former glory. Aware of popular sentiment in Egypt, the British took care to represent the Arab revolt to Egyptians as a rebellion not against the caliph but against the "impious, godless" Young Turks who were oppressing "the Arabs."

At the end of the war the British invited the leaders of the Arabs to the Versailles conference but refused to permit the Egyptian leaders to attend. Still, the Arabs reaped no benefits. In a series of treaties the European powers (Britain and France) dismantled the Ottoman Empire and distributed among themselves its former territories. For the British, having induced the Arabs to fight with them against the Turks by promising them independence, had also signed a secret treaty with the French (the Sykes-Picot agreement) undertaking to divide between them after the war "the spoils of the Ottoman Empire." Formalizing their control over the territories that they had just captured from the Ottomans, France took Syria and divided it into two countries, Lebanon and Syria, and Britain took Iraq and

Palestine. Britain was, of course, already occupying Egypt. Similarly the Balfour Declaration, promising Palestine, a land obviously with its own inhabitants, to people living elsewhere—designating it a national homeland for the Jews—had been issued earlier, in 1917, when the British first captured Palestine. (There were, of course, Jews as well as Muslims and Christians among the population of Palestine when the British captured it, but it was not out of concern for Palestinian Jews that the British now declared Palestine a homeland for the Jews but rather—as is well known—in response to the desires and hopes of European Jewry for a homeland in Palestine.)

Some of this I knew already. I knew about T. E. Lawrence and the Arab revolt, and I had known in a general way that Arab nationalism was a recent idea. But only now, putting together the Christian and missionary-inspired origins of Arab nationalism in Syria and the use the British made of the idea to mobilize the "Arabs" against the Ottomans, did I realize the extent to which Arab nationalism had emerged as a way of opposing the Islamic Empire. And only now did I realize the extent to which Egypt had not only *not* been Arab but actually had been mostly on the opposite side to that of the Arabs. The exiled khedive and political leaders of Egypt supported the Ottomans and hated the British, and so apparently did the "masses." And even the modernizing intellectuals, who wanted political independence from the Ottomans, had all their cultural, intellectual, and personal ties with Turks and with Istanbul, which many of them regularly visited.

And so already my understanding of Egypt and its relation to the Arabs was beginning to shift. Already I was beginning to feel that the world was not as I had assumed it to be and its seas and continents not after all where I had thought they were. Still, whatever internal shifts and readjustments were involved for me in what I had learned thus far, they were nothing to the geologic shifts and turmoil and upheaval that I would find myself flung up or cast down by as I read on, trying to piece together what happened next—and reading now about the history of the Jews in Egypt and about Egypt's relations to Zionism and the Palestinians.

Eventually things would calm down. Eventually I would come to see that these facts, too, were part of the history of Egypt and that after all they fitted quite intelligibly into that history. But to begin with, with almost every new detail I learned I found myself precipitated into a state of general agitation, my feelings running the gamut of shock, disbelief, shame, despair, and exhilaration—why exhilaration?—and finally, finally understanding. Physically I could not sit still, I could only read a paragraph or two at a time, at least whenever I stumbled upon one or the other of these, to me, completely mind-blowing facts. I'd jump up and walk and walk, repeating to myself whatever it was I'd just read. Egyptians, I'd be rushing around saying to myself, joined their Zionist friends in Cairo and Alexandria to celebrate the Balfour Declaration? There were Zionist associations in Cairo and Alexandria then? It was okay in Egypt to be a Zionist? The governor of Alexandria, Ahmad Ziyour Pasha—later prime minister of Egypt—went to a party in the city celebrating the Balfour Declaration that culminated in their sending a telegram to Lord Balfour to thank him?

Hours and hours and days of this, then, would be interspersed with enormous, crashing, paralyzing anxieties at the very thought of writing about Arabness. There was no question I couldn't do it. I'd just have to leave it out. Just forget it—Arab, not Arab—just forget it. It was much too complicated. How could I possibly deal with all this history?

The first Jewish flag to fly over Jerusalem after its capture by the British was made in Egypt? Joseph Cicurel of the house of Cicurel (a department store I remembered from my childhood, the Harrods of Cairo) had had it made in his Alexandria workshops. Cicurel was president of the Zionist association of Cairo. And at the same time he was an Egyptian nationalist? He was also a trustee of the Bank of Egypt, the bank founded by the Muslim nationalist Talaat Harb with the object of wresting control of the Egyptian economy from Europeans and placing it in Egyptian hands. The same was true of Leon Castro, the vice president of the same Zionist association and likewise an Egyptian nationalist. A member of the Wafd, the party leading the struggle for independence from the British, he was also a friend and staunch supporter of Saad Zaghloul, leader of the Wafd and *the* hero of the Egyptian nationalist struggle.

On and on, more such extraordinary facts about Egyptians' relationship to Zionism—and also to the Palestinians. The Egyptian government sent a representative—we are now in 1925—to the celebrations for the inauguration of the Hebrew University in Jerusalem. This representative was none other than Ahmad Lutfi al-Sayyid, the editor of *al-Jarida*, the paper that shaped the political consciousness of a generation of Egyptians—my father's generation —and the man who would later facilitate women's entry into the Egyptian University. In the late 1920s and early 1930s, when Palestinians began publishing a paper in Egypt advocating their cause, the Egyptian government several times closed the paper down and banned the publication of "Palestinian propaganda." And in the wake of conflict over the Wailing Wall and Muslim fears about rights of access to the al-Aqsa mosque, also in the early 1930s, it even banned the invocation of the name of Palestine in mosques on Fridays. Meanwhile several Zionist papers continued publication and Zionism was not banned.

Reading such facts as these and observing my own feelings and the paralyzing anxiety I felt at the mere thought of writing about such things, I came to conclude that this sort of information did not ordinarily figure in history books on Egypt precisely because, according to the political alignments of our day, alignments that we consider to be entirely obvious and natural, they seemed so shamefully unpatriotic, and so disloyal and unfeeling toward the Palestinians.

In the ensuing days I would begin to understand how it was that Egyptian attitudes had been so profoundly different from what they are today, and I would come to understand also my own connection to that past and the ways in which it was interwoven with my own early life. But even then, even when I'd understood all this, I would still find myself completely stalled and unable to imagine how I could possibly write about these things.

Still feeling totally paralyzed, I began to analyze my paralysis as a product probably of my having internalized the taboos against questioning Arabness that had been part, after all, of my adolescence. But this insight—if it was an insight—did me no good. I was still perfectly capable of silencing myself without any external prohibitions.

Quite a number of remarkable Egyptians, I discovered along the way, had been suspected or accused of being either too pro-Jewish, too conciliatory, and too weak on Zionism or deficient in their Arabness or their loyalty to Arabness. Among those whose actions or words or positions one way or another laid them open to such charges were Saad Zaghloul, hero of Egyptian nationalism. And Taha Husain and Tewfik al-Hakim and Naguib Mahfouz, three of Egypt's finest writers. Major figures in the country's history. The equivalent in American terms would be to find that Harry Truman, William Faulkner, F. Scott Fitzgerald, and Eugene O'Neill had all been suspected of un-American inclinations. And of course there was Anwar Sadat, gunned down in part for his retreat—and all that such a retreat implied—from Nasser's position as to Egypt's fundamental Arabness.

But knowing this made no difference either. Nothing unfroze me.

Then one evening as I was walking home, something began to shift. I am not sure quite why or how things began to change but I know that the shift was connected to, or, more exactly, was the direct outcome of, the preceding perfectly pleasant but uneventful few hours. I was in Cambridge for the year on a fellowship (it was here that I pursued and pieced together this history) and had gone out to hear a talk by the Lebanese novelist Hanan al-Shaykh. She'd come down from London to speak at the Oriental Studies Faculty. Hanan was already there when I arrived and rose to greet me, which took me by surprise: we had met only once, briefly and in a crowd, and I hadn't expected her to recognize me. It had felt good, I realized, sitting down and looking around me, to be recognized and to be greeted in the way that, in the world in which I had once lived, one automatically greeted people—or at least other women. The room was more crowded than it had been for the previous lecturers. Aside from Tareef and Bassim, who were the professors at the Oriental Faculty, and some students, the audience did not seem the usual academic crowd that I'd seen at other lectures. Hanan's reputation had clearly drawn out from wherever they were in their separate spaces a good number of the town's Arab and, I guessed from their looks, specifically Lebanese community. There were several older people there, many of them women, living, for whatever reason, in this exile. Here now to honor one of their own, to take pride in her, to listen to her words—and to remember.

Hanan, a slight, beautiful woman, began to read in a clear, soft voice and the room fell quiet, a look of intentness and pleasure and anticipation already on people's faces. Her paper, about how she became a writer, was full of evocations of the streets and cafés of Beirut, and of its dusty, cluttered, narrow bookshops, and of her youthful discoveries of the classics of contemporary Arabic literature, and of poetry read and heard and ideas exchanged under the apple trees. It began, almost at once, to work its enchantment. As the minutes passed, the faces around me grew perceptibly happier, mellower, more relaxed. Even Bassim and Tareef, sitting facing me on either side of her—dear colleagues both but men who, as I knew, were somewhat skeptical of the fame of Arab women writers—were looking mellow and happy and relaxed. They had clearly been won over.

I found myself thinking enviously that this was what I would like to be writing, something that would affirm my community in exile. Something that would remind its members of how lovely our lives, our countries, our ways are. How lovely our literature. What a fine thing, whatever it is people say of us, what a fine thing it is, in spite of them all, to be Arab; what a wonderful heritage we have. Something that would sustain them. Sustain us. What wouldn't I give, I sat there thinking, listening to her quote Arab poets, to have had that in my past, all that wealth of Arabic literature that nurtured her as writer; what wouldn't I give now to have all those poets and writers to remember and write about and remind people of? I loved the lines she was quoting—but I appreciated them, I realized, only the way I might the poetry of a foreign tongue that I only somewhat knew. They did not have for me the resonances of lines learned long ago. Nor, of course, since they were in literary Arabic, did they have the charge and redolence and burdened evocativeness of a language spoken in childhood and youth and in love and anger and just in the ordinary moments of living. But on the other hand they didn't have that wealth and redolence for her, either. Even though she clearly loved the literature and language and was herself a fine Arabic writer, for her too it was a language she had not spoken in childhood and did not speak now. Nobody speaks literary Arabic—or maybe just some pedant somewhere.

We went afterward—Hanan, Tareef, Bassim, Zeeba (another colleague), and I—for drinks at King's. The mood of the lecture stayed with us, our talk pleasant, relaxed, easy. At some point Hanan asked me what I was working on. I was vague, evasive, guilty. I even lied a little. "I'm looking at Egypt's history," I said, "twentieth century." And then for the rest of the evening I felt guilty, sitting there like a Judas among these friends. I felt like a betrayer. Was it even imaginable that I could have responded, sitting there among them—two Lebanese, one Palestinian, one Iranian, three of the four of them having been made homeless one way or another by Israeli aggression or by some spin-off of that conflict—was it conceivable that I could say, "Well, actually I am looking into this whole question of the Arabness of Egyptian identity, I am trying to really look at it, deconstruct it. You see I remember . . ." It was completely unimaginable, impossible, inconceivable.

I felt like a betrayer.

Coming out onto King's Parade, afterwards, the night suddenly balmy, the street almost empty though it wasn't that late, people's voices carrying clear, loud, the way they do sometimes on summer nights—but not usually now, in winter, winter on the point of turning to spring—I walked on homeward, down Senate House Passage and along the narrow road onto the bridge. There was a crescent moon over the trees in a deep, deep sky.

I did feel kin, of course, and I did feel that I was among people who were, in some quite real sense, my community. But was this because of "Arabness"? Was I, for instance, really likely to feel more kin, more at home, with someone from Saudi Arabia than with someone, say, from Istanbul? I doubted it. (Saudis speak Arabic, Turks don't.) This, though, was not the issue now. I realized that my feelings of being completely prohibited from writing about Arabness were not, or not only, a response to old prohibitions or a fear of breaking some mental taboo internalized in adolescence. No, my fear that I would, in this act of unraveling, cross over the line into betrayal was about real, not abstract betrayal. I'd been so set on this act of unraveling, this taking apart of the notion of Arabness. It had seemed to me so essential, so necessary to understanding what it was that I'd lived through, and essential and necessary also to freeing myself from the unbearable lies that I'd forever felt trapped in. Essential and necessary in one sense, and yet to proceed would inevitably, as it now felt, take me over the line into betrayal. And so, thinking about it now, from the context of having been with people I liked and felt in some sense kin with, I wondered what it could possibly matter, when weighed against the reality of people's being driven from their homes or penned into impossible lives, that I had felt myself coerced into being something that I did not feel I was. A small, trivial nothing of a detail to put up with as a way of conveying to them solidarity and support.

But I am not here to betray, I said, waiting at the traffic lights. Had I said it out loud? I looked around—there was nobody there anyway.

I am not here to betray. I just do not want to live any longer with a lie about who I am. I don't want any longer to live with lies and manipulations, I can't stand to be caught up like this forever in other people's inventions, imputations, false constructions of who I am—what I think, believe, feel, or ought to think or believe or feel.

But how—if I don't directly address this—how will I ever free myself from lies?

If I didn't live where I live, I thought to myself, if I were still living in Egypt, I probably wouldn't feel that it was so absolutely necessary to extricate myself from this enmeshment of lies. In Egypt the sense of falseness and coercion would be there in a political sense, but at least in ordinary daily life I'd be just another Egyptian, whereas in the West it's impossible for me ever to escape, forget this false constructed Arabness. It's almost always somehow there, the notion that I am Arab, in any and every interaction. And sometimes it's quite grossly and offensively present, depending on how bigoted or ignorant the person I am confronting is.

But this is a problem, I realized now, arising out of *their* notion of Arab, the Western, not the Arab, notion of Arab. So there are two different notions of Arab that I am trapped in—both false, both heavily weighted and cargoed with another and silent freight. Both imputing to me feelings and beliefs that aren't mine. They overlap in some ways, but they are not, I am sure, identical. But this was a piece of the puzzle—the fact that there were two different notions of Arab—that for the moment I would have to defer figuring out.

Anyway, the long and short of it is that I am not here to betray. I am taking apart the notion of Arabness and following out the history of when and how we became Arab just to know—not with the object of, or as code for, the betrayal of anybody. For Egyptians to debate or question their Arabness ("search" for their identity) is usually code, as I realize now, for debating the extent of our responsibility toward the Palestinians. And it is accordingly read by Arabs and by Egyptians as a covert way of advocating either support for or abandonment of the Palestinians. But my own exploration of the question here is not code for anything. My sole object here is only to see things, as clearly and exactly as I know how, for what they are. And to free myself of lies.

⟿

And so in any case one reason that Zionism was permitted to be overtly present in Egypt in the late 1920s and early 1930s and that prominent members of the government and of the governing classes were sympathetic to Zionism was that Egyptians seemed not to know what is obvious to us in hindsight—that making Palestine into a homeland for the Jews would eventually entail the expulsion and dispossession of the Palestinians. There had as yet been no large-scale immigration of Europeans to Palestine and, at the end of the 1910s and through most of the 1920s, when troubles broke out intermittently in Palestine the government and media in Egypt typically reacted by exhorting the Jews and Muslims and Christians of Palestine to work together to find a peaceful solution, offering themselves as mediators, and worrying that this reprehensible interreligious, intercommunal violence would spread to their own country. Because of this last concern, newspapers (or at least some newspapers) and the government responded to news of outbreaks of violence in Palestine by reiterating their own total commitment to preserving religious pluralism, and the government in addition took such measures as banning Palestinian "propaganda"—in fear that interreligious hostilities and in particular anti-Jewish violence, as yet unknown in Egypt, would spread to their own land.

For, as of 1918, the modernizing intellectuals and their party, the Wafd, had begun to become the uncontested political leaders of the nation. And in the early twenties their political goals and platform—democracy, a constitution guaranteeing, among other things, the rights of the individual, pluralism, and an implicit secularism committed to the equal rights of all Egyptians, regardless of religion—won the support of the nation in a landslide election that carried small villages as well as major cities. These goals, conceived and defined by the country's political and intellectual leadership, received the endorsement of the populace as a whole.

Egypt's experiment in democracy would be conducted under difficult circumstances. The British, refusing to grant Egypt complete independence, retained important powers and sometimes interfered outright in the democratic process, at one point later forcing Egypt's king, literally at gunpoint (surrounding his palace with their tanks), to appoint the prime minister they wanted. The king, for his part, plotted to wrest power back from the government to himself. Despite these difficulties the country did make political progress and there were even some exhilarating times and significant achievements, among them the promulgation of a constitution in 1923, article 3 of which granted equal rights to all Egyptians, "without distinction of race, language, or religion." The same principles were reiterated in

Egypt's Nationality Laws, which went into effect in 1929 with the formal dissolution of the Ottoman Empire and the replacement of Ottoman citizenship with a brand-new nationality, the Egyptian nationality. These principles and a commitment to Egypt as a multireligious community were furthermore made clear and visible to all in the composition of the government. When, in 1924, Zaghloul became Egypt's first elected prime minister, Jews as well as Copts served in his cabinet—and indeed both Jews and Copts would continue to serve in the Egyptian government in the following decades.

As all this shows, then, not only was the country's political leadership deeply committed to the goal of preserving Egypt as a pluralist society; in addition, Jews were integrally part of the community of Egypt and of its political and cultural leadership, and they were the friends and colleagues and co-workers of Muslim and Coptic Egyptians. Then there were other factors, too, influencing how Egyptians related to the issue of Palestine. Most obviously, there were no Palestinians then (or very few) in Egypt and certainly there was no historical community of Palestinians as there was a historical Jewish community. In this era about half the Jewish community of Egypt— a community of about 75,000—were Egyptian Jews. The rest were recent immigrants from other territories of the Ottoman Empire and from Europe. (These latter often looked down on the local Jewish community, particularly the Jewish working classes, who were indistinguishable in culture and ways from working-class Muslims and Copts. Middle- and upper-class Jews, like Copts and Muslims of their class, were fast becoming Europeanized.)

And then finally there was the fact that Egyptians at this point did not (and at any class level) see themselves as Arab or as having any special connection with the Arabs, nor did they think that they had any particular interest in or special responsibility for what transpired in Palestine.

Egyptian attitudes began to shift toward a sympathy with the Palestinians in the thirties, as the situation in Palestine began to change when, with the rise of Fascism in Europe, European Jewish immigration to Palestine increased enormously. Palestinian political activism also increased. Through the thirties Palestinian strikes and rebellions against the British and their struggles with Zionists were constantly in the news. By the late thirties the Palestinians had won the sympathies of Egyptians. Fund-raisers and various other events in support of Palestine and in aid of Palestinian relief were held at all class levels, including by Huda Shaarawi's Feminist Union, among the first associations to organize a regionwide conference in support of the Palestinians.

Most important, in terms of publicizing the situation of Palestinians and mobilizing popular support for them, the Muslim Brotherhood, dedicated to instituting an Islamic government in Egypt and to freeing all Muslim lands from imperialists, vigorously took up the Palestinian cause. It began to hold protest demonstrations on Balfour Day and to address the issue of Palestine in Friday sermons.

It was these sorts of activities that, as I mentioned earlier, the government had been attempting to suppress, out of its commitment to a pluralist Egypt and its desire to prevent the spread of interreligious strife. And the government continued through the thirties to try to suppress inflammatory pro-Palestinian activities and to keep Egypt out of direct involvement in the question of Palestine. This was the position assumed not only by the Wafd when it was in power but by the several governments formed by different parties in this era. This view represented, in other words, the consensus position of the governing classes across party lines. And so a rift began to form in Egypt on the issue of Palestine, not on the matter of sympathy for the Palestinians but as to what Egypt's political involvement should be: a rift, initially, not so much between the governing classes and the "masses" as between the government and governing classes on the one hand and the Brotherhood on the other.

Through the thirties the demonstrations the Brotherhood organized grew steadily more massive, and they began to take the direction that the government had, all along, feared they would take. In 1936, the Brotherhood called for a boycott of Jewish businesses. In the same year, the first anti-Jewish graffiti to be reported in Egypt appeared in Port Said. In 1938, police clashed with Brotherhood demonstrators —some of whom were shouting "Down with the Jews"—and tried to prevent them from entering the Jewish quarter of Old Cairo.

It was in the thirties that a few intellectuals—two or three men to begin with, all of whom had links with the Arabs—began to express the idea that Egypt should align itself with the Arabs and regard itself as Arab. But it was probably the emphasis the Muslim Brotherhood now placed on this idea that helped spread it most effectively. While the government had emphasized Egypt's heritage as quintessentially and indissolubly multicultural (Pharaonic, Mediterranean, and Islamic, as they put it in those days) as a way of legitimizing its determined emphasis on pluralism as a fundamental goal for this country, the Brotherhood countered by asserting that Islam and only Islam constituted Egypt's defining identity. It was Islam, they declared, that had saved Egypt from its pagan past (thereby conveniently erasing from history the fact that the majority of Egyptians had been Christian at the time of the Muslim invasion)—an Islam brought to the country, they stressed, by the Arabs. All Egyptians, therefore, and all Muslims owed a particular debt to the Arabs and had an obligation to help liberate Arab lands from infidel imperialists.

By the end of the thirties the popularity of the Palestinian cause and the growing influence of the Brotherhood were forcing the government and dominant political parties to slant their message differently. In 1939, a prominent member of the Wafd made headlines by writing an article declaring "Egypt is Arab!"

Through World War II overt political activism and demonstrations were banned under the Emergencies Act. When they resumed after the war, the pro-Palestinian demonstrations organized by the Muslim Brotherhood took the course of ever greater intercommunal tensions and anti-Jewish violence that the government and the different political parties had all along feared. Huge demonstrations held on Balfour Day in 1945 and again in 1947 spilled over into violent attacks on Jews and now on any other group deemed "foreign." Jewish, European, and Coptic shops were looted, and synagogues and Catholic, Greek Orthodox, and Coptic churches and schools vandalized. One synagogue was set on fire.

~

The unraveling of that old world and its society are just dimly part of the fabric of my own memories.

I remember being at play in the garden one dusk when the news came that al-Na'rashi, the prime minister, had been shot. *"Atalu al-Na'rashi!"* They killed al-Na'rashi! "They," I know now, were the Muslim Brothers. There was somberness then in our home. My parents, I believe, knew the Na'rashis. But not only somberness—there was something electric, still there even now in my memory, about how they uttered the words and how they spoke of this death. Now I imagine them saying to one another, the adults, living through these crises and troubled times, what next for the country, what next?

And I remember the midnight-blue paper on the windows, purplish when the daylight came through it, during the 1948 war with Israel, and being woken in the night and taken downstairs to the entree, a room with no windows and only a heavy glass and ironwork door, where everyone was gathered in the darkness, talking, listening to the bombs fall.

This was a few months before the assassination of Na'rashi (al-Nuqrashi)—as the history books, not my memory, tell me.

And then, in retaliation for Na'rashi's murder, Hasan al-Banna, the founder of the Muslim Brotherhood and its Supreme Guide, was gunned down. This I do not remember. The Muslim Brotherhood, by now an enormously powerful organization in the country with a vast membership and its own secret military units, was engaged through the forties in a terrorist and counterterrorist war with the political establishment. Al-Banna died in the hospital to which he was brought and where, by order of King Farouk, he was given no medical treatment.

It was by order of Farouk, too, that Egypt went to war with Israel. After the United Nations resolution to partition Palestine and Israel's declaration of statehood in 1948, the Egyptian political establishment—both government and opposition—had favored a cautious re-

sponse, a verbal, not a military, response. But Farouk harbored
dreams, now that the Ottoman Empire was gone, of having himself
declared caliph of Islam. He worried that, if Egypt did not go to war
now, King Abdullah of Jordan, who had declared that Jordan would
go to war, would reap glory on the battlefield and put an end to his
own dreams. And so, pre-empting the Egyptian government's decision
and in violation of the constitution, he ordered military units to cross
into Palestine. After the fact, the government hastily convened a
meeting to bestow a semblance of legality on the king's orders. The
opposition, however, and in particular the Liberal Constitutionalists
—who (as the history books put it), out of a "narrow Egyptian secular
nationalism" were "most impervious to Palestinian appeals"—were
fiercely critical of this government action.

But of course it was not that Farouk had been pervious to Palestinian appeals. Nor was it only Farouk for whom from now on taking
up the Palestinian cause was essentially an avenue to the fulfillment
of his political ambitions. While Na'rashi was making speeches cau-
tioning against a hasty military response, Hasan al-Banna was declaring in mosques the Muslim Brotherhood's readiness for a jihad against
the Zionists. But he, too, was in reality furthering his own cause. In
the forties the Brotherhood, historians have speculated, had a trained
secret army of about 75,000 men. But they reportedly sent to the
Palestine campaign just 600. The movement was hoping, say historians, to reserve most of its secret units for its Egyptian war—its war
on the cities of Egypt.

By this point, that is, Palestine and the Palestinian cause had
begun to be what they have been ever since in the politics of the Arab
world: an issue that the Middle East's villains and heroes would use
to manipulate people's sympathies and to further their own political
ends and fantasies of power—with what costs or benefits to the Palestinian people only the Palestinians themselves can say.

Where did my parents stand in all this? I don't know. I was too
young and do not remember. It would be quite impossible for me to

have grasped what they said enough to be able to say, now, they said this or believed that.

And yet also now I think I know.

But the evidence I have is so vague, so insubstantial, so inconclusive. Some things I do know and do remember beyond a shadow of a doubt. For instance, I know that they definitely did not like the Muslim Brothers. I don't remember any particular thing that they said about them, but I remember this as a general feeling. And I remember that a man who was a relative by marriage (a younger man beholden in some way, looking in some way to my father) was a Muslim Brother and that he emerged from prison at some point (still, now, in the days of King Farouk) and that he had tuberculosis and that he came to our house and that my father, making clear to him (and evidently to all of us) his total disapproval of his politics, helped him get treatment.

I don't remember in any way that I would now be able to reproduce what my parents were saying as they lived through these wrenching times in the history of Egypt. But I was there, obviously, and heard them talk and no doubt in some sense absorbed what they were saying. And they *were* people who talked politics. Over lunch when my father came home from work and on weekends when we were home from school and joined our parents. Over tea and the papers in the early morning, sitting in my mother's huge bed, where we half listened to them talk. What exactly was the content of that grief and somberness that descended over our home and the feeling of charged tension that I remember when Na'rashi was shot? What exactly did they say to each other? And what did they say when al-Banna was shot—and allowed to die, untreated, by order of the king?

That's another thing I incontrovertibly know and remember: they did not like King Farouk.

And what did they say when there were riots in Egypt and attacks on synagogues and churches? And what did they say as we sat in the dark in the entree, listening to the sound of distant bombs and antiaircraft fire and then a nearer, louder, more frightening explosion? What were they saying about the war with Israel? Could they have been among those who condemned the king for getting us into this war? Could they have been among those who, like the government opposition, condemned the government for "lending any semblance of legitimacy" to the king's action? Could they have been among those who, like the Liberal Constitutionalists, out of a "narrow Egyptian secular nationalism" opposed the war? Could they have been among those "impervious to Palestinian appeals" who believed that Egypt should not go to war with Israel? Could they have been among those for whom grief about what was happening to Egypt overrode and took priority over what was happening to the Palestinians?

Though I do not remember their words, I would have picked up the import of what they were saying, and their attitudes would certainly have shaped my responses to whatever I encountered at school.

Including, of course, Miss Nabih.

I did not know, until I read into this history and learned what I have here set down, that there had been Egyptians—perfectly ordinary, decent, upright, principled citizens of Egypt, not disloyal, unpatriotic, unfeeling people—who believed in something else, some other idea of Egypt and its society and future, and who openly argued against getting involved in supporting the Palestinians and going to war with Israel.

My parents were the people that they were. Of the class that they were, the milieu that they were, the era that they were. And they had the feelings and beliefs about Egypt that they had, and the hopes for Egypt that they had. Not indifference toward the Palestinians and their sufferings, nor commitment to some "narrow Egyptian secular nationalism," but quite simply loyalty to their own community and to the people—Copts, Jews and Muslims—who made up that community had been what my parents had steadfastly held on to and had refused to be moved from. Loyalty to their actual community—over and above some fictive, politically created community that the politicians ordered them to be loyal to. And, yes, their overall position reflected too their particular hopes for Egypt, and their commitment to what we today call "pluralism." But "pluralism" after all is merely a modern version of what had been, in another world, another era, their tradition and heritage, from generation to generation to generation, in Cairo and Alexandria and Spain and Morocco and Istanbul.

And so this, then, had been the source of those moments of inexplicable exhilaration in the midst of turbulence—my beginning to glimpse finally what had been the history and prehistory of my own conflicted feelings. They taught me so well, instilled in me so deeply their notion of what it was to be Egyptian, that I still mourn and am always still and all over again filled with an enormous sense of loss at the thought of the destruction of the multireligious Egyptian community that I knew. And still now news of intercommunal violence in Egypt and of attacks on Copts (there are no Jews now) and of attacks on Muslims too, of course—but it is the Copts who are the beleaguered community—is almost the bleakest news I know of coming out of there.

In 1941, Anthony Eden, the British foreign minister, proposed the creation of an Arab League, to include Egypt. This British proposal precipitated an intense debate that polarized Egyptians. Was Egypt Arab? Mediterranean? Pharaonic? Britain had put forward the idea as a counterproposal to an idea that Iraq had been advancing: the creation of a federated Arab state, to consist of Iraq, Syria, Jordan, and Palestine. Such a federation, should it occur, could lead to the rise of a formidable new power in the Middle East, and this was something Britain did not want. It was something Egypt did not want, either. As the region began to adjust to the disappearance of Turkey as the center of empire and the newly emergent countries began to vie for regional dominance, Egypt—at that point the richest, most developed and most populous nation in the region—had no intention of ceding power and influence to Iraq or Jordan or to any federation of these. Thus, in 1943, the Egyptian government agreed to the British proposal and the Arab League was formed in 1945.

And so here we are in 1945, and Egypt, for reasons of regional strategy, officially becomes an Arab country, although not as yet exclusively Arab, as it would become under Nasser. And again, curiously, Britain played the role of instigator, and of midwife, as it were, to the birth of yet another Arab nation. Once more, as with its leadership of the Arab revolt, Britain's purpose in urging Egypt to define itself as Arab was, of course, the furtherance of British political interests.

It was as if we had become Arab, and all the region gradually had become Arab (when, once, only Arabia had been Arab), because the Europeans saw us as Arabs—all of us as just Arabs. And because, to serve their own political interests and in pursuit of their own ends—the dismantling of the Ottoman Empire, the acquisition of new colonial territories, retaining control of territories under their mandate—it was strategically and politically useful to them, in this particular era in history, to define us, and to have us define ourselves, as Arabs. And gradually over this era we had all complied, imagining this, correctly or not, to be in our own interest, too.

The Europeans were defining us and we, falling in with their ideas, agreed to define ourselves as Arab in the dictionary sense: "a member of the Semitic people of the Arabian peninsula; a member of an Arabic-speaking people." But the Europeans were also defining us as Arab in quite another sense. Just as with the word "African"—"a native or inhabitant of Africa; a person of immediate or remote African ancestry; esp: Negro"—there is no trace in the dictionary definition of the word's pejorative connotations. There is nothing here of what anyone who has heard of O. J. Simpson or *The Bell Curve* or who knows anything about American history *knows* that that word means. This is the case also with the word "Arab," which similarly comes, in European tongues, internally loaded in the negative.

Such words carry within them entire landscapes, entire histories.

The European powers defined us as "Arab" in this other sense by what they did. They defined us as "Arab" in this sense when they made an agreement with Sheikh Abdullah and those who fought alongside Lawrence, promising them independence—and then broke the agreement. They defined us as "Arab" at the Peace conferences of Versailles and Sèvres when they dealt with Middle Eastern territories as mere spoils of the Ottoman Empire, to be divided between France and Britain as booty, bargaining with one another for this bit or that, drawing lines and borders on their maps with little concern for the people and lands they were carving up. And they defined us as "Arab" when they designated an already inhabited land as a homeland for people living, then, elsewhere. They defined us as "Arab" when they led Egyptians to believe that in return for neutrality during the war they would get independence—and failed to keep their promise and exiled leaders and fired on demonstrators who dared protest. They defined us as "Arab" when they set aside the results of elections and forced the appointment of their chosen prime minister.

"Arabs" meant people with whom you made treaties that you did not have to honor, arabs being by definition people of a lesser humanity and there being no need to honor treaties with people of lesser humanity. It meant people whose lands you could carve up and apportion as you wished, because they were of a lesser humanity. It meant people whose democracies you could obstruct at will, because you did not have to behave justly toward people of a lesser humanity. And what could mere arabs, anyway, know of democracy and democratic process?

Until now, all who had come to this land of Egypt—Greeks, Romans, Arabs, Turks—had known that they were coming to a place of civilization. All, until now, had come knowing that they had as much to learn here as to teach, as much to take, in terms of knowledge and ways of understanding and of living, as to give. That, until now, was how it had been.

The Europeans began writing their meaning of the word "arab" freely and indiscriminately all over the Middle East from about 1918 on, when the region as a whole fell into their hands. Prior to this, during their rule in Egypt, that meaning of the word had occasionally surfaced—at Dinshwai, for instance—but it had not been the dominant, consistent hallmark of their conduct.

And so in those years they scribbled their meaning of "arab" all over the landscape, in their acts and in the lines they drew on maps, tracing out their meaning in a script at once cryptic and universal: as cryptic and universal as the mark of a snake or the trail of deer on a blank page of snow.

And in time, quite soon, their meaning of the word "arab" would enter our meaning of it, too. Not etymologically, in the way that dictionaries trace meanings through transformations from word to word to word. No. It entered it corrosively, changing it from within, as if the European meaning were a kind of virus eating up the inside of the word "Arab," replacing it with itself—leaving it unchanged on the outside. Think of what it did to the words "African," "Africa": somehow, somehow, loading those words in the negative.

The European meaning of "arab," then, hollowed out our word, replacing it entirely with itself. Except that now ours is their meaning of the word "arab" in reverse. Like "black" and "Black," as in "Black is beautiful."

It is this sense of "arab," the European sense, with its cargo of negativities, that I, living in the West, so often encounter and feel myself trapped in. This is the meaning of "arab," still very much alive, still very much around, that prompted me, for instance, to quickly hide my Arabic newspaper in my shopping bag so that people would not know I was Arab—and so react to me, possibly, in some bigoted fashion, as people all too commonly do when they discover I am Arab. Like the man—more extreme than usual—who spat at me on the bus in Cambridge when I was a student: smiling at first, asking me if I was Israeli, and then, leaning toward me, seeing that the medallion I wore was after all Arabic, spitting right at me. And it is the meaning of "arab" that is there in my students' understanding when, as they grow more at ease with me, they disarmingly reveal that they would never have thought of calling me an Arab until I had called myself one, because, until then, they had thought the word was an insult. And it is there in the countless microaggressions (as the noted author and legal scholar Patricia Williams calls them) that ordinarily and daily are part of the fabric of living for those of us in the West who belong to a "race" charged, in this culture, in the negative.

And it is there in the meanings threading Western books and films and newspapers and so on. I, like many I know who are Arab, never go to a film in which I know that Arabs or Muslims figure. Naturally—why would I want to subject myself to the lies and racism that all too often are part of such things? This goes, too, for popular books on Arabs—their very popularity is usually an index of the fact that they are filled with bigotries and dehumanizations masquerading as truth.

⌁

But it would be another generation, not my parents' generation, not the generation who had grown up admiring European civilization, who would come to see clearly and to decipher for themselves what it was that the Europeans had scrawled across the landscape.

Nasser, born in 1917 and coming to consciousness, then, entirely after the watershed year of 1918, was perhaps among the first to figure out (for he was, whatever his flaws, an astute man) the meaning of what they had traced there—and to respond to it by crystallizing the identity "arab" into its obverse, "Arab," although even he, as I discovered to my surprise, fully grasped that he was Arab only a few years before I got slapped for not knowing that I was Arab. For Nasser seems to have understood that he was Arab precisely by intently studying the marks and runes the imperialists had made upon the landscape. Reflecting himself on when it was exactly that he understood that he was Arab, he singles out the study of the recent history of the region, and above all (he repeatedly returns to this) the history of Palestine, as critical to his understanding of himself as an Arab. He wrote in his *Philosophy of the Revolution*: "As far as I am concerned I remember the first elements of Arab consciousness began to filter into my mind as a student in secondary school, when I went out with my fellow schoolboys . . . every year as a protest against the Balfour Declaration whereby England gave the Jews a national home usurped unjustly from its legal owners. When I asked myself at the time," Nasser goes on, "why I left my school so enthusiastically and why I was angry for this land which I never saw I could not find an answer except the echoes of sentiment." Gradually "a form of comprehension" began when he studied "the Palestine campaigns and the history of the region in general" in military college, and finally that comprehension crystallized "when the Palestine crisis loomed on the horizon."

"When I asked myself . . . why I was so angry." Anger, as Nasser's own choice of words makes clear, was the key emotion in the early formation of his nascent identity as an Arab.

Spring is here.

The crocuses are out on the Backs. Rivulets of blue, all along the pathways, vividest, vividest blue, and gashes and splashes of it on the verges and under the trees.

Why then, walking through this, did I suddenly feel this sense of loss—measureless, measureless loss—sweep through me?

And so that, O my daughter, is what happened. That, in those years, is what happened to us.

$\mathcal{F}$ROM $\mathcal{A}$BU $\mathcal{D}$HABI TO $\mathcal{A}$MERICA

Recently I was asked, "What country are you from?" I said Egypt, and the man said, "Do you consider Egypt to be in Africa?" So I found Egypt being uprooted from Africa too, after it had ceased to be part of the Arab world. Now I no longer know the continent in which Egypt can be found, nor do I know if I am Arab, or African . . .

Nawal El Saadawi, Egyptian feminist

THE UNITED ARAB EMIRATES, a small country of spectacular deserts, mountains, and oases on the shallow, vivid blue Persian Gulf, was, at the time that I arrived, undergoing the most momentous transformation of its history. A few years earlier Zayed, the sheikh of Abu Dhabi, had offered to use his oil wealth to finance education, housing, and medical treatment for all the people of the region, including in neighboring emirates, which now united under his titular leadership. And thus the people of the region, who were principally a Bedu, nomadic people, were in the process of being settled and the country as a whole was being catapulted almost instantaneously into modernity.

To provide its people with these new amenities, the country had had to look to other countries for skilled personnel, and they looked above all to other Arab countries. When I got there the foreign population of non-local Arabs, consisting of Egyptians and Palestinians but also of Syrians, Jordanians, and others, outnumbered the local Bedu population by six to one. These other Arabs were the doctors and nurses, the architects and teachers and headmasters and headmistresses. The need to house this vast and, as it were, invading population of foreign Arabs, as well as to house the local people, cities, and in particular Abu Dhabi, had arisen almost overnight out of the sands. Ten years earlier there had been no constructed building in Abu Dhabi, which was now the capital, only tents and reed huts; no building other than the whitewashed fortress that stood now in the middle of a city of towering high-rises.

And Abu Dhabi did somehow have the air of a place conjured up overnight out of the sands. Silhouettes of cranes stood against the horizon whichever direction one looked, two or three buildings going up at once alongside each other. Nearby would be other new-looking buildings and ones alongside them that were, at one and the same moment, both new-looking and derelict eyesores. Blocks had gone up too fast and were poorly built. Many buildings were habitable for just two or three years and then had to be abandoned. There was one such apartment block that I passed in my afternoon walks along the corniche: a grand blue-and-white tower block standing like a ship with a commanding view of the sea, gleamingly new—and derelict. I would hear the sea wind that always blew here, whistling and moaning through its gaping, darkening windows and doors, whining and whistling and tugging and fidgeting at it, as if to pick it apart.

I was often conscious in Abu Dhabi of the foreignness of all this—modern buildings, higgledy-piggledy city, construction cranes, new and derelict buildings, and also the invasion of other Arabs and their cultures smothering and overwhelming the local Bedu culture —all in the name of modernity and education. It often seemed like something—dream, nightmare—conjured up just yesterday out of the sands and that surely like a dream would any moment pass away. Left to the workings of nature, to the deft, steady pickings and fidgetings of desert, sea, wind, all of this surely, I'd find myself thinking, would quickly disappear and the old desert simplicity once more be restored. It was not an unpleasing thought.

In all of Abu Dhabi there was only one place that had its own intrinsic loveliness: the old whitewashed fortress built, with its ancient, studded wood door, in the local style, beside it a cluster of sheltering palms and a small thicket of vivid, yellow-flowering shrubs.

And so I sensed even then that I was witnessing loss: the vanishing of Bedu culture, its banishment to the edges of life, its smothering by a supposedly superior culture bringing, supposedly, "education." I sensed this but I didn't quite understand or trust what I was sensing. After all, wasn't all this—education, modernity, improvement—a necessary and incontrovertible good? I don't know the answer even now. But I do believe that I was right in my feeling that I was witnessing the imposition of a profoundly different and in many ways inferior culture. In coming to this understanding I would find myself suddenly also understanding one more piece in that central enigma in my own life of Arabness, identity, language, culture. My understanding of the meaning of mother tongue and mother culture in my own life would, as I reflected on Abu Dhabi, be forever changed.

I was placed, as soon as I arrived in the country, on a committee whose task it was to oversee the development and reform of education throughout the Emirates. In the preceding few years schools had opened fast and without much planning, and we were required now to revise and rationalize the curricula and plan the future of education. My fellow committee members were all Egyptians and Palestinians. There were no locals on the committee, although we reported as a committee to the minister of education, who was a local. This arrangement was typical. Advisers and advisory committees were made up of foreign Arabs, and the people to whom they reported and who held the highest posts were locals. The latter were drawn from among those few who had had a formal education—and there was only a small handful in the country—and from among the sons of important families.

All the other members of the committee were men. In those days there were no more than three or four people in the entire country with Ph.D.'s, and I was one of them. It was this that had made it possible to appoint me, a woman, to this high-level committee.

We began our work by polling the locals about how they wanted to see education developed. Meanwhile we all also visited schools, observed classes, and interviewed teachers and students. In my case I also began to meet with local women to hear directly from them how they felt about women's education. Of course I was the only member of the committee who could do this, since local Bedu society was strictly segregated and local women did not meet with men who were not relatives.

One of the first women I interviewed was Mariam, from one of the ruling families of the Emirates. I sat waiting for her in the reception room at the Women's Center with my companion, Gameela, an Egyptian who had been in the Gulf for several years and had been assigned to be my interpreter, for to begin with, Gulf Arabic was scarcely intelligible to me. In the corner sat a heavy woman completely hidden in a black ʿabaya, (the Gulf word for *milayya*). We both assumed that this was some simple woman waiting, like us, to meet with Mariam, but she turned out to be Mariam herself. I went through the questionnaire, asking her about women and education. She was probably in her fifties and was nonliterate.

Of course, she said, women should have the right to education up to the highest levels and of course they should be able to pursue whatever profession they wished.

What about—I asked, going on to the next item on the questionnaire—women's role in Islam and the requirements of Islam?

Who had founded Islam, Mariam instantly retorted, was it a man or a woman?

Startled, my companion, who was dressed in the Egyptian-style robes and head veil of strict piety, murmured, "The Prophet Muhammad, peace and mercy be upon him!"

"Exactly!" said Mariam. "And whose side d'you think he was on?"

Mariam was engaged right then, she told us, in an argument with Fatima, the principal wife of Zayed, the ruler, and with other women, as to what should be the emblem of women's centers in the Emirates. A gazelle had been proposed, partly to honor Zayed, whose emirate, Abu Dhabi, meant "father of [place of] the gazelle." Mariam wanted it to be the face of an unveiled woman with some sign indicating that she was a doctor or engineer. A gazelle sounded like a nice idea but in effect, she said, what it was really doing was insidiously associating women with animals and nonhuman creatures, and that was a dangerous thing to do.

Mariam was among the most remarkable and forthright of the women I would meet but all, like her, were firm and passionate about the importance of education for women, and many had, though in different ways, those same qualities of strength, directness, clarity, and a secure confidence in their own vision. Moza, for example, a cousin of the ruler: in her late twenties and too old to have benefited from the country's educational revolution, she attended literacy classes and would continue to attend to within days of giving birth. She had herself founded and endowed the Women's Adult Education Center where she took the classes. A woman of enormous wealth in her own right, she wanted other women who craved education to be able to pursue it. Women's centers offering literacy classes (and child care for the women taking the classes) existed throughout the Emirates, many of them funded by local notable women.

Those qualities of resolve, spiritedness, and passion were there too in the new generation. Hissa, for example, who was a youngster of fifteen when I met her, had been removed from school and married off against her will when she was twelve—and had then appealed her case to the president, through his wife Sheikha Fatima. Islam gave her the right, she'd insisted, not to be married without her consent and the right to education, and she demanded both. She won. She intended, she told me as we strolled in the school yard, with its white colonnades and splashes of bougainvillea, to become a petroleum engineer. Hissa's story was unusual, but the schools were full of young women as spirited as she who had every intention of going on to become engineers, architects, scientists. Few wanted to major in literature and the humanities, the subjects that in other countries girls are culturally steered toward. Here it seems they were steered by their culture in quite another direction.

Soon it became ordinary for me to be in the company of these extraordinary women, to observe the clarity and forthrightness with which they expressed their opinions and went about their lives, and also the sense of humor and laughter that they frequently brought to their gatherings and to their perceptions of their situation. Only a handful of local women had had formal education. Like the local men, they held responsible positions, though less public and powerful ones, as headmistresses, say, or regional educational directors. It became ordinary too, then, to wait in an office or reception room and observe one of these younger formally educated women arrive, wrapped in the black ʿabaya. Once in the privacy of an all-women's space, she would let it drop or cast it off altogether to reveal an elegant pantsuit.

Naturally it was soon quite obvious to me that, for whatever reason, the local culture bred people who were intellectually strong and unafraid, including confident, clear-minded, utterly tenacious women who needed no instruction from anyone in the qualities of strength, clarity, vision, understanding, imagination.

❧

As the responses to our questionnaire began to come in, it quickly became evident that it was not only the women here who staunchly supported women's education. Overwhelmingly the local men, too, were in favor of equal education for women. They believed that women should be able to qualify for any profession. Whatever either sex felt about segregation and about women's pursuing professional lives within a segregated context, they clearly did not want to see women held back intellectually or prevented from pursuing the professions they wished.

These views, though, I soon discovered, were not echoed on the committee. Dr. Haydar, the chair of the committee, instructed us, as we reviewed the responses and prepared to reformulate the country's educational goals, to set aside the local people's views regarding equal education for women. The majority of our respondents were uneducated people, he pointed out, and most in fact were illiterate. They had these nice hopes and wishes about equal education for women but their lack of education meant they didn't have the knowledge or capacity to foresee the consequences of policies in the way that we educated people could. That was why they had us here, to tell them of those consequences and to tell them how, rationally, to develop their society.

Haydar, a Lebanese who had studied in Egypt and America, was a complicated person. The notion of women's equality was clearly in some way deeply antithetical to him; a tone of sneering bitterness crept into his words whenever he spoke of it. Invariably his example of how things spun out of control and into destructive chaos when societies treated women as equal was America, where perhaps, I surmised, he had suffered some awful rejection—but who knows, perhaps not. In America, he said on one occasion, they had either given or were about to give women the right to serve in the army, including in positions in which they would have men serving under them.

"Can you imagine a pregnant woman," he said, making the gesture of a swollen belly before him, "giving orders to her soldiers!" He looked round at us, laughing a humorless, scandalized laugh. Laughter ensued from all around me. For some reason that moment has stuck with me.

If women had degrees in engineering or some such subject, he asked, would they be willing to be the servants of society? If we, the committee, did what the locals said they wanted, the entire basis of society, which rested on women's role in the family and, frankly, on their being willing to be the servants to men, would be destroyed. Had these people thought of such things? Of course not!

Our job was exactly to think of these things and to plan an educational future for the country that was consonant with the Islamic principles on which, as the national constitution declared, this society was based. He was himself, Haydar told us, an atheist. (I knew no one else in the Emirates who openly declared his atheism and this was, here, a courageous act.) His personal beliefs, however, were irrelevant, he said, it was simply his professional duty to see to it that we came up with an educational program that conformed to the principles to which the country declared itself committed, and Islamic principles were completely clear as to the role of women.

Haydar's comments met with nods and general approval from all around me. We should begin, Haydar then proposed, by cutting down on the math and science classes being offered in girls' schools and substituting, say, home economics.

Of course all this was appalling to me and the situation seemed hopeless—I was totally outnumbered. But there would be a satisfying resolution.

Brooding on all this and on the gray-faced men on the committee, who were so casually preparing to blight the hopes of the local women, and on the fact that these men were nonlocals from other Arab cultures who were now imposing the narrow, bigoted ideas of their own backgrounds on the locals, I decided to talk to Ibrahim, the director of education. He was a local and my immediate boss. He had been the person responsible for my being appointed to the committee.

Ibrahim, I knew, was strongly in favor of equal education for women. As a boy he had attended the only school available in the region before oil wealth, an English school funded by the British government. Then he had won a scholarship to England, where he earned a B.A.

He listened to what I had to say and then suggested that I tell Moza and the other local women what the committee was planning. (It had been he who had suggested in the first place that I should get to know the local women.) So I dropped in that evening at the Women's Center, and over a glass of tea I told Moza about the math and science classes. Within a week or two, we on the committee got a directive from above instructing us to drop this scheme. Thereafter I didn't much worry when Haydar came up with some similar idea. I'd listen and mildly demur or even at times appear to agree—and then just let one of the women know what was afoot. It always worked. I did, I confess, enjoy the bemused look on Haydar's face whenever he announced—as if despairing of these foolish, unpredictable locals— that he had got a call or a note from the minister telling him that the committee was not to do this or that.

I am sure now that in appointing me to that committee Ibrahim hoped that I would come to serve precisely the role that I did. I believe that I was in fact recruited to be an ally of Ibrahim's against the stifling attitudes that had inundated the Emirates from other Arab countries. It had been Ibrahim's mentor, Mr. Taylor, who had been responsible for hiring me. One cold day in England, settling down at the end of a long day's teaching to prepare the next day's classes, I'd fallen to worrying about my finances. My part-time job, which actually took up all my time, paid very meagerly. And so on an impulse I picked up that day's *Times*, where I'd noticed an ad for a job in the Emirates, and applied.

Mr. Taylor, the Emirates' educational representative in England, had responded at once, inviting me down to London. He was thrilled to have my application, he said quite openly. Their whole school system was suffocating, he told me, under the by-rote Arabic educational system that they had imported wholesale (along with teachers, teaching methods, syllabi) from other Arab countries, particularly Egypt. Now Ibrahim, a brilliant young man whom he had known all his life, had been appointed director of education and meant to change all this—and someone of my background could be of enormous help to him in this task. Mr. Taylor had been headmaster of the school that Ibrahim attended and had been in the Emirates several years before oil was discovered.

As director of education, Ibrahim had considerable power, but he was not a member of an important family and, as these things still counted, he had to use his wits to bring about the outcomes he wanted. His superior, the minister of education, who was from a prominent family and had a B.A. from Cairo, had the power to override his decisions and to accept the recommendations of our committee. He was much more ambivalent than Ibrahim on the question of equal education for women.

The divide on this question, as I gradually came to understand, was not at all a straightforward divide between women and men. While the nonlocal Arab men on the committee were opposed to equal education, the local men as a group were not. Ibrahim, educated in England, was in favor of it—but so also were others, among them the nonliterate and the barely literate, including Zayed, the president of the country and a nonliterate man, who had committed funding in equal measure to men's and women's education.

Among local men the divide was between men who were ambivalent about or even opposed to equal education for women—mostly men educated in the Arabic and primarily in the Egyptian educational system—and men who supported equal education. A small minority of the latter group had been educated in the English system; the rest were nonliterate or barely literate—in other words, they were men who belonged fully to the oral, living culture of the region.

At the time all that was clear to me was that there seemed to be something distinctly more oppressive toward women in the attitudes of non-local Arab men and that the Arabic, Egyptian-inspired educational system seemed to have a perceptibly negative effect intellectually. It seemed to close down the minds of people who'd been through it instead of opening them up—closing them down in all sorts of ways but particularly in regard to women.

What I was observing, I realize now, was the profound gulf between the oral culture of the region on the one hand and the Arabic culture of literacy on the other. Oral cultures here in the Gulf, as indeed everywhere else, are the creations of living communities of men and women and represent the ongoing interactions of these communities with their heritage of beliefs, outlook, circumstances and so on. But the Arabic culture of literacy, a culture whose language nobody, no living community, ordinarily speaks, clearly was not the product, as oral cultures are, of people living their lives and creatively and continuously interacting with their environment and heritage. Ngũgĩ wa Thiong'o, the Kenyan writer who has pondered with great depth and imagination this question of the relation between mother tongue and culture and the written language, describes his mother tongue as the language that people used as they worked in the fields, the language that they used to tell stories in the evenings around the fireside. It was a language alive therefore with "the words and images and with the inflection of the voices" of the people who made up his community, and a language whose words had "a suggestive power well beyond the immediate and lexical meanings. Our appreciation of the suggestive magical power of language was reinforced by the games we played with words through riddles, proverbs, transpositions of syllables, or through nonsensical but musically arranged words. So we learned the music of our language on top of the content. The language, through images and symbols, gave us a view of the world."

All of Ngũgĩ's words apply to Gulf Arabic and Egyptian Arabic and to all the varieties of vernacular Arabic, none of which at the moment has a written form. But Ngũgĩ's words do not apply to standard Arabic, the only written form of Arabic that there is. Nobody in the world—except maybe academics and textbook writers—sits around the fireside telling stories in standard Arabic, no one working in a field anywhere in the Arab world speaks that language, and no children anywhere play word games and tell riddles and proverbs in standard Arabic.

But if this language and its culture are not the language and culture of a living community, whose culture is it that is being disseminated through the culture of literacy that Arab governments are zealously imposing on their populations through schools and universities throughout the Arab world? Rooted in no particular place and in no living culture, from whom does this culture emanate and whose values do its texts embody? Presumably they are the values and worldviews of government bureaucrats and textbook writers and of the literate elites of today, along with those of the Arabic textual heritage through the ages on which textbooks and the contemporary culture of literacy continue to draw. The Arabic literary heritage, like the medieval Islamic heritage that I discussed in chapter 5, was produced over the centuries primarily by men and, by and large, by middle-class men who lived in deeply misogynist societies. Presumably it is their perspective, recycled today in textbooks and continuing to feed into the Arabic culture of literacy, that imparts to that culture its distinctly negative flavor in relation to women. But here I am only speculating. I have not researched the sources, origins, and creators of this Arabic culture of literacy.

Whatever its sources and whoever its creators, it is, as I observed it, a sterile and oppressive culture. I remember my uneasy feeling in Abu Dhabi, as I watched Egyptians and Palestinians trained in this prevailing culture of literacy inculcate it in their young charges, that I was witnessing the tragic imposition of a sterile, inferior bureaucratic culture on young minds and the gradual erasure of their own vital and vibrant and much richer and more humane local Bedu culture. And this was being done in the name of education.

Ironically enough, the steady spread and imposition of this culture of literacy throughout the Arab world seems to represent a kind of linguistic and cultural imperialism—a linguistic, cultural, and also a class imperialism that is being conducted in the name of education and of Arab unity and of the oneness of the Arab nation. Steadily throughout the Arab world, as this Arab culture of literacy marches inexorably onward, local cultures continue to be erased and their linguistic and cultural creativity condemned to permanent, unwritten silence. And we are supposed to applaud this, not protest it as we would if it were any other form of imperialism or political domination. This variety of domination goes by the name of "nationalism," and we are supposed to support it.

As I came to understand all this, another piece of the puzzle making up my own history suddenly fell into place. For I realized that, just as Gulf Arabic and Gulf culture were different from standard Arabic and the Arab culture of literacy, so also were the language and culture in which I grew up, Cairene Egyptian culture and language. For me too, then, this language of standard Arabic was not my mother tongue and the values purveyed by the Arabic texts that we read were not those of my mother culture. The characteristic, defining flavor of that culture, my native Cairene culture, was perhaps above all that it so richly and easily blended into its own unique Cairo brew a wealth of traditions and provenances and ways and histories and memories: Islam, Christianity, Judaism, Morocco, Istanbul, Alexandria, a village in Croatia.

In all of Egypt there was no school that I could have attended where I could have read books and learned to write in my mother tongue, the language that we spoke at home, that everybody in Cairo spoke, and that I was completely fluent in, its words rich for me with the inflections and music of the voices that I loved and with the images and riddles and syllables of our games. There is no linguistic reason why Egyptian Arabic could not be a written language, only political reasons. The situation would be parallel to Italians or French people, say, finding themselves unable to write in Italian or French and being compelled instead to write only in Latin.

Whatever school my parents sent me to, Arabic or English, I would have found myself imbibing a culture and studying a language and learning attitudes that were different from those of the world in which I lived at home in Cairo and Alexandria. The choice either way entailed alienation from my home culture and home language and from the language and oral culture of other Cairenes. In short, the choice was always only a choice between colonialism and colonialism, or at any rate between domination and domination.

This was, for me, a liberatory understanding. Surely now I would be able to cast off completely the guilt laid on me by the Nasser-Nabih combination for not being more fluent in standard Arabic. It also enabled me to understand something that had previously seemed completely illogical. I had always felt that English was somehow closer and more kin to Egyptian Arabic than was standard Arabic. Until now this had seemed to me to be a nonsensical, unreasonable feeling. Now I realized that in fact English *felt* more like Egyptian Arabic because it *was* more like it: both are living languages and both have that quickness and pliancy and vitality that living spoken languages have and that the written Arabic of our day does not. I have yet to hear or read any piece of Arabic poetry or prose by a modern writer that, however gorgeous and delicate and poetic and moving, is not also stilted and artificial. There is a very high price to pay for having a written language that is only a language of literature and that has only a distant, attenuated connection to the living language.

I am not, I should say, implicitly arguing that we should do away with or stop teaching standard Arabic, for of course I recognize its usefulness as a lingua franca. And I know too how complicated the issue is, among other reasons because Classical Arabic (albeit different again from Standard Arabic) is the language of the Quran, and I know that many major writers of literary Arabic—including Naguib Mahfouz—consider literary Arabic, the Arabic of the educated classes, to be the only acceptable vehicle for literature. So I am certainly not arguing against our continuing to teach, study and learn literary Arabic. I am, however, making a plea for a recognition of the enormous linguistic and cultural diversity that makes up the Arab world. And I am arguing for our developing a creative approach that, instead of silencing and erasing the tremendous wealth that this diversity represents, would foster it and foster the development, on at least an equal footing with standard Arabic, of written forms of Moroccan, Gulf, Egyptian, Iraqi, Palestinian, and other Arabics, and also of the non-Arabic living languages of the region, such as Nubian and Berber. European nationalisms have devastated their own local languages—Welsh, Scots, Breton—languages now struggling to make a comeback. Let us avoid that history. Let us find a way to celebrate, and rejoice in, this wealth and diversity that is ours, instead of setting out to suppress it.

Public space in the Emirates was overwhelmingly men's space and one felt in it—I felt—like an intruder. This was particularly true in al-Ain, the town to which I now moved to take up an appointment at the newly opened university. I remember looking out longingly in the afternoons onto the empty desert avenue on which my bungalow stood, weighing whether I could set off on a long walk out here. Occasionally I saw a male figure trudging along this road, but never a woman alone. If I walked along in plain sight of passing cars (not that there were that many; it would have felt safer had it been a busy road), would this be construed as a flouting of local custom? Might it be interpreted, say, by someone speeding by in a car as a provocation? And what would I wear? I would stand out too distinctively in this landscape. My normal dress here was conservative Western-style clothing—no head veil, no long gown. That was how I went to work. More casually I wore pants—taking care that they were on the loose, baggy side—and long-sleeved blouses. It felt too risky, too exposed to walk along that road, and so I never did, instead taking my walks in the oasis behind my bungalow. There, for one thing, I very rarely encountered men, except for old men. I'd come across young women there sometimes, tending to the land or bathing with their children in the spring reserved for women, but never young men. Presumably they had left behind this traditional way of life for the opportunities of the city. In the oasis, moreover, with its footpaths winding among the fruit groves, I did not feel exposed to people passing in cars.

Sometimes, too, I would take my walks in the zoo. Zayed, the country's president, a passionate falconer, was passionate also about the preservation of the wildlife of the region—oryx, gazelle—and an avid animal enthusiast generally. And so al-Ain, his native town, had a fine zoo. For some reason I found it enormously comforting to stroll there, hearing the animal sounds, stopping to observe giraffe, chimpanzees, zebra—zebra, those creatures whose magicalness Jahangir captures so perfectly. "It is as if the painter of fate," he writes, "with a strange brush, had left it on the page of the world." Like Rumi, Jahangir, a Mogul king, wrote in Persian.

This was a time of great solitude. I had social acquaintances, of course, but no intimate friends in al-Ain. When I was not teaching, attending meetings, or going to some school or college event, I spent most of my time alone. Living in that bungalow perched on the edge of the desert, I had, whichever way I turned, the beauty of al-Ain's setting always before me. To the west were the ribbed, windswept dunes of the ancient Arabian Desert, mesmerizingly perfect in their formations. At sunset their rose-beige crests and hollows (in which nestled just one solitary thorn tree) turned a startling fiery red. To the south was the rock face of the great mountain Gabal Akhdar, Green Mountain. And in the distance below the mountain were lush oases. From my back window I had a view of the tops of palm trees in the sunken oasis behind my house from which came, every morning and evening, a loud burst of birdsong.

And yet in some ways too, ways that were partly imaginative and partly real, I felt connected with not just one community but two.

And both enriched my solitude and made this a time, indeed, not of loneliness but of solitude.

The immediate and real community with which I was connected was that of the local women. And it was a community that, just as Girton's had been, was at once new and unfamiliar but also, in its underlying ways and rhythms, deeply familiar. Outwardly some of these ways were extremely novel, enough for me to be riveted by it all, as when I visited Fatima, the president's principal wife, for the first time and observed how things were at her palace. Most striking of all was the informality of the gathering and the feeling that social rank wasn't of much consequence. The British ambassador's wife and Fatima's chauffeur, a young Egyptian woman in a pantsuit, were equally part of the company, sitting about on the sofas around the room and apparently conversing on equal footing. Even the coffee servers, standing by ready to top up our cups, joined—not timidly but vehemently and forthrightly—in the general talk whenever they felt moved to.

Fatima and other prominent local women were very much part of the ordinary community of women in this small country where people like them were the patrons of the women's schools and the women's college (which was part of the university)—and they were often the chief guests at school and college celebrations. On these occasions the students often presented plays they had written. They would strut about on stage with painted mustaches and the white robes of men and utter vacuous and hilarious pomposities that would make the audience, consisting entirely of women and girls (and little boys) in this segregated society, dissolve in laughter, guffawing and applauding. Informality reigned here, too. The chief guests, Fatima and her entourage, say, would often arrive late, the festivities of course awaiting them, and once the dances, prize awards, plays, and musical performances began, the atmosphere would continue to be informal, people chatting, nobody sitting rigidly attentive, children running to the front of the hall and joining in the dancing, nobody telling them to sit still.

And this, I realize now, was familiar space. Like Grandmother's corner room at Zatoun, like the balcony at Alexandria, this was space not at the center but on the margins of society, a place with its own perspective, its own rather skeptical, often amused view of all the grand, important, and self-important people who occupied center space. My aunts Aisha and Nazli and Farida, too, had leaped to seemingly reverent attention in Grandfather's presence—and then, when he was gone, had done, in Grandmother's room, wonderful, hilarious imitations and send-ups of his imperious ways. (Laughter, that refuge and consolation of the powerless. Vehicle of scathing and skeptical critiques sometimes, but slipped in simply as entirely harmless humor.) This space was space in which, at some fundamental level and perhaps without my even recognizing it, I felt deeply at home.

It was also a place of respite and sanctuary that, I am sure, must have helped sustain me when I had to venture once more into what was the very visibly and palpably masculine space of the public world. Overwhelmingly the people in the street were men. Passing a mosque on a Friday at the end of prayers, one saw men, only men, flowing out from its doors. Even in the market one saw mostly men, although in al-Ain, a place less totally modern than Abu Dhabi, a place where the older ways of living were still present in the surrounding oases and mountains, there was a small women's market on the outskirts of town. Local women brought their produce there to sell, sitting masked on the ground beside baskets of dried peppers or spices, the edges of the brilliant silver-edged pantaloons that they wore (magenta, orange, green) just showing under their outer garments.

But simply stepping out into the street then, one became instantaneously aware of the masculine domination that defined this society and of the restrictions that hemmed in women's lives in a way that I, at any rate, had not observed and experienced as so blatant a fact either in England or in Egypt. I can understand, having had that experience, why Western women coming to Egypt, say, in the nineteenth century, were convinced that the oppression of women there was so much worse than in their own countries—when it was not necessarily or uniformly so at all—simply because dress and other visual signals made the gender division of society so obvious. This was how I, too, reacted in the Gulf. For the moment one stepped into the street, there it was, literally in black and white. The local men wore white and the women black. And in this often unimaginably hot, unimaginably humid climate, men wore light airy robes and women went about masked and in layers of clothes, muffled also in an outer layer of heavy black.

My connection with the second community that buoyed and sustained me was entirely imaginary. In my first months working with the local women and learning from them, learning from their attitudes and perspectives and from their clear-sightedness and determination, I had begun to have my consciousness raised as a feminist. When I returned to Cambridge for the summer vacation, I searched the bookstores for feminist books. I brought back with me a good number of such recently published books and in my free time immersed myself in them. They were all, at least all those that I found exciting and illuminating, Americans—Kate Millett, Elaine Showalter, Patricia Spacks, Adrienne Rich, and Mary Daly, among others. Academic things, as I read on, no longer seemed, as they did by the end of my graduate years in Cambridge, distant and irrelevant and merely "academic." Things began to fall into place. I began to see the point of theory. And I began to learn from these writers what I had begun to learn already from the women of Abu Dhabi, women like Mariam: that it was from here, from this vantage point on the margins, that I could begin to examine, analyze, and think about the world of which I was part in a way that finally, for me, would begin to make sense.

Other moments from those days that have remained in my mind as marking, somehow, turning points:

I was coming out of the oasis after one of my walks, just as the sun was setting. Coming toward me, on the dune just ahead, was the figure of a woman carrying a huge bundle of firewood on her head. It was exactly that moment of translucent luminosity which, in that latitude, comes immediately after sunset, and for an instant her form, outlined against the sky, was caught up in that luminosity.

"Cursed be she, the bearer of firewood!" The words come involuntarily into my mind—words, as I remembered them, from the Quran. Just then, as we drew closer, she called out to me, "*Salam aleikum!*"—"Peace be with you!"—and then, unexpectedly, she smiled warmly, as if we were friends.

"*Aleikum a-salam!*" I responded. It is thus, I found myself thinking, that she enters the scripted world of Arabic, woman, bearer of firewood: she enters it cursed. It is thus that she is forever captured. In fact I had slightly misremembered the words. The verses curse first of all Abu Lahab, an enemy of the Prophet's, then his wife, the "carrier of firewood," an enemy, too. How exactly had it come about, I wondered, that these words, this curse—a curse in some sense attaching itself forever to woman, bearer of firewood—was judged to be part of the Quran, part of the sacred eternal word of God? I knew, of course, that Muhammad himself was nonliterate and that a complete final written version of the Quran did not exist during his lifetime or even for a good number of years afterwards. So who, then, had decided which words exactly, which utterances of the Prophet, were to be regarded as part of the Quran, part of the eternal sacred word of God, and which not? Who had had the power to make these decisions, and how exactly had they made them?

Another moment. I was in a lecture hall at the university, at a public lecture on women in early Islam. It was a timely moment for such a lecture. Just across the Gulf, the Iranian revolution was in full flood and cresting, it seemed, to success. Iran, like Iraq, was a powerful, frightening neighbor, always apparently harboring predatory desires for the small, vulnerable states along the Gulf with their tremendous oil wealth, and it was a country, therefore, always cautiously to be watched. The possibility of the Islamic revolution's success in Iran triggered anxiety in the Emirates and a move toward conservatism with regard to women—toward, for example, the imposition of veiling on nonlocal women, women like myself. Above all, it seemed, the Emirates feared that if they did not move in that direction Iran might use local noncompliance with this and similar "Islamic" practices as an excuse to invade the country.

The lecture was being delivered by one of the professors in the

Islamic studies department, an Iraqi who, as I happened to know, had recently divorced his wife and exercised his right in Islamic law to take custody of his young children, even though it meant that his wife, who had no option now but to return to Iraq, would hardly ever see them. She, as I knew, had been utterly distraught. The audience consisted mainly of men, but in the back of the hall were some young college women, two or three of them my students. I sat with them. It was not proper for us to sit anywhere except at the back.

When the speaker drew his lecture to a close—he was both an eloquent and a handsome man—one of the young women rose and challenged his reading of history. She challenged it on two grounds. For one thing, she said, he was giving the Sunni perspective as opposed to the Shi'a (Sunni and Shi'a are the two main branches of Islam—somewhat like, but also not like, the Catholic-Protestant divide). Consequently the very same women whom he had chosen to praise could be represented negatively, and vice versa. For another thing, he had chosen to focus on women whose virtues were as good wives and mothers, whereas he had left out women who were great leaders, great warriors. The lecturer's response, whatever it was, was unmemorable.

We exited—into the public world, the world where the presence and imposition of a purely masculine order on everything is so profoundly in evidence. The women students took the college bus back to the women's college, which, like Girton and for the same reasons as Girton, was located on the very outskirts of town and well into the desert. And I drove off first to the market to pick up some provisions and then home. The mosque, as I drove past, was letting out a knot of men.

Somewhere in that time I began to form the idea of looking into all this, this history of Muslim women, and of sifting through the material to understand what our history had been and what our situation was and what future we could look to as Muslim women. And somewhere in that time I began to form the project of going to America. In America I would be able to read and research freely and to acquire the tools and methods of research that women there were developing and using so brilliantly. Because of the Iranian revolution, I was, in any case, thinking that I could not stay in the Gulf much longer. America rather than England was the natural place now for me to think of, for all three of my siblings had settled there. All three had found that in Europe (England, Switzerland, and Germany had been their bases) they simply could not advance in their professions beyond a certain point. In America, they told me, things were different. Even though people had their prejudices, if you had the ability and the qualifications you could move forward in America. And I had been carefully putting aside part of my salary so that I would be able to finance such a move.

It was no easy transition, the transition to America and to women's studies.

First of all, live American feminism was not anything like what I had imagined. Reading its thoughtful texts in the quiet of the desert, I had, I suppose, formed a notion of feminism as tranquil, lucid, meditative—whereas, of course, the living feminism I encountered once on these shores was anything but a lucid, tranquil, meditative affair. Militant, vital, tempestuous, passionate, visionary, turbulent— any or all of these might be more apt. In the gatherings of feminists —at the various conferences, meetings, and public lectures that I now single-mindedly threw myself into attending—there was a kind of raw, exhilarating energy and a sense, intellectually, of freewheeling anarchy. Almost as if people felt themselves caught up in some holy purifying fire that was burning away the dross and obscurities from their minds, freeing them to dream dreams and see visions and to gather themselves up and prepare to unmake and remake the world, remake it as it had never been made before.

And all this *was* tremendously exhilarating and exciting. But along with exhilaration came shock. For I naturally made a point at these conferences of attending, and often participating in, sessions and panels on Muslim women. Not that these were common. The women's studies conferences I attended when I first came in 1980—I remember one at Barnard, and another in Bloomington, Indiana—focused primarily on white women and were overwhelmingly attended by white women. But such sessions on Muslim women as there were left me nearly speechless and certainly in shock at the combination of hostility and sheer ignorance that the Muslim panelists, myself included, almost invariably encountered. We could not pursue the investigation of our heritage, traditions, religion in the way that white women were investigating and rethinking theirs. Whatever aspect of our history or religion each of us had been trying to reflect on, we would be besieged, at the end of our presentations, with furious questions and declarations openly dismissive of Islam. People quite commonly did not even seem to know that there was some connection between the patriarchal vision to be found in Islam and that in Judaism and Christianity. Regularly we would be asked belligerently, "Well, what about the veil" or "What about clitoridectomy?" when none of us had mentioned either subject for the simple reason that it was completely irrelevant to the topics of our papers. The implication was that, in trying to examine and rethink our traditions rather than dismissing them out of hand, we were implicitly defending whatever our audience considered to be indefensible. And the further implication and presumption was that, whereas they—white women, Christian women, Jewish women—could rethink their heritage and religions and traditions, we had to abandon ours because they were just intrinsically, essentially, and irredeemably misogynist and patriarchal in a way that theirs (apparently) were not. In contrast to their situation, our salvation entailed not arguing with and working to change our traditions but giving up our cultures, religions, and traditions and adopting theirs.

And so the first thing I wrote after my arrival and within months of being in America was an article addressing the extraordinary barrage of hostility and ignorance with which I found myself besieged as I moved among this community of women. They were women who were engaged in radically rejecting, contesting, and rethinking their own traditions and heritage and the ingrained prejudices against women that formed part of that heritage but who turned on me a gaze completely structured and hidebound by that heritage; in their attitudes and beliefs about Islam and women in Islam, they plainly revealed their unquestioning faith in and acceptance of the prejudiced, hostile, and often ridiculous notions that their heritage had constructed about Islam and its women. I had come wanting to read and think and write about Muslim women, but it was this that commanded my attention as the subject that I desperately had to address. The first piece I wrote, "Western Ethnocentrism and Perceptions of the Harem," still rings for me with the shocked and furious tones of that initial encounter.

My first year in America, 1979, was also the year of the Iran hostage crisis, and I am sure now that the hostility toward Islam by which I felt myself besieged was more pronounced than usual because of that situation. But as I would learn soon enough, the task of addressing racism for feminists of color in the West is, and has to be, an ongoing and central part of the work and the thinking that we ordinarily do, no less so than the work of addressing male dominance. And so my first experience of American feminism was a kind of initiation and baptism by fire into what has indeed been an ongoing part of my thought and work ever since. Back then, though, it was still early in our understanding of the racist gaze the white feminist movement turned on women of other cultures and races. Audre Lorde, at a conference in 1976 (in a presentation much-anthologized since), was among the first to identify, and speak out against, this strand in white feminist thought, and June Jordan, Bell Hooks, and others followed up with work on the subject.

Also making my initial experience of America a more arduous experience than it might otherwise have been was the fact that I took a job in women's studies. I had come intent on working in this field and had applied for an advertised position as a part-time lecturer at the University of Massachusetts at Amherst. Although the pay was low, I felt that a part-time job was the sensible way into the field, whose scholarly productions I'd been reading out in the desert but about which I had still an enormous amount to learn. A part-time job would give me the time, I thought, to do all the extra reading that I no doubt needed to do.

Of course I found that my part-time job, as is so often the case, was only technically part-time. In fact, preparing classes, teaching, and attending meetings took up every moment of my waking life. I have never worked so hard in my life as in my first couple of years in America. Of course, too, the fact that everything was new to me contributed to making those years so tough. Teaching in a new academic system in a new country must always entail demanding transitions, but I am sure that my having joined a women's studies program, particularly at that moment in the history of women's studies in America, rather than, say, taking a job in a more established department, created a whole set of unique hurdles and difficulties.

Women's studies programs in that era, including the program that I joined, had an embattled and precarious relationship with the university. There was sometimes open hostility from faculty members in other departments and, occasionally, condescension and a presumption that the women's studies faculty must be ignorant, undereducated fanatical women. For me, as someone coming from abroad who had not been part of the American feminist movement, there was one very particular difficulty that I had not anticipated when I imagined that, by working hard and reading widely, I could quickly master the ideas, theories, perspectives that I needed to be familiar with. I could *not* quickly master them through reading, for the simple reason that a lot of them had not yet found their way into print. The ideas that I heard passionately voiced and argued around me by faculty and also by students were part of a rich, vibrant, diverse, and internally contentious cargo of debates that had been generated by an intellectually vital social movement. This was what I had stepped into in joining women's studies—a living social movement of quite extraordinary but as yet mainly oral intellectual vitality, about to spill over and become a predominantly intellectual, academic, and theoretical force rather than, as it had in part been in its beginnings, an activist social movement. It was the ideas that people had developed in their encounters and meetings and exchanges in their involvement in this movement, and the continuing evolution of these ideas, that were providing the foundations of women's studies. I stepped, that is to say, too, into the stream of what was as yet a largely unwritten oral culture—the oral, living culture of the feminist movement, a culture to which there were as yet almost no guides, no maps, no books.

There were often passionate debates, both among my colleagues and in the feminist community more widely, between, say, Radical feminists and Marxist feminists, debates that could become quite furious. It was clear that there was a history here, a common, shared evolution, in the course of which particular positions, in relation to this or that issue, had been progressively defined and sometimes had become polarized. But to someone arriving from the Arab Gulf, what these positions and issues were and why they should generate such passion was, at first anyway, profoundly unfathomable. And there was nothing, or very little, in those days, that I could read that would enlighten me and make the issues, debates, and history accessible. Moreover, this culture and history that I had not been part of informed nearly everything in women's studies, not only intellectual issues but also ordinary routines and exchanges and conversations. It was this culture, for instance, that determined that all decisions were to be made by consensus and not by vote. It determined, too, the code of dress—as strict here, in its way, as in Abu Dhabi. For those were the days when whether you shaved your legs or wore a bra signaled where you stood on the internal feminist battlelines and/or your degree of feminist enlightenment. In Abu Dhabi it had been easy to ask about appropriate dress and the meaning of this or that style, but here not only were you supposed to just *know*, but supposedly there was no dress code and people here—as I was emphatically told when I ventured the question in my early innocent days—simply dressed exactly how they wished. And so there were many ways in which the women's studies culture in which I found myself was an unknown culture to me to which I had no key and maps. But, as with any other culture, after a period of intense immersion, my confusion naturally resolved into comprehension.

Another difficulty arising from my being in women's studies was one I shared with my colleagues. An essentially new field, women's studies as yet had no set syllabi, no texts, no solid, extensive body of scholarship to draw on. And so even devising courses and syllabi and putting them together from photocopies was a demanding task. Even the novels and stories by women that were already being used and that would soon be the staples of feminist courses in literature were not yet in readily accessible form or were just being published and reissued, in large part thanks to the feminist movement and the demand created by women's studies. And the kind of material that a few years later would begin to be available on feminist theory, on women of color in America, on women in Islam, and so on, was also not yet available. In short, women's studies was still in the process of being invented, created, and developed as a field. My colleagues as well as I, a newcomer, were still groping our way forward in this as yet unstudied, uncharted, and indeed uninvented territory, for the most part without textbooks, without established syllabi, without a body of scholarship raising the questions that needed to be raised, setting them out, analyzing them, complicating them.

We are now, of course, in quite another place.

And I am now at the end point of the story I set out to tell here.

For thereafter my life becomes part of other stories, American stories. It becomes part of the story of feminism in America, the story of women in America, the story of people of color in America, the story of Arabs in America, the story of Muslims in America, and part of the story of America itself and of American lives in a world of dissolving boundaries and vanishing borders.

There are more Muslims today in America, it is said, than Episcopalians. We did not have, on these shores, an auspicious beginning. I think of Bilalia Fula, buried here, after his years of slavery, with his prayer rug and his Quran. I think of Al-Hajj Omar ibn Said, brought to this country in shackles when he was thirty-seven, as he wrote in his autobiography—one of the first Muslim autobiographies written in America. I think of the countless others brought here in the same way, who held on in their minds as long as they could to the world they were from, passing on to children and grandchildren, however they might, their vanishing memories.

～

But this now is another time. We are on the point of a new beginning.

$\mathscr{C}$AIRO $\mathscr{M}$OMENTS

I WAS AT the Hilton, where my host, the American University of Cairo, had put me up. I was waiting for my old friend Hala to pick me up. Hala, now a distinguished economist, was taking me to stay with her for my remaining days in Cairo, in the apartment in Zamalek that she shared with her mother.

When she arrived we sat out for a while on the balcony over drinks, enjoying the spectacular views of the Nile and of the island of Zamalek just opposite. Beyond it, on the Nile's western bank, the city extended now almost to the pyramids. Most of Cairo—the heart of the modern city and Old Cairo—was behind us. But standing in a corner of the balcony and looking back, one could see just a little of the old city and, past it, the purple outline of the Mu'attam hills and the Citadel, with its famous pencil-thin minarets against the lilac sunset sky, a sky perceptibly more polluted now than when I lived here all those many years ago.

Cairo's traffic problems were enormous. (A city that in my day had a population of perhaps a million was now home to nearly ten million.) I abandoned any thought of nostalgic expeditions that, before arriving, I had thought I might make—to Ain Shams, for instance, even though house and garden were gone, or Zatoun, still there and still a school. Given Cairo's traffic, just getting there would have been a major undertaking. Having plunged at once into the business of preparing, revising, and delivering lectures, I in fact had little time for nostalgia or for comparing how things had been and how different it all was now—which was probably all to the good.

And, of course, it *was* quite different. Particularly striking to me was the prevalence among women of some form of Islamic dress—but all of it now modern Islamic dress. There were no *milayyas* to be seen in the streets, no simple way like that by which you could immediately tell class difference. As I knew, the veil no longer meant what it had in my day. The women wearing it were quite likely to be educated professional women, working women, upwardly mobile women. The veil did not connote for them, as it had for my grandmother, women's seclusion, invisibility, confinement to the home. Quite the contrary—it meant exactly the opposite: it was affirmation of their right to work and to be in the public world pursuing professional and working lives. Why? It would take a chapter or two to explain this, let alone the rest of the tremendous cultural transformation going on in Egypt.

Despite this enormous change—change that was visually very striking simply because people were dressed so differently now—and the many other ones just in the appearance of the city, with its highrise buildings and overpasses and various other features new to me, there was a feel to Cairo that harked back not to Nasser's days but to the pre-Nasser era. It was a sense of the enormous intellectual vitality and cultural richness of this city and a sense of an almost palpable vibrancy and ferment: this place that was (as it has been for millennia) a meeting place of so many histories, so many ways of thought, so many forms of belief. And this sense of the complexity and mental aliveness of the place was there despite the growing presence of fundamentalism and fundamentalism's deadly intent to curtail freedom of thought.

Everywhere I went I experienced this vibrancy. Almost everyone I met seemed passionately engaged in trying to understand this complicated moment of history and in analyzing all the different strands that went into making it and all its conceivable outcomes. And almost everyone was utterly committed to standing against the tide of fundamentalism and to fighting for and preserving their freedom to speak, to write, to think. Here, moreover, commitment to ideas and to the right to think and speak freely had an edge that it didn't necessarily have in other places. It could mean being willing literally to put your life on the line for your beliefs. At least one of the journalists I met, Galal Amin, who along with his intellectual acuity and courage also had a tremendous capacity to laugh, had had his life repeatedly threatened by fundamentalists simply for his being forthrightly critical of their positions. Of course, though, the community I had tapped into through the American University included some of Cairo's most lively and distinguished intellectuals. Still, the exhilarating intellectual vibrancy of almost every party and gathering (almost every time, I'd come away feeling the way one does after a particularly exhilarating conference) was so remarkable that I began to wonder whether there weren't perhaps some unintended benefits to having one's freedom of thought and speech threatened—in the way that hanging, as they say, wonderfully focuses the mind. Perhaps it not only focused the mind but made one prize and understand all the more acutely how important, how vital, indeed, to one's life and well-being it is to question and reflect on and openly share one's ideas.

Hala pointed out to me, as we sat in the fading light, where Embaba was. Embaba was reputedly the "hotbed" of Islamic fundamentalism. Municipal services to the district were appallingly poor. Rubbish was left to pile up and rot in the streets for months, water pipes broke and were not repaired for weeks. Police regularly conducted antifundamentalist raids there, arresting people nearly indiscriminately—a man might be arrested and left to languish in jail simply because he had a beard. These kinds of conditions and government behavior would drive almost any population crazy, cause almost anybody to turn violent. What was the government thinking of? Hala asked. What did it expect?

Clearly, nothing was simple.

She pointed out also the houseboat on the river where Naguib Mahfouz, the novelist, held his weekly open gatherings. The fundamentalists (I use the word "fundamentalist" in the way that it is commonly used, although there are enormous academic debates raging as to its appropriateness) had announced that they considered his work blasphemous and that they meant to kill him. Mahfouz had a well-known beaten path that he took daily and always at exactly the same time, walking from his house to the café he frequented and back. He was advised after this threat to change his routine but refused. He was not now, in his eighties, he said, going to change the habits of a lifetime and the routines whose rhythms were the rhythms of his writing life for the sake of these fanatical people. And then one morning, as he was making his punctual way along his route, he was attacked and stabbed—but fortunately survived.

It's impossible not to be affected by these incidents and threats, nationally and internationally. There is probably no writer of Muslim background who is engaged in seriously thinking and writing about anything touching on Islam who is not perennially conscious of this awful element that now makes up the world in which we live.

The next morning at Hala's, Nini Shaarawi called to say that she would be accompanying a friend the following day to visit the friend's mother's grave at the Arafa, Cairo's City of the Dead. It had occurred to her, she said, that I might like to go with them, for afterward they could take me to visit my parents' graves.

Nini is Huda Shaarawi's great-granddaughter. She had come to hear my lectures, and when we chatted afterward we instantly connected. In no time we were talking like old friends.

I immediately accepted her offer. It had been very much on my mind to visit my parents' graves but I had been wondering how. The Arafa is a vast, mazelike place and I needed to go with people who knew their way around. It seemed a nice coincidence that, just as I was beginning to feel quite concerned about finding someone, Nini would spontaneously offer herself. It seemed right, too, that it should be Nini—in whose great-grandmother's words I had sensed a deep affinity with my own mother—who would be accompanying me to visit my mother's and father's graves.

Hala went off to work, dropping me off at the house of one of her friends to do an interview. I'd found myself embarked on the project of doing video interviews with Cairo women almost accidentally, and certainly without having originally planned it. I'd brought a video camera with me to Cairo, intending to interview my aunts and the mothers of friends so as to record how life had been for that older generation. But once I began interviewing people I found myself completely riveted by the process: by the unexpectedly intimate atmosphere that comes into being as people reflect on their lives in response to the questions of a stranger and, even more, by the revelations of the profoundly different Cairo lives I was learning of. So I decided to give my remaining days in Cairo to these interviews. By the time I left I had interviewed women at all sorts of social levels and in various walks of life: writers, artists, intellectuals, maids, secretaries, accountants, doctors—and one businesswoman, a self-made millionaire.

That morning I was interviewing Nadia, who worked as a maid. A reserved, thoughtful-looking woman, she sat on the sofa in the living room where, the previous day, her mistress had also sat for an interview. Nadia wore a handsome blue dress donned specially for the occasion and a *mandil*, a decorative scarf tied tightly round the head that is conventional dress for maids. She began responding to my questions self-consciously but gradually lost her awkwardness as she became absorbed in thinking about and looking back at her life. Her father had died when she was six, leaving her mother with five children. They left their home to live in a room on the roof of a relative's house. Her mother went to work as a maid, during the day locking the children up in the room on the roof for safety. The youngest, an infant, was left in Nadia's care. Later Nadia went to school for a couple of years, then at ten to work as a live-in maid in a relative's house. She had worked ever since. At twenty she married, but when her husband took a second wife, she divorced. She was left with two young children whom she alone supported from then on, raising them with the help of her mother. Her daughter was just completing her schooling; she was very smart and was going to be a teacher. Her son, who was also smart but not academically inclined, had dropped out of school and was an apprentice mechanic. She didn't live in where she worked, because of her children. The family had a two-room apartment, which they shared with her mother, in the suburb of Boula' Da'rour, about an hour by bus from where she worked. She loved to read, she told me. And only at that point—not when she'd been talking of the hardships she'd overcome, but now, only now— did she cry, tears quietly running down her face.

We made our way across Cairo in Nini's car, Nini at the wheel, along the long straight avenue that is the final stretch of the route to the Arafa. Directly ahead of us, dusty and barren, were the Mu'attam hills. Below them were the beige, ochre, and dust-colored low flat roofs and domes and occasional minarets that make up the Arafa, the City of the Dead. It is, in fact, a vast city unto itself, with its own different districts, the region of the mausoleums of the Mamluk royalty standing out distinctively against the horizon because of its density of minarets and its grander, browner, more ancient buildings.

People stood on the roadside holding up flowers for sale, and along some stretches there were just baskets of flowers, mostly of marigolds, no one attending them.

I had only been to the Arafa once as a young girl, when I'd accompanied my school friend Nawal for the burial of her father, and I had found it utterly gruesome and terrifying. The place looked like a city, a bizarre and macabre city: there were streets and avenues and alleys, alleys that got narrower and narrower and more and more mazelike as you wound your way farther and farther in. But it was unlike a city in that all the houses were unnaturally low, because everybody here, of course, was dead and underground. A parody of a city. In fact, the Arafa housed a huge population of the living. First of all, those who tended to the graves lived there; then there were the poor, who depended for their livelihood on the customary charities at a death (*shureik*, a special kind of plaited, sweetish bread, dates, silver coins). Today the Arafa is also where the new homeless of Cairo, often recent migrants from the countryside, live. Cairo's City of the Dead houses, it is said, a million or two (nobody really knows) of the living.

Some parts of it were more populous than others. The alleyways into which we turned as we made our way toward the plot belonging to the family of Nini's friend, Amna, were quiet and almost deserted. But as soon as we pulled up, people somehow materialized as if from nowhere and immediately formed a knot around the car, invoking God's mercy on our dead and reaching out their hands for alms.

Once inside the enclosure, all was quiet again. In one corner stood a small open-sided mosque and beside it a beautiful, delicate-leaved tree. The couple who lived in the room over the portals and tended to the plot brought in the flowers that Amna had brought— white gladioli and white roses—placing them in vases on the white marble markers with gold lettering (giving the names and dates of the dead) that were in the center of the mosque.

On the back wall were inscribed several verses from the Quran. We took our places on a bench within and listened as three men, sitting cross-legged on mats on the floor, chanted in turn from the Quran.

I caught the words *"nur ʿala nur,"* light upon light. Recognizing the verse from which they came, a favorite verse among Sufis, I wondered if Amna had herself selected the passages and if she, like Nini, had a particular interest in Sufism. Nini had told me of undergoing a transforming religious experience and had hinted that she had been initiated on the Sufi path during a period when she lived in France. Some Sufi orders do not permit initiates to reveal openly that they are Sufis and I took this to be the reason underlying Nini's ambiguous words. The Shaarawis had lost their wealth in the Nasser revolution and Nini had at one time been homeless and alone. I do not know the exact circumstances. For a stretch of time she had survived by sleeping at night in the different mosques of Cairo. Then the family of one of her friends had taken her in and, soon after, she had received a scholarship and been able to go on to college.

After the visit at Amna's mother's tomb we began to drive slowly through the Arafa's narrow alleys, looking for my own family's (and more exactly my mother's family's) burial plot and enclosure. We stopped many times to inquire, but we had no success and in the end had to give up. It was disappointing but we had not been enormously hopeful to begin with, for I had not managed to get much information other than the name of the general district. Calling my aunts for directions I'd discovered that my aunt Nazli did not know how to get there herself, having always relied on other people to take her. And Aunt Aisha, who did know, was in great pain from a backache and unable not only to accompany us but even to do much more than give the most cursory, vague directions through this very complicated territory. I even called my paternal cousin, just in case she knew. She did not, but I got from her, instead, a long account of how my father's family had at first insisted that he be buried in Alexandria in his own family's burial plot and then had relented because of Mother's protestations that they should be buried together. I had not known until then that people were supposed to be buried back with their natal families. (And perhaps they are not; perhaps this was just a matter of family pride.) My parents could not, in any case, have been buried side by side because, as I understand it, in the labyrinth of underground corridors and chambers with which burial plots in the Arafa are honeycombed, men are buried in chambers along one side of a corridor and women in chambers along the other. These practices of burial chambers and so on are those only of Egyptians, perhaps only of Egyptians buried in the Arafa. Supposedly they go back to Pharaonic times and have nothing to do with Islam, although those practicing them believe that they are thoroughly Islamic.

≈

*This is how it always is
when I finish a poem.*

*A great silence overcomes me,
and I wonder why I ever thought
to use language.*

Jalaluddin Rumi, the poet whose words these are and whom I have quoted a couple of times in the preceding pages, lived in Konya, in Anatolia, and died in 1273. At his death all of Konya mourned. Jews, Christians, Buddhists, and Hindus, as well as Muslims, walked in his procession, weeping.

Rumi's cat, who had meowed piteously through his last illness, refused to eat after his death and died a week later. Rumi's daughter buried her at his side. Symbol, she said, of Rumi's deep connection with all beings.

JUL 12
AUG 2
AUG 31
JAN 25
JAN 29

0135 1

305.42
AHME   Ahmed, Leila

          A border passage

7/99

        Elkins Park Free Library
        563 East Church Road
        Elkins Park, PA 19027-2499

                              GAYLORD FG